SOCIAL PSYCHOLOGY

A Complete Introduction

To Holly, with all my love as always.

To Mum, Dad and Nikki, thanks for all your love and support over the years. I couldn't have done it without you.

Teach Yourself®

SOCIAL PSYCHOLOGY
A Complete Introduction

Dr Paul Seager

First published in Great Britain in 2014 by Hodder & Stoughton. An Hachette UK company.

First published in US in 2014 by The McGraw-Hill Companies, Inc.

This edition published 2014

Copyright © Paul Seager 2014

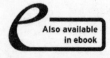

Contents

Introduction

When asked the question, 'What is social psychology?' many people's initial response is along the lines of, 'Oh, it's just common sense, isn't it?'. Certainly many students perceive social psychology to be the easy option in their academic year. As a social psychologist, I can tell you that both of these views are not true – and here are the reasons why.

First, what exactly is common sense? If common sense is defined by collective wisdom, then we should turn perhaps to proverbs to give us a view on the world. For example, 'Opposites attract' would tell us about interpersonal relationships, and 'Many hands make light work' would give us insight into group behaviour. But wait, I hear you cry, what about 'Birds of a feather flock together' contradicting our first common sense pearl of wisdom, and 'Too many cooks spoil the broth' as a counterpoint for the second. And this is exactly my point: common sense can be very contradictory at times, and may simply be one person's point of view.

It is often the case that we may only remember the time we met a happy couple who seemed to be opposite in every way, but have forgotten the countless times that we encountered happy couples that were very alike. Of course, there is no doubting that some of the areas dealt with by social psychology do seem obvious to us now, but my counter-argument here would be that this is only because social psychologists have done their job so well in the past, by investigating areas of interest and giving some definitive answers through the application of good research.

To address the second issue, with regard to students' views of social psychology, it is probably because the topics covered by social psychology are so linked to us as individuals. Take any chapter in this book, and it is likely that each of us will have had a personal experience related to it. This closeness can lead us to believe that we understand it completely, and this in turn may lead us to conclude that we don't need to work any further at understanding it; we simply use our personal views and experiences to explain the topic (and heaven knows I've read many exam scripts over the years that have done just that). However, social psychologists work very hard to give an objective (as opposed to subjective) view of the social world, and this involves using a number of different research methods to address some tricky issues. Many students don't appreciate the amount of work required to tackle the subjects that comprise social psychology.

So, having (hopefully) justified the existence of social psychologists, it begs the questions as to just what is social psychology.

What is social psychology?

One of the classic definitions of social psychology was given by Gordon Allport (1954a), who defined it as: 'the attempt to understand and explain how the thoughts, feelings and behaviour of individuals are influenced by the actual, imagined or implied presence of other human beings' (p. 5). To be quite honest, definitions of social psychology don't get too much better than this. It seems then that social psychology is all about the interaction with, and influence by, others. When talking of other human beings, this could mean a reference to individuals or groups, and groups certainly play an important part in European social psychology (see below).

Social psychology is also about the context of the interactions, and the way in which the situation can influence the behaviour of an individual. In this regard, it becomes clearer as to what social psychology isn't, and this would be that it isn't so much about the personality of individuals – certainly not according to Allport's view.

There will certainly be times throughout the book when we look at how personality characteristics might influence behaviour, such as leadership, but much of the time this is not the case (for instance, Milgram was more interested in the context in which an authority was situated, and less interested in how obedience was accounted for by individual differences – but we're getting a little ahead of ourselves here, though you could skip to Chapter 6 to learn more about Milgram if you really can't wait). Typically, social psychologists view personality characteristics as moderators of behaviour rather than a sole cause.

There can be no doubt that the field of social psychology has changed over the years, and is changing still, with other disciplines and theoretical perspectives, such as cognitive psychology, neuroscience and evolutionary theory, exerting some degree of influence on it. Whilst this book aims to give an overview of some of the more traditional areas covered by social psychology, by way of introduction to the topic, the reader should certainly be aware that the field is currently evolving, in much the same way as it has always done, as a brief historical survey of the field will show.

A brief history of social psychology

It is difficult to know exactly from where social psychology sprang originally: some say that the German scholars known as the 'folk psychologists' were an early influence with their idea of a collective mind. Others claim that Auguste Comte's idea of using scientific principles to study social processes was also an influence. In all likelihood, there were probably a number of different factors that contributed to its birth. However, in terms of the earliest social psychology experiment, this distinction normally goes to Normal Triplett (1898), who conducted a study investigating what we would now refer to as 'social facilitation' (see Chapter 11 for more details).

With regards to the first social psychological textbooks, some claim that 1908 is the key year. Textbooks by both Ross and McDougal are acknowledged by many as the first of their kind; however, others argue that their content bears very little resemblance to what we recognize today as being social psychology (which is likely a fair comment as McDougal's text seems to be based in biology and, as Ross was a sociologist, his text focuses more on topics such as crowd behaviour and culture). A better claim to the first social psychology text probably comes from Floyd Allport who published his book

Social Psychology in 1924. The book, which was a strong advocate of the experimental method, put forth an agenda for this emerging field of study.

Experimental psychology facilities were being created in a number of American universities around the beginning of the twentieth century, following on from Wundt's establishment of such a laboratory in Leipzig, Germany in 1879; it is likely that such facilities provided the breeding ground for social psychologists.

Perhaps a little surprisingly, there was a quiet period of about twenty years for the discipline following the publication of Allport's work, though this time frame probably marked the bedding-in of the topic. However, that's not to say that important work wasn't being conducted, as there are one or two key publications of note that emerged during this time (for example, a text by Sherif in 1936 detailing the use of the autokinetic effect to look at the formation and development of group norms and its effect on conformity – see Chapter 6). Nevertheless, it seems that the onset of the Second World War marked a turning point for social psychology.

The war is generally credited for furthering the cause of social psychology on three fronts, though it was mainly in America that the benefits were felt initially. First, the military took an interest in what the field could tell them about, amongst other things, propaganda and its effects on morale. Attitude change was also high on the agenda, both on the front lines and the home front; for example, how could people be persuaded to make do with less as rationing began to take hold. Secondly, there was an influx of academics, both Jewish and non-Jewish to United States' universities, and some of these went on to become highly influential figures in the field: for example Kurt Lewin, who went on to inspire a generation of social psychologists. Thirdly, people started to take an interest in important topics such as obedience and authoritarianism. For instance, why didn't German soldiers just say 'no' when ordered to carry out atrocities? Was it the power of the situation, or was it the personality of the German people? Together, these three factors helped promote the importance of social psychology, and soon no university was without such a department.

But where was European social psychology in all of this? Well, there were certainly a number of European academics who played an important role in helping the field to develop pre-war. For example, Hugo Munsterberg played a key role in introducing social psychology into the legal arena, as well as influencing a number of other individuals, such as Floyd Allport (see above). However, by the end of the war there was very little in the way of a European social psychological movement.

Whilst America tried to revive the field in Europe after the war, it was probably more in the way of self-interest (in an attempt to prevent the spread of Communism to places like Britain) than altruism. Certainly European social psychology remained a fractured movement into the 1960s, with any links being mainly via American scientists rather than directly with each other. However, slowly but surely, a European movement began to emerge, and one which was moving in a slightly different direction to that of their transatlantic cousins: whilst America was interested in a more 'individual' focus, investigating areas such as interpersonal factors, the Europeans, perhaps as a direct consequence of the post-war rebuilding effort going on across the continent, were more interested in groups and intergroup processes.

To a certain extent, these differences persist in the present, and this is perhaps evidenced by the way that this book devotes a number of chapters to group processes and intergroup relationships (a trend that may not be found in some North American texts). The likes of Henri Tajfel and Serge Moscovici were important players in the development of the European social psychology agenda in the 1960s, which led to the formation of what is currently known as the European Association of Social Psychology. Today, there is a flourishing social psychology culture on both sides of the Atlantic.

'The Second World War proved to be something of an intellectual watershed for theory and research into intergroup relations. The publication of Dollard et al.'s (1939) Frustration and Aggression *and Adorno et al.'s (1950)* The Authoritarian Personality *were enormously influential in kindling social psychologists' interest in the factors that determine the attitudes and behavior of members of one group toward those of another.'*

(Brewer & Brown, 1998, p. 554).

The aim of this book

This book aims to give you a glimpse into a new world. Imagine this book as the wardrobe into the Narnia-like world of social psychology. It will act as a starting place for your journey of exploration. Some of you may have been here before, but are now looking to explore the world more fully; but for some of you, this will be your first encounter with social psychology. You've probably picked up the book because you're curious. And curiosity is an excellent trait for any budding social psychologist.

This book will introduce you to many areas of social psychology. Chapter 1 will give you an overview of how social psychologists go about doing their research. Chapter 2 aims to take a look at the 'self'. When embarking on a journey filled with individuals and groups, there's no better place to start than at home – finding out about yourself, and what makes 'you' tick. Chapter 3 looks at how we make sense of the people around us; the attributions we make about others and their behaviour. Chapter 4 investigates why the decisions we make with regards to the world around us can sometimes be flawed, or, at the very least, not optimal. Welcome to the world of social cognition. Chapter 5 looks at the relationships we build with others – from casual acquaintances, through friendship, to love – and what happens when they break down. Chapter 6 begins to look at how our actions can be influenced by other people, and Chapter 7 continues the theme by investigating the extent to which our attitudes guide our behaviour, and how those attitudes can be changed through persuasion techniques. Chapters 8 and 9 look at two opposite ends of the spectrum in terms of our social behaviour – why and when we might help other people (even in the most adverse of circumstances), and why and when we might behave aggressively towards others. Chapter 10 will be the starting point on your journey to explore groups: what they are and how they work. If you've ever thought about forming a group (perhaps a rock band, perhaps a neighbourhood watch group, or perhaps even a social psychology society), then this chapter should prove to be illuminating. Chapter 11 looks at some of the processes that go on within a group, and Chapter 12 looks at one specific component of groups – their leaders. Chapter 13 looks at the thorny issue of prejudice and how this can be propagated by group membership. The journey through all things 'groups' ends with Chapter 14 which looks at intergroup relationships, why they sometimes descend into conflict and ways that social psychologists have devised to reduce, and potentially resolve, such conflict. Chapter 15 reiterates the very applied nature of social psychology, a theme that has run through just about all of the chapters, and looks at how it impacts on the world on a daily basis.

Each chapter provides you with a clear and concise introduction to each topic. It will define key terms as appropriate, and will give you a detailed look at a number of studies that have been conducted in the area. Some important names and dates are dropped in to give you a sense of when significant concepts were formalized and by who: it will also allow you to build a historical timeline of the development of different areas of social psychology. However, in order to avoid getting bogged down and bamboozled by a multitude of names and dates (which so many students do) and potentially missing the messages delivered by each chapter, not all studies or concepts are referenced (although there is a list of references at the back of the book for the quotes used in each chapter). However, it should be fairly straightforward – using the power of Google Scholar (or another academic search engine of your choice) – to follow up on these as you see fit.

Each chapter ends with a summary, and a 'Food for thought' section which invites you to think about how the topic of the chapter can be applied to a particular aspect of the real world. It also lists a small number of sources for further reading which will help you to explore the topic of each chapter in more detail if you are so inclined. And just to check that you were paying attention (and more importantly, to help you formalize your new-found knowledge), each chapter ends with ten 'Fact-check' questions to quiz you on its content.

So, that's the aim of the book – a complete introduction to social psychology. Of course, what this book therefore doesn't do is to tell you everything there is to know about social psychology, or even everything about the topics of each chapter. There was simply not enough room to do this. What I have aimed to do though is to give you a good overview of each topic, and introduce you to some of the key concepts and studies involved. There may be bits missing which you were expecting, and for this I apologize (but I did try to include everything which I thought you might find interesting); but I do hope that this book will motivate you to explore each topic further. My aim then is to whet your appetite for social psychology, and I hope you will be prompted to go on to feast further on this fascinating subject.

Summary

Social psychology is so much more than common sense, but to get to grips with it fully does require a little application. And the first step on this journey is to understand exactly what social psychology is and isn't: the definition supplied by Gordon Allport certainly provides an excellent starting point. The chapter aimed to show that social psychology has a rich and interesting history, a fascinating present and the promise of an exciting future.

Food for thought

Pick up a copy of one of today's newspapers, flick through the first ten to twenty pages and make a note of the major stories. Then, when you have read this book, come back to your list and try to marry up the stories with a relevant chapter. If the stories involve people or groups, it is highly likely that you will be able to make a match in most cases. When you have done this, think about the content of the relevant chapter and how it might be applied to the story. For example, there is bound to be a war going on somewhere (though I'd be more than happy to be proved wrong) – turn to Chapter 14 (intergroup relations) and look at the strategies for reducing intergroup conflict. How could these be applied to the war?

How to use this book

This Complete Introduction from Teach Yourself ® includes a number of special boxed features, which have been developed to help you understand the subject more quickly and remember it more effectively. Throughout the book, you will find these indicated by the following icons.

The book includes concise **quotes** from other key sources. These will be useful for helping you understand different viewpoints on the subject, and they are fully referenced so that you can include them in essays if you are unable to get your hands on the source.

The **case study** is a more in-depth introduction to a particular example. There is at least one in most chapters, and hopefully they will provide good material for essays and class discussions.

The **key ideas** are highlighted throughout the book. If you only have half an hour to go before your exam, scanning through these would be a very good way of spending your time.

The **fact-check** questions at the end of each chapter, are designed to help you ensure you have taken in the most important concepts from the chapter. If you find you are consistently getting several answers wrong, it may be worth trying to read more slowly, or taking notes as you go.

The **dig deeper** boxes give you ways to explore topics in greater depth than we are able to go to in this introductory level book.

1

Doing research in social psychology

Imagine you are having a debate with a friend about relationships, and about what types of people get together. Your friend claims that 'opposite attracts' and points out that a couple he knows are happily married but they are like chalk and cheese; she is very extroverted and likes to host parties whereas he is very introverted and likes nothing better than a quiet night in with a cup of cocoa and a good book. But no you say, surely 'birds of a feather flock together', and you point out a couple you know who are both introverts, and both like cycling; and what's more you say, you once knew of a friend who was an extrovert who started dating an introvert but it never lasted – after six months they split up because they were too dissimilar.

The chances are that you will both claim you are right ... but how could we test which of these two contradictory proverbs is actually correct? Well, this is what social psychologists do – they formulate interesting questions and then test them to find an answer. However, the way in which they do so can vary greatly (depending on the question) but the manner in which they do it is a careful one to ensure that the answer they arrive at is valid. There are many books that deal in depth with how social psychologists go about doing research, but the aim of this chapter is to give you a very simple overview of the area so that you are able to understand some of the different methods and terminology used in the studies described in the coming chapters.

The scientific method

Most social psychologists consider the discipline of social psychology to be a science, and to reflect this, many of their studies employ what is known as the scientific method. This involves a number of steps:

1 **Observe**: social psychologists observe the world around them, and when they find something interesting they put it to the test. This book is full of areas in which they have been testing over the years. In the case of relationships, the interesting question is whether birds of a feather flock together or whether opposite attracts.

2 **Hypothesize**: the next step is to make a prediction – called a **hypothesis**. This is a statement that can be measured in some way and potentially falsified. For our example, the hypothesis could be something along the lines of: 'There will be a difference in the length of time couples stay married dependent on their levels of similarity'.

3 **Test**: The hypothesis is then operationalized in some way; that is to say, it is turned into something that can be tested. For example, for our hypothesis the terms need to be defined – what do we mean by 'levels of similarity' (e.g. will we be testing personality traits of both individuals, such as Introversion/Extraversion; Agreeableness; Openness, Conscientiousness, etc., or will we define similarity in some other way.). Once this has been done, we set about collecting our data.

4 **Analyse**: once the data has been collected, we analyse it to see if there is any truth in the theory that we are testing; to state it more formally, we look to see whether we can accept or reject our hypothesis. If we accept it, then we are suggesting that the data we have collected supports our theory, but if we reject it, our theory might need some modification (before we reject it totally).

5 **Modify**: whilst the data might support our initial idea, our hypothesis might still be too general, or perhaps too specific. We might then modify our theory to tell us more.

For example, when we referred to married couples, we might only have tested heterosexual couples, and therefore be unable to say whether it applies to same-sex couples. We would therefore modify our hypothesis, or perhaps generate a number of new hypotheses, and run our study again by collecting more data to incorporate our new parameters.

6 **Repeat:** if we have modified our hypotheses, we would run a new study. However, even if we were happy with our study, other researchers might not be. They might see something in our research that they consider to be a methodological flaw (perhaps we only collected data in a specific area of the country and they might feel that this is not a representative sample of married couples); or they might feel that our findings are so unusual that they want to repeat our study just to check that we haven't falsified our data. One of the strengths of the scientific method is replication. If someone else, in a different university or a different country, can take our methodology, repeat our study and find the same results, this will give our theory even more credibility. If they were to find something different, then perhaps further work would be needed on our theory.

Key idea: Hypothesis

A statement that is falsifiable through some form of testing employing the scientific method.

There are a number of different methods through which scientists test their hypotheses, and they are generally broken down into two broad categories: experimental methods and non-experimental methods. Both have their strengths and weaknesses, and many hypotheses can be tested in more than one way.

Experimental methods

The experiment is a traditional method employed by scientists and it is usually conducted within a controlled 'laboratory' environment. It consists of a situation where the researcher manipulates something (called an **independent variable**) and observes its effects on something else (called the **dependent variable**). For example, if we were interested in whether viewing violence on television increased aggressive behaviour, we might create an experiment to test our idea. We could assign participants to one of two different conditions: in one they watch a television clip containing violent acts, and in one they watch a television clip containing no violent acts. After they have watched their clip, any subsequent acts of aggression are measured (for example, we might ask them to wait in a room that contains a punch bag and secretly monitor if, and how often, they hit the bag whilst waiting).

Key idea: Independent variable (IV)

The variable or variables that are manipulated to see whether they produce an effect on one or more dependent variables.

Key idea: Dependent variable (DV)

The variable which is expected to change as a result of the manipulation of an independent variable.

When designing our experiment, there are a number of elements that we need to consider:

1 Who are our **participants**? These are the people who take part in our experiment (or our research in general). They can be drawn from the general population, or they can have specific characteristics (e.g. children). Generally, participants are randomly allocated to different experimental conditions to equalize any individual differences exhibited by specific individuals (e.g. intelligence). Where participants cannot be randomly assigned to conditions, for example, if gender or nationality is an independent variable, then this is referred to as a *quasi-experiment*.

Key idea: Participants

The individuals, or groups, who take part in studies to allow researchers to collect data to test hypotheses.

2 The role of the *experimenter* and/or any confederates. It is necessary to ensure that there is no chance of the experimenter inadvertently influencing the outcome of the experiment (known as *experimenter effects*). Additionally, one experimenter may not be able to run a complicated experiment alone and may require confederates (also called stooges) to act out certain roles within the study.

3 What are our *independent and dependant variables*? Many experiments have more than one of each type of variable. The independent variable (which can lead to a number of 'conditions') is something that is manipulated to see if it produces a desired effect on what we are measuring, which in turn is called the dependent variable. In our proposed experiment, the independent variable would be the type of television clip viewed (aggressive or non-aggressive) and the dependent variable would be the number of times that they hit the punch bag in the waiting room.

4 We must decide whether there are any *ethical considerations* that we need to consider for our experiment (see below for a more detailed discussion). For example, if watching a television clip with violent content does make a person more aggressive, do we (as the researcher) really want to be responsible for sending a violent person back out into the world where they might harm another individual.

Our experimental design to test our research question ('Does watching violence on TV make people more aggressive') allows us to look for a causal relationship (our IV affects our DV). In our simple design, we would test the hypothesis by analysing our data to see whether the participants watching the violent clip hit the punch bag more than those watching the non-violent clip. If they did, we might accept our hypothesis and claim that our theory was correct. However, I'm sure you've already spotted a number of flaws in the design of the experiment (e.g. is hitting a punch bag in a waiting room a sign of aggression or boredom? How hard would the bag have to be hit to be classified as an aggressive act?). To minimize these flaws, we would perhaps need to design a slightly more elaborate experiment (or perhaps use a different research method – see below).

There are a number of advantages to the experimental method:

1 It allows us to attribute cause and effect.

2 It allows us to carefully control the conditions of our study, and control is very important to ensure that there are no **confounding variables** that might also explain our findings.

3 Experiments are more straightforward to replicate than some other methods.

'The great advantage of the experimental method is that the causal relationship between variables can be determined with much greater certainty. This is done in two ways: by controlling all factors except the independent variable and by randomly assigning people to condition.'
(Aronson, Wilson & Brewer, 1998)

Key idea: Confounding variables

Anything that is not the IV which might also affect the DV; some other uncontrolled factor(s) that might account for the findings of a study.

However, there are also a number of problems with the experimental method. These include:

▶ Experiments can be difficult to design, and sometimes they are simply unethical to conduct.

▶ Experiments are sometimes highly artificial and don't reflect what happens in the real world (they lack external validity).

- They only measure a small snapshot in time and may not capture longer-term effects.

- They are susceptible to reactivity effects whereby participants act in a certain way because they know they are part of an experiment (though if they don't know they are part of an experiment, there may be ethical issues to consider).

Related to the experiment is the *field experiment*; this is a study conducted outside of a controlled laboratory setting but which satisfies the criteria for an experiment. For example, experiments carried out in a school or a shopping centre would be considered to be field experiments. There have been a number of notable social psychology field experiments, and two of my favourites include one conducted on a rickety bridge over a deep ravine (Dutton & Aron, 1974) and one in a men's lavatory (Middlemist, Knowles & Matter, 1976). Such studies represent the inventiveness of social psychologists (read up on these studies to find out more).

However, on many occasions, the research question requires a method other than an experiment to be applied.

Non-experimental methods

There are a number of non-experimental methods, and these include:

FIELD STUDIES

Usually conducted outside of a laboratory setting, these types of studies attempt to investigate social phenomena in the real-world. It may include the naturalistic observation of a specific population (e.g. schoolchildren in the playground, or football crowds) in an attempt to record and explain the behaviour of individuals or groups. This type of method circumnavigates some of the problems with a lab-based study in that it avoids the problem of artificial reactive behaviour on the part of the participants, but it does raise some ethical questions (e.g. the idea of informed consent – see below). Field studies can include methods (such as the experiment or the survey) other than observation. Generally, this method has the advantage in that it has a greater level of **ecological validity**, but the downside is that it usually lacks control, and some of the findings of such research may be accounted for by factors of which the researcher is unaware.

Key idea: Ecological validity

The degree to which research findings can be generalized to a real-world setting.

SURVEYS

This method involves asking a series of questions (for example, via a paper-based questionnaire, a phone poll or, increasingly, a web-based survey) to tap into the beliefs, attitudes and behaviour of a given population. One advantage to this type of methodology is that it allows a large number of participants to be recruited quite easily and quickly, which allows the researcher to be confident that the findings of any such study can be generalized to a large population. However, there are also a number of disadvantages, such as the need for the questions to be worded very carefully to avoid any misinterpretation of their intention, and the worry that participants will not respond truthfully, but will instead answer in such a way that paints themselves in the best possible light (a **'social desirability'** bias). Additionally, because the researcher is typically not present when participants complete questionnaires, the method lacks the control of an experiment.

Key idea: Social desirability

The way in which participants may modify their responses or behaviour to ensure that they 'look good' and are portrayed in the best possible way.

ARCHIVAL RESEARCH

It is possible that a set of data, which is of interest to social psychologists, already exists in some form; in which case they will simply reanalyse the data in such a way to give them answers to a question that is of interest. For example, if they were interested in whether female defendants in a jury trial were treated more leniently than male defendants, and whether this varied by type of crime (e.g. murder vs. shoplifting), they might seek permission to access the archives of a number of Crown courts and pull out the data they need from existing records. This method has the advantage that it is real-world data and thus possesses a good degree of ecological validity (in a way that experimental lab-based data may not), but has the disadvantage that the data may be incomplete (e.g. missing data that the researcher needs) or lacking in context (for example, the exact circumstances in which the data was collected). Typically archival data is used to formulate a hypothesis that is then tested using a more controlled method.

CASE STUDIES

A case study typically involves collecting some form of data about a single individual or group. A particularly interesting case study was conducted by Festinger and his colleagues with regard to a small group who prophesized the end of the world (chronicled in his fascinating book 'When prophecy fails' – well worth a read); it details the group dynamics both in the lead up to the predicted event and after the event fails to happen, and looks at the way the individuals react. It has the advantage of being able to take a very detailed and intricate look at behaviour in a naturalistic setting, but lacks control of confounding variables, may be very difficult to replicate and potentially hard to generalize to a wider population. However, such studies usually facilitate the production of specific hypotheses which can be tested under more controlled conditions.

Having looked at a number of different methods that might be employed, it is important to note that no one method is necessarily better than another. They all have strengths and weaknesses, and it may be possible to employ more than one method to address a research question (e.g. we could employ a survey method and/or an experimental method to address our question of whether 'birds of a feather flock together').

There are certainly many additional issues that should be considered with regards to the design and implementation of studies, and it is beyond the scope of this chapter, or indeed this book, to cover them all. However, one question that does crop up from time to time in the forthcoming chapters is whether or not a study, a method, or a tool (such as a questionnaire) is a valid one; thus it will be useful to introduce briefly the notion of 'validity'.

Types of validity

There are a number of different types of validity that relate to research. In general, if an individual asks about the validity of a study, they are just questioning whether the study is doing what it purports to do. For example, if a study claims that it is testing the effect of type of leadership on group productivity, then this is what it must do, and in this particular instance, for the study to be valid, steps should have been taken to ensure that the productivity of the group cannot have been affected by anything else other than the type of leadership. However, there are other more specific types of validity and these include:

▶ **Face validity:** the extent to which it is clear as to what the study is testing. The advantage of this type of validity is that it can motivate participants to engage with a study if they can see its purpose. However, in some cases, if a study has too much face validity, the responses of participants may be affected. For instance, if a questionnaire distributed to participants states in the opening sentence of its instructions that it intends to measure how racist the individual is, this will almost certainly have an effect on participant answers;

▶ **Internal validity:** the degree to which confidence can be maintained that the independent variable actually influences the dependent variable, thus reflecting a real effect;

▶ **Content validity:** the extent to which a test used in a study covers the specific topic area, and to which it has been verified by an expert. Some intelligence tests have been scrutinized with regards to their content validity: do they actually measure intelligence (whatever that might be).

There are many other types of validity, such as predictive validity, construct validity, concurrent validity, external validity and so forth. These may refer to either the study itself or the tools (e.g. questionnaires) employed by the study.

This chapter then has looked at the different methods that social psychologists employ to study social phenomena, and there are certainly many different areas for them to study and many questions to answer. However, the ways in which they go about obtaining these answers must be ethical ones, and hence the final section of this chapter deals with the sometimes tricky issue of ethics within social psychological research.

Ethics

When conducting research, social psychologists are bound by a set of ethical guidelines in order to protect their participants. These guidelines are usually set by the governing body for psychologists in whatever country they practice: for example, in Britain it is the British Psychological Society (BPS), and in America it is the American Psychological Association (APA). It should be noted that not all psychologists will necessarily belong to a governing body: it is usual that they do, but it is not a legal requirement.

The full BPS code of ethics and conduct can be accessed from: http://www.bps.org.uk. The structure of the code is based around four ethical principles (see Spotlight below). However, whilst these four principles are indeed the cornerstones of the ethical code, there are five key factors that every student, who plans to carry out some form of research, has drummed in to them:

1 Informed consent

2 Respect for privacy (anonymity and confidentiality)

3 Use of deception

4 Welfare of participants

5 Debriefing

Informed consent refers to the fact that every potential participant has the right to know what the researcher will be asking them to do before they agree to take part in a study. Occasionally, it is necessary to employ deception (see below) in a study whereby participants are not informed about the true nature of the study until it has concluded. However, it is important that participants are informed of the exact nature of the study at the earliest possible opportunity (see debriefing below).

It is important that researchers have a *respect for privacy* of their participants. As a general rule, all participants can expect to remain anonymous with regards to the data that they are providing by taking part in a study; likewise, any responses they give to the researcher should be treated as confidential. If for any reason *anonymity and confidentiality* are unable to be preserved, the researcher must inform the participant at the earliest possible opportunity so that they can decide whether or not to take part in the study, or, if they have already completed the study, whether or not they want to withdraw their data – a decision that must be accepted unconditionally by the researcher.

Probably the most (in)famous use of *deception* in a study was by Stanley Milgram in his obedience experiments (see Chapter 6 for further details). Deception is usually used in order to get a snapshot of a participant's true behaviour in a given situation; in some situations, if participants were told about the exact nature of the study in advance, it is unlikely that the researcher could have confidence that their results were a true reflection of what would really happen in the situation. Where possible the use of deception should be avoided unless the integrity of the study depends upon its use. If deception is used within a study, the researcher must inform the participants of the nature of the deception as soon as possible (usually at the conclusion of the study via the debriefing – see below).

The physical and psychological *welfare of participants* is of paramount importance. Any research must be carefully considered to ensure that the potential for harm to participants has been reduced as much as possible. Additionally, participants should be told that even if they agree to take part in a study, they have the *right to withdraw* from it at any point, especially if they are experiencing any form of distress. Where any possible distress is anticipated in advance (no matter how small), such as when asking participants to complete questionnaires regarding difficult topics (for example, studies investigating child abuse or rape myths), the researcher needs to have a support mechanism in place. It is not unusual for a participant to be given a list of support help lines, or websites, at the end of a questionnaire study.

Debriefing must occur at the end of any study, its purpose being to inform participants of the nature of the study (or the true nature of the study if deception has been used). It is also the ideal time to tell participants of any support networks that are available to them, and to answer any questions that they may have about the study in which they have just participated. Where the study may appear to the participant to be evaluative in nature (e.g. a test of an ability, such as intelligence, reasoning or lie detection), it is important that they are reassured of their anonymity, the confidentiality of their data, that the results are merely a snapshot at one specific moment in time and therefore perhaps are not a true reflection of their actual ability (if appropriate). A final consideration of the debriefing is to ensure that the participant leaves the study in the same condition (e.g. mood) as when they started the study.

Spotlight: British Psychological Society: Four ethical principles

According to the BPS code of ethics and conduct published in August 2009, which is current at the time of the publication of this book, there are four guiding principles. All members of the BPS are bound by these principles, and the statement of values attached to each; these are stated verbatim below:

1 **'Respect:** Psychologists value the dignity and worth of all persons, with sensitivity to the dynamics of perceived authority or influence over clients, and with particular regard to people's rights including those of privacy and self-determination.

2 **Competence:** Psychologists value the continuing development and maintenance of high standards of competence in their professional work, and the importance

of preserving their ability to function optimally within the recognized limits of their knowledge, skill, training, education and experience.

3 Responsibility: Psychologists value their responsibilities to clients, to the general public, and to the profession and science of Psychology, including the avoidance of harm and the prevention of misuse or abuse of their contributions to society.

4 Integrity: Psychologists value honesty, accuracy, clarity, and fairness in their interactions with all persons, and seek to promote integrity in all facets of their scientific and professional endeavours.'

Summary

This chapter looked at the different ways in which social psychologists conduct research. The basic tenets of the scientific method (which underlies such research) were described, as were a number of different popular methods that they use, such as experiments and surveys. Advantages and disadvantages of the different methods were highlighted, and it became clear that it was possible to use different methods to address different (or even the same) research questions. The importance of ethics in research was also addressed.

Food for thought

As you work your way through this book and read about different studies, try to think about whether there might have been alternative ways in which the research could have been conducted. Assess the advantages and disadvantages of these alternative methods and consider any ethical issues that might need to be addressed. If you're feeling really brave, design a study to test whether 'Many hands make light work' or whether actually 'Too many cooks spoil the broth'.

Dig deeper

British Psychological Society. (2009). *Code of Ethics and Conduct.* Guidance published by the ethics committee of the British Psychological Society. Accessed via: www.bps.org.uk

Coolican, H. (2014) *Research Methods and Statistics in Psychology.* Sixth Edition. Hodder & Stoughton.

Robson, C. (2011) *Real World Research.* Third Edition. Wiley & Sons.

Fact-check

1 A statement that can be measured in some way, and which is potentially falsifiable, is referred to as:

   a A hypothesis

   b An independent variable

   c A dependent variable

   d A theory

2 With regard to the scientific method, which is the correct order for the sequence of steps employed?

   a Hypothesize, observe, test, analyse, repeat, modify

   b Observe, hypothesize, test, analyse, modify, repeat

   c Hypothesize, observe, test, modify, analyse, repeat

   d Observe, test, hypothesize, modify, analyse, repeat

3 A study is conducted that aims to investigate whether or not 'Opposites attract'. University students who have recently started dating are asked to complete a number of personality tests. Six months later, the couples are contacted again by the researcher to find out whether they are still together. It is expected that couples who show different personality traits are more likely to still be together than couples who show similar personality traits. The independent variable for this study is:

   a Participants are university students

   b Whether the couple are still together after six months

   c Whether or not couples share the same personality traits

   d The different type of personality tests used

4 With regards to the study above, the dependent variable is:

   a Participants are university students

   b Whether the couple are still together after six months

   c Whether or not couples share the same personality traits

   d The different type of personality tests used

5 With regards to the study above, is it:

   a A survey

   b A case study

   c An experiment

   d A quasi-experiment

6 If we modify our study slightly and decide to test both same-sex couples and heterosexual couples, what type of study is it?
   a A survey
   b A case study
   c An experiment
   d A quasi-experiment

7 Which of the following is not an advantage of an experiment?
   a It allows us to determine cause and effect
   b It allows us to control the conditions and reduce the influence of confounding variables
   c It is easier to replicate than some other methods
   d It measures a small snapshot in time

8 Which of the following is not a true statement?
   a Field studies are high in ecological validity but lack a degree of control
   b Surveys can recruit large numbers of participants quite quickly whilst retaining a good level of control
   c Archival research gives the researcher access to existing data which saves time, but the data may be incomplete
   d Cases studies allow a very detailed look at one individual or group, but lack generalizability to a wider population

9 The extent to which a study appears to be investigating what it claims to be investigating is referred to as:
   a Face validity
   b External validity
   c Internal validity
   d Ecological validity

10 Which of the following is not one of the four ethical principles of the British Psychological Society?
   a Respect
   b Competence
   c Vision
   d Integrity

2

The Self

'Who am I?' It's a question that we have probably all asked ourselves at several points throughout our lives. And it is a question that is quite difficult to answer. If you were given a piece of paper which had 'Who am I?' written at the top of it, and you were asked to write twenty things to answer the question, your answers would be quite different to the next person asked to do it; in fact, your answers might be quite different to the ones that you might give if asked to do the same task in a week, a month or a year's time.

As humans, we try to make sense of the world, and such understanding inevitably starts with trying to understand ourselves. To do this, we have to ask some difficult questions: for example, what makes us who we are? How do we make sense of the information that we hold about ourselves? How do we feel about ourselves? How does who we are make us do what we do. This chapter looks at how social psychologists have attempted to answer these questions.

Understanding the Self

To begin to understand ourselves, we must first become self-aware, and this is not something that happens immediately upon our birth. For example, if you were to paint a spot on the nose of a baby and place them in front of a mirror, their behaviour would depend on their age. A very young child (up until the age of about 12 months) would not reach for their nose to investigate the spot; instead they would likely assume that they were seeing another child. However, at around 18 months, they would probably identify the image in the mirror as being themselves and consequently reach out to investigate the spot on their nose. This is taken as the first indication of self-awareness, and with this awakening comes the beginning of the desire to understand more about oneself – a desire that remains with most people for the rest of their lives.

Generally speaking, there are three ways in which we can gather information about our self:

1 We can do it ourselves (self-understanding).

2 We can rely on another person to do it (other-understanding).

3 We can use groups to define ourselves (group understanding).

SELF-UNDERSTANDING

There are two main routes to self-understanding: **introspection** and the observation of our own behaviour (self-perception).

Key idea: Introspection

The way an individual watches and monitors their internal states to understand themselves; to comprehend who they are and why they do what they do.

It seems like a truism that the best person to understand oneself is indeed oneself, and the best way to do so is to monitor one's own thoughts and feelings, referred to as introspection. However, whilst it can be useful at times, this is a potentially problematic method for understanding the self fully as research has shown that individuals are not very accurate when it comes to understanding what they are thinking or why they are thinking it (see Case study below).

Case study: Inaccuracies with understanding the self

When we look inwards to try to understand why we are thinking something or behaving in a certain way, we assume that this will give us accurate knowledge about our self. However, a study by Wilson and Nisbett (1978) cleverly illustrated that this is not always the case. Female shoppers were given a number of samples of nylon stockings and asked to rate their quality. The key to this study was that all of the stockings were identical (though the shoppers did not know this). When asked why they rated some stockings more highly than others, the participants claimed that their decisions were made based on attributes such as 'softness' or 'workmanship'. However, the results of the study showed that generally the highest ratings were given to the stockings that were simply seen last. This highlights quite clearly that the reasons we think we do something may be very different from the actual reasons we do something.

Ultimately, there are a number of key problems with introspection:

1 We are processing so much information at the same time, some consciously and some unconsciously, that we don't really know which of this information is causing our thoughts or behaviours.

2 We overestimate the positive facets of our character. For example, if asked to rate yourself for the quality of physical attractiveness, you are more likely to say that you are 'above average'; in fact, research has shown that most people say this, and this is simply not possible. This can also be problematic when we need a more accurate view of ourselves, such as when we are choosing which job would be best for us to apply for, or when deciding who would be an ideal partner based on our character and traits.

3 For self-protective reasons, we are sometimes driven both to keep unwanted thoughts out of our heads, and not to dwell on bad past experiences. This can be an issue if we are attempting to learn from past mistakes.

This is not to say that introspection cannot be used to understand who we are as individuals, as some research suggests that writing about ourselves does tend to give us good insight into ourselves; rather it is important to understand its limitations in providing us with self-knowledge. Such forewarning can itself be of some use in self-understanding.

Another way to understand oneself is to observe one's own behaviour (**self-perception**), and from this behaviour we can perhaps observe how we are feeling and what we are thinking. For example, if a student comes out of an exam smiling (and that does happen more often than you might believe!), they might reasonably conclude that this behaviour is evidence that they think they have done well in the exam. This 'self-perception' theory was put forward by Bem (1972). However, these self-observations need to be tempered by the 'context' of the behaviours; that is, the circumstances under which the behaviour occurs. If the situation seems to account for our behaviour (e.g. smiling after an exam), then we are unlikely to draw any definite conclusions about our self; however, if the situation doesn't account for our actions (e.g. we smile all the time), then we are more likely to infer that our behaviour was due to who we are (e.g. we smile because we are a naturally happy person). For example, if you went to the theatre because your partner wanted you to, then you wouldn't draw conclusions about yourself as being a theatre-goer; but if you went of your own volition, and perhaps even on your own, then you would be more confident in drawing conclusions about yourself (e.g. you are a lover of the theatre).

Similarly, our self-perception may have important implications for motivation. If we perceive our behaviour in a given instance as being 'internally' driven (e.g. playing a sport for the love of the game) then our motivation will likely be stronger than if it is 'externally' driven (e.g. playing a sport just to win a prize, or to please someone else). This can have important implications for how we motivate ourselves and others (especially children) to perform well. It may be that offering prizes for performing well (e.g. at school) is not the best way forward. Instead fostering an internal motivation will often lead to better and more sustained performances. For example, one study showed that independent judges rated an artist's work to be of a higher quality when it was a non-commissioned piece (internally driven – they did it because they wanted to do it) than when it was commissioned (externally driven – they did it because they were paid to do it).

However, self-perception theory is still a little limited as many things may lead to our behaviour (as with introspection) and we are not always able to pinpoint exactly the most important of them in terms of accounting for our behaviour.

Key idea: Self-perception

The way in which an individual understands their inner states by observing and interpreting their own behaviour.

OTHER-UNDERSTANDING

Understanding of ourselves can also come through observing how others react to us and by processing what they tell us. For example, if a person acts in a more friendly way towards us after we have donated to charity, or if they tell us that it was a kind thing that we did, then we are more likely to think of ourselves as a kind person.

One of the first people we look to in order to understand ourselves is likely to be our primary caregiver; this relationship will certainly have an effect on whether or not we develop high or low self-esteem (see below). Our levels of self-esteem will have a significant effect on how our model of self begins to develop. If our caregivers (e.g. parents, teachers) provide us with consistent and responsive feedback, then our self-concept is more likely to be a positive one; conversely, a lack of responsiveness, and negligence, on behalf of the caregiver will more likely lead to an individual developing a negative self-concept. Thus, the attachments we form with our caregivers at an early age can significantly affect how we view ourselves.

The reactions of others (who are not caregivers) towards us will also help us to understand ourselves, and it has been suggested that we use an amalgamation of the views of others to do so. However, there seems to be limited support for this idea as research suggests that this generalized view is not a good match with how people actually see us. Generally, we're not very good at figuring out how other people see us, as others have a tendency to hide any undesirable views of us which they hold. And even if we were to ask them, they may not be forthcoming with any unpalatable opinions.

Additionally, a *confirmation bias* might also influence how we use the views of others to understand our self. That is, we may have a tendency only to seek out, or remember, the views of others that coincide with our own views of ourselves; we conveniently ignore the times when they contradict our own views. Overall, any feedback that we get from others about our self tends to be filtered to some level, with greater filtering applied when we receive adverse feedback (to which we are not always receptive).

A further way in which we can use others to help us define our self is to compare ourselves with them (referred to as **social comparison**). This helps us define our abilities and our opinions. We do, however, tend to do this with 'similar' others. For example, if an individual wanted to understand how good they were at football or chess, they wouldn't necessarily compare themselves to Wayne Rooney or Gary Kasparov; they are much more likely to use a member of their own football or chess team for comparison.

As individuals, we tend to make these comparisons automatically, and much of the time we don't actually realize that we're doing it. Often, when trying to improve a skill, an individual might make *upward comparisons* to see how far they have to go before attaining their next goal; *downward comparisons* tend to be made when they are lacking in confidence, and perhaps feeling low, in order to make them feel better about themselves.

Finally, we also look to significant others in our life to help us understand ourselves. This can occur both when they are, and are not, present, and it can happen consciously or unconsciously. One study exposed Catholic women to subliminal pictures (of either the Pope or a psychologist) and then asked them to rate themselves on levels of morality and anxiety (i.e. their self-conception). The findings showed that the devout (i.e. practising) Catholic women were more likely to conceive of themselves as less moral when exposed to a picture of the Pope (i.e. a significant person in their life) than a psychologist (i.e. not a significant person in their life). This suggests that people important to an individual do impact strongly on how they see themselves.

Key idea: Social comparison

The way in which we compare ourselves to others in order to understand our own beliefs, opinions, abilities and behaviours.

GROUP UNDERSTANDING

A final way in which we understand ourselves is through the groups to which we belong and with which we identify. This is the basis for *social identity theory*. This idea was formulated by Tajfel and Turner and suggests that part of our self-understanding is derived from our group memberships (referred to as ingroups). These groups can be chosen (e.g. belonging to a sports team, being a supporter of a sports team, belonging to a recreational group such as a chess club, being a member of a formalized group such as a trade union, or an informal group of friends) or thrust upon us (e.g. our gender, nationality, ethnicity and perhaps even our religion). The assumption of social identity theory is that people need to feel good about themselves (possess a positive self-identity), and that they will therefore draw favourable comparisons between their ingroups and the groups to which they do not belong (referred to as outgroups). Social identity theory is an important concept when we look at aggression (see Chapter 9), prejudice (see Chapter 13), and intergroup relations (see Chapter 14).

In terms of how we feel about ourselves, social identity can help to explain how an individual will feel about themselves, and how they might act. If, for example, we view ourselves as English and our football or cricket team are performing well and have just won a World Cup (forgive me for being overly optimistic – but I feel the need to bolster my social identity!), then we will feel good about ourselves because we see our ingroup as being better than outgroups; however, if our team is performing poorly (no comment) then we might not feel so good about ourselves. However, even in this latter case, it is possible to improve the way we feel about ourselves by choosing which outgroups to use as a comparison (hence we might compare ourselves with the French – assuming they were knocked out of the World Cup before us – as opposed to the Germans – who won it).

It is important, however, to draw a distinction between our social identity (gained through the groups to which we belong or don't belong) and our *personal identity*, which refers to our individual characteristics and personality traits. Our personal identity views us as a unique individual distinct from others; our social identity views us as sharing many similarities with other people who belong to the same group(s) that we do. Sometimes our personal identity will be most important to us, and at other times our social identity will be the most important. A key point of social identity theory is how the groups to which we belong can affect how we view ourselves.

Overall, it is possible to see how all three sources (self, others, groups) can play pivotal roles in how we construct our self-identity. Some of the sources we use are more reliable than others, and sometimes our construction is more explicit and conscious than at others. However, having gained this knowledge about ourselves, the question then becomes how we store it and how we use it to understand ourselves.

Self-knowledge

One way in which we can organize knowledge about ourselves in our minds is through the use of **self-schemas**. This has been shown in a number of studies. For example, in one piece of research, individuals were asked to rate themselves on certain attributes related to the dimension of independence-dependence, and then asked to rate how important these attributes were to their self-concept. Those who considered the related attributes as important in describing themselves were classified as being schematic; those who didn't were rated as being aschematic (i.e. they didn't have a self-schema for being either dependent or independent). Later, the same set of individuals was asked to judged schema-congruent traits as being true or not true of themselves. The findings suggested that schematic individuals were much quicker at making the judgements than the aschematic individuals, and more easily remembered past behaviour related to the trait. This suggests that we are more sensitive to information relevant to our self-concept in that we process it more quickly and thoroughly than information not related to our self-concept: this is referred to as the **self-reference effect**.

Key idea: Self-reference effect

This refers to the idea that an individual processes information more quickly and thoroughly when it relates to their self-concept than when it doesn't.

Our self-schemas have also been shown to be important in the way that we use them to process information about other people: because they are of great importance to ourselves, we are more likely to judge other people by them (personally I always get very frustrated if people arrive late for meetings as time-keeping is very important to me). Of course, not all of the vast number of our self-schemas will be active at any one time; the situation in which we find ourselves will tend to dictate which ones are active, and this is referred to as our *working self-concept*. This of course begs the question of how easy it is to turn on our different self-schemas, and this is still a matter of some debate. It has however been noted that there are large individual differences with respect to which self-schemas are activated by which situations.

Key idea: Self-schemas

Mental representations in the mind used to store and organize information about the self, and which in turn aid an individual to understand how they should feel, think, and behave in a given situation.

As well as holding beliefs about ourselves in the present (our 'actual' self), we also project about how we might *like* to be (our 'ideal' self) and how we think we *should* be (our 'ought' self). *Self-discrepancy theory* argues that people compare themselves using these different forms of selves, and strive to maintain a match between their 'actual' self and both their 'ideal' and 'ought' selves. Any difference between them will lead to some form of psychological distress, with greater perceived distance leading to greater distress. In terms of emotions, discrepancy between an individual's actual and ideal self (a lack of positive outcome) is predicted to lead to feelings such as disappointment and sadness, whereas discrepancy between actual and ought selves (the presence of negative outcomes) is more likely to lead to feelings of fear, anger or nervousness, dependent on the exact context.

Having looked at the different ways in which we try to determine who we are, psychologists have also investigated ways in which people determine how they feel about themselves; that is, whether we regard our self-concept positively or negatively.

Self-esteem

Self-esteem refers to an individual's subjective evaluation of themselves in terms of positivity or negativity. How an individual feels about themselves can have a profound effect on how they function psychologically. Self-esteem can also be used as a measure of how an individual feels they are doing in the eyes of others. As with other aspects of the self, it can vary across time and context.

Key idea: Self-esteem

Self-esteem refers to an individual's subjective assessment of themselves in terms of their own qualities. It is seen as a vital component in the psychological well-being of a person.

The development of self-esteem is thought to originate to some extent from the parenting style to which an individual is subjected as a child. An authoritative parenting style, which is characterized by showing strict control over the child whilst being warm and supportive, is more likely to lead to higher levels of self-esteem than children subjected to either an authoritarian (strict control but lacking in support) or permissive (lacking in control but more supportive) parenting style.

'Arguably, the most important thing in one's life is the self. Given the importance of evaluative responding, it is no wonder then that the evaluation of self, or self-esteem, is a topic that has occupied social psychologists almost from the beginning of the discipline in its present form ...'
(Abraham Tesser, 2001, p. 479)

Self-esteem can be measured either explicitly through the use of questionnaires, or implicitly, through response time measures (see Spotlight below). Additionally it has been proposed that while measures, such as that of Rosenberg, assess general levels of self-esteem of an individual (*trait self-esteem*), it may also vary according to the situation in which an individual finds themselves (*state self-esteem*). However, there are individual differences in the stability of self-esteem, with instability tending to indicate greater levels of anger and hostility in response to criticism, and an increased likelihood of depression in response to the general vagaries of life.

Spotlight: Measuring self-esteem

Explicit measurement of self-esteem typically uses questionnaires, such as the one developed by Rosenberg (1965) which includes items such as:

▶ I feel that I have a number of good qualities.
▶ At times I feel that I am no good at all.
▶ On the whole, I am satisfied with myself.

In this case, an individual is asked to indicate whether each statement is true or false with regard to themselves, and the pattern of their answers gives an indication of their level of self-esteem. This level of measurement can be subject to a social desirability bias (see Chapter 1). Implicit measurements of self-esteem are used in an attempt to avoid such biases and can be based on tests involving measures of whether or not an individual values the letters in their name, or the speed with which they link themselves to positive adjectives.

Some research has suggested that whilst there are differences in the behaviour of people showing high and low levels of self-esteem, the developmental course of an individual can show varying levels of self-esteem at different ages. It shows signs of instability in the very young (pre-teens), more stability in the early twenties onwards, but around the age of sixty, the stability once again decreases. Overall, low self-esteem is associated with negative consequences such as mood swings, susceptibility to influence, and there is a belief that individuals with lowered self-esteem are more likely to be violent and show criminal tendencies. Individuals with higher levels of self-esteem on the other hand are generally seen as more self-confident, optimistic, emotionally stable, and more resistant to stress and depression. Overall, the perception is that high self-esteem is good and low self-esteem is bad.

However, the reality is not so simple. First, research suggests that people tend to have relative levels of self-esteem rather than absolute levels: people show higher or lower levels but rarely high or low. Secondly, research suggests there is very little truth in the belief that low self-esteem tends to lead to greater levels of violence or criminality. Finally, if anything, it is the highest levels of self-esteem that tend to be most problematic. For example, some research suggests that if levels of self-esteem are very high, whereby individuals believe that they are in some way special and superior to others (thus evidencing the trait of Narcissism), it can lead to individual instability. This, in turn, can lead to aggressive behaviour if such an individual perceives that others are threatening their identity in some way, for example through criticism: in these cases, violent outbursts are not uncommon.

The effect of culture on identity

Another factor that has been shown to have an effect on an individual's self-perception is the culture in which they grow up. Typically people from more Western cultures (individualistic cultures) identify with a more *independent self,* whereas those from East Asia, Latin America and Southern Europe (collectivistic cultures) identify more with an *interdependent self*.

The independent self is typified by individuals who think of themselves as being unique and individual in some way; they view themselves as possessing greater self-autonomy, and are perhaps defined more by their inner thoughts. On the other hand, the interdependent self is exemplified by individuals who tend to have greater links with, and more respect for, groups, such as the family or society. Overall, they tend to be more defined by their relationships with others.

With respect to the question posed at the beginning of the chapter ('Who am I?'), those evidencing an independent self typically tend to write a statement to characterize themselves as individuals (for example, I am cautious), whereas those with an interdependent self write statements that characterize themselves as part of a greater whole (for example, I am a Christian). Of course, in today's multi-cultural society, an individual may be required to hold more than one self-identity (for example a Chinese migrant living in New York), and some studies suggest that such bicultural individuals who are able to balance their different cultural identities may show improved communication and problem-solving skills.

Self-regulation

Having established how an individual's self-esteem can affect their psychological functioning, and how their culture can influence how they view themselves, research has also looked at how the self affects an individual's behaviour. Theories of *self-regulation* attempt to explain a person's behaviour in terms of their inner dynamic processes (e.g. self-awareness and self-focussing), and how their knowledge is translated into goal-setting and actual behaviour. For instance, if we feel that we are overweight and could do with shedding a few pounds, we all know how to go about losing the weight (we should eat less and exercise more), but transforming such knowledge into action is somewhat trickier.

> 'Self-regulation, broadly, is defined by setting a standard to achieve a goal, investing the necessary effort to move toward reaching the goal, and monitoring one's progress in order to shield the goal against temptation or obstacles ...'
>
> (Cortes, Kammrath, Scholer & Peetz, 2014, p. 380)

One proposed method of self-regulation suggests that an individual applies a TOTE (test-operate-test-exit) loop to their behaviour. For example, a student might reflect on their academic performance and consider whether they are working hard enough. Using the TOTE loop, they might measure how many hours a week they spend studying (test): if they conclude that the number of hours is not sufficient to produce a good academic performance, they might decide to change their daily routine (for example, by going out with their friends an hour later than usual) to incorporate an extra hour of study a day (operate). At some point in the future, they would again measure their behaviour to determine if they are now working hard enough (test); if they are, then they will maintain the new level of behaviour and pay no further attention to the issue (exit); if they are not, then further behaviour change may be planned. In essence, this idea suggests that an individual self-regulates their behaviour by monitoring it against a set of standards and modifying their behaviour to match the desired standards more closely. In order to monitor their behaviour, an individual initially relies on self-awareness.

Self-awareness theory proposes that some of our behaviour is the result of one of our inner processes, namely the ability to self-focus. When we self-focus, we become the object of our own scrutiny; this can be made to occur consciously (e.g. looking at yourself in a mirror, or watching a video-recording of yourself) or may happen unconsciously as a product of the situation in which we find ourselves (for example, you are in the presence of a number of people who you perceive to be very different to yourself).

By scrutinizing ourselves, we start to assess (and become self-aware of) how we are performing against an appropriate set of norms for a given behaviour (for example, our job, as a partner in a relationship, or as a parent). If the assessment is a negative one, which is to say that you realize that you are not measuring up to the expected behaviour, then unpleasant feelings are likely to arise. In order to alleviate these unpleasant feelings, you will be motivated to change your behaviour in some way. Of course, this behaviour change is contingent on an individual believing that they are capable of producing the required behaviour. Self-awareness and self-focus contribute to the test phases of the TOTE loop.

Having decided to self-focus on a particular behaviour, the question arises as to which standards should be used to test the behaviour against. There are a number of sources that might set such a standard, for example:

1 The individual – it may be a form of personal goal.

2 Others – friends, loved ones or even a boss.

3 An institution – e.g. university or company requirements.

4 Society – rules to which an individual must adhere.

These standards help an individual to determine the goal of the 'operate' phase of the TOTE loop.

The question of how (and if) an individual attains their goal behaviour is a tricky one. It might typically be thought of as requiring 'willpower' or the like, and people are fond of referring to the amount of willpower they have ('Oh, I can't resist another biscuit – I have so little willpower). Some research does suggest that an individual has limited resources to use in order to effect behaviour change. Thus when an individual tries to regulate a given behaviour, they only have a limited ability to regulate any other behaviour. However, it is difficult to know whether failure to change one's behaviour is due to limited resources, or whether it might be due to a lack of self-monitoring. There is evidence to suggest that increasing an individual's self-monitoring (for example, monitoring one's study hours each day) can facilitate reaching a goal.

Overall, self-regulation accounts quite well for how an individual behaves, and therefore it appears that self-regulation is a good thing. Certainly research findings generally suggest that when an individual freely sets their own goals, they are more likely to be successfully achieved than when they feel pressured to set a goal, or when another person sets goals for them. However, in some situations, too much of a good thing can become a bad thing. Too much self-focussing can lead to an over-analysis of our behaviour, and if such behaviour is already well-learned, such as driving a car, it can lead to a disruption in our behaviour and a decline in performance (please don't put this idea to the test on a busy road!).

Summary

The chapter identified the ways in which we use ourselves, other individuals and groups to create our notion of self and how we use this to understand who we are. It showed how we organize information about ourselves, how this information may determine the way we behave at any given moment, and how the culture in which we grow up can affect our self-identity. It also looked at how we evaluate ourselves subjectively and introduced the concept of self-esteem, discussing how this may affect our outlook on life. The chapter concluded by introducing the concept of self-regulation and showed how this might account for our behaviour.

Food for thought

The next time that you try to change your behaviour in some way, whether to go on a diet, or to become more punctual, it is worth considering, in light of the content of the chapter, exactly how your self will facilitate, and respond to, such a change. This may help you to be more successful, or it may prompt you to rethink your plans.

Dig deeper

Baumeister, R. F. (Ed.) (1999). *The Self in Social Psychology. Key Readings in Social Psychology*. Psychology Press.

Carver, C. S. & Scheier, M. F. (2001). *On the Self-regulation of Behaviour*. Cambridge University Press.

Swann, W. B., Chang-Schneider, C. & Larsen McClarty, K. (2007). 'Do people's self-views matter? Self-concept and self-esteem in everyday life'. *American Psychologist*, **62**, 84–94.

Vohs, K. D. & Baumeister, R. F. (Eds.) (2013). *Handbook of Self-Regulation*. Second Edition. Guilford Press.

Zeigler-Hill, V. (Ed.) (2013). *Self-Esteem. Current issues in Social Psychology*. Psychology Press.

Fact-check

1 At approximately what age do we first become self-aware?
 a At birth
 b Between 0–6 months old
 c Between 6–12 months old
 d Between 12–18 months old

2 Which of the following is not a valid source for gathering information about our self?
 a Our self
 b Other people
 c Other groups
 d They are all valid sources
 e None of them are valid sources

3 Which of the following is not a problem with using introspection to understand our self?
 a We don't process enough information
 b We underestimate the positive facets of our character
 c We strive to think about bad past experiences
 d They are all problems with introspection
 e None of them are problems with introspection

4 Understanding oneself through the observation of one's own behaviour is referred to as:
 a Introspection
 b Self-perception
 c Self-confirmation
 d Self-comparison

5 Contrasting another person's performance on a task with our own performance on the same task, in order to understand our own ability, is referred to as:
 a Social comparison
 b Self-comparison
 c Social perception
 d Social identity

6 How we define ourselves in terms of our personality characteristics and traits is referred to as our:
- **a** Comparative identity
- **b** Social identity
- **c** Personal identity
- **d** None of the above

7 An individual will process information more quickly when it is related to their self-concept than when it is not. This is referred to as the:
- **a** Self-schema effect
- **b** Self-discrepancy outcome
- **c** Self-reference effect
- **d** Working self-concept

8 Higher levels of self-esteem tend to be shown by children who are subjected to which one of the following styles of parenting?
- **a** Laissez-faire
- **b** Permissive
- **c** Authoritarian
- **d** Authoritative

9 With regards to self-esteem, which of the following statements is not true?
- **a** Self-esteem is most stable in the early teens
- **b** Low self-esteem is more likely to be linked with violent outbursts and aggressive behaviour
- **c** Implicit measures of self-esteem are more prone to a social desirability bias
- **d** Actually, they are all true
- **e** Actually, none of them are true

10 Which of the following is not a valid source for producing a desired standard to use when self-regulating one's behaviour?
- **a** Oneself
- **b** Trusted others
- **c** Societal norms
- **d** Actually they are all valid sources
- **e** Actually none of them are valid sources

3

Attributions

This chapter tackles the problem of how we make sense of the actions of others. For example, imagine it is your first day at university (or in a new job) and as you are walking down the corridor, you see one of your lecturers (or a colleague) walking down the corridor towards you. As they pass you, they smile at you, say 'Good morning', and carry on their way. 'Hmmm …' you might think, 'They seem to be a friendly person'. However, imagine that you are serving on a jury, and you are sitting in court. The defendant walks into the witness box, and before he starts to answer any question, he smiles at the jury. 'Hmmm …' you think, 'That seems a little arrogant and over-confident'. Now, whether or not your judgements might be correct is the topic of another chapter (see Chapter 4 on social cognition). However, *why* and *how* you make these judgements about others – how you attribute meaning to their behaviour – is what we will deal with here.

Heider's (1958) naïve scientist theory

As human beings, we have a need for understanding, a desire to make sense of things. If we can create a sense of order in our environment, then this gives us a greater confidence in our surroundings, and allows us to impose control on our environment. To do this, as we are social animals, we need to understand people, whether they are strangers, acquaintances, friends, or loved ones.

For example, imagine that your old neighbours move out and new ones move in. You will seek to understand them, even if you don't have the opportunity to talk to them immediately. You will start to attribute traits and motives to them immediately based on what you see and hear. Similarly, if you start a new job, or a new university course, you will come into contact with new people and will immediately start to try to understand them.

Fritz Heider was a key figure in the area of **attribution** theory (some even claim he was the 'founding father'). He believed that, as individuals, people formulate reasons for human behaviour, in much the same way that scientists formulate theories about how and why things work (whether it be the universe or a new chemical compound).

Key idea: Attribution

The way in which a person assigns a cause to the behaviour of another, or to themselves.

To this end, Heider referred to people as 'naïve scientists'. His theory was based on three main ideas:

1 As an individual, we know that our own behaviour has a reason, therefore it likely follows that other people's behaviour does too. Therefore it is not unreasonable to try to discover these reasons. Heider and a colleague demonstrated this notion with a simple experiment where they showed

participants a film of three moving geometric shapes (a large and small triangle and a disc) and asked them to describe what was happening. Instead of talking in terms of geometry, speed and distance, the majority of participants attributed human characteristics and motive to each shape; they were given personality and reasons for their actions (movements), even though there was none.

2 Individuals attempt to find stable traits in others that can account for the behaviour that they observe. This helps to bring predictability to a potentially unstable situation, and with this predictability comes control.

3 In attempting to find reasons for the behaviour of others, we look for both 'personal' and 'environmental' causes – what social psychologists call **internal attributions** or 'dispositions', and **external attributions** or 'situational'.

Key idea: Internal attributions and external attributions

An internal attribution is a judgement of another's behaviours (or our own) based on a perceived internal cause, such as a motive or personality trait.

An external attribution is a judgement of another's behaviour (or our own) based on a perceived 'environmental' cause outside of the person's control.

According to Heider, it is difficult to see 'internal' causes for behaviour, and we should only look for these if there are no 'overt' explanations for the behaviour of another. However, humans tend to be biased towards internal attributions, even when external causes are present; we have a flawed tendency to attribute the behaviour of another to stable internal dispositions. So, if a person walks past us in a corridor without saying 'hello', we are more likely to consider that they have a rude 'disposition' rather than seeking alternative 'situational' explanations (e.g. they are having a bad day, or their eyesight is terrible and they need new glasses).

Some research suggests that we make such judgements on the
basis of very little information indeed. For example, one study
asked individuals to talk to other individuals on the phone,
and then describe the people that they had talked to. The
results showed that the participants made judgements about
the stranger's personality trait just based on hearing their voice.
Imagine that you are talking to a person on the phone for the
very first time (whether it be a customer for your business, or a
person on a sales help line) – it is likely that by the time you put
the phone down, you will have started to 'form a picture' (make
attributions) of that person.

Heider laid many of the foundations of modern attribution
theory on which more formal theories of attribution have
sought to build. We will now look in more depth at two such
theories.

Jones and Davis (1965) theory of correspondent inference

One of the first theories to be proposed was by Jones and Davis
(1965) who wanted to show how people make a connection
between an intentional overt action and an internal trait; how
an individual infers that a deliberate action by another person
corresponds to an underlying disposition. For example, if a
lecturer is always shouting at students in seminars, or a co-
worker is always shouting at his colleagues (we assume that
the lecturer or co-worker chooses to perform this behaviour),
then we are likely to infer that they have an 'angry' disposition.
Again we do this because we like things to be neat and tidy, and
as simple as possible – it's easier to 'pigeonhole' somebody ('He
is an angry person') than to deal with the reality that things

might be a bit more complex. It's easier to deal with someone if we 'know' what they are like. It gives us the control over our world to which Heider was referring.

Key idea: Correspondent inference theory

The idea that an overt action (behaviour) of another person is causally related to an internal disposition that they possess.

According to Jones and Davis' theory, we attempt to link an action to a specific internal cause, and to make these **correspondent inferences**, we use a number of sources of information:

1 IS THE BEHAVIOUR FREELY CHOSEN?

If a person's behaviour appears to be 'freely chosen', then it is more likely to correspond to an underlying disposition. For example, if we see Celia in the park playing football in the rain, we are more likely to judge that she likes football, as we assume that very few people would choose to play in the rain without such a liking. However, if we judge that a person's actions are due to an external source, then we are less likely to infer that the behaviour corresponds to a disposition. For example, if we see Celia walking a dog in the rain, but we know that her Mum insists that she take her turn to walk the dog, we wouldn't necessarily infer that Celia is a dog-lover, or someone who likes to walk pets in the rain. Of course, we won't always know whether an action is freely chosen or not.

2 DOES THE BEHAVIOUR LEAD TO A SPECIFIC EFFECT?

If a person's behaviour has a very unique outcome (a non-common effect), as opposed to a range of possible consequences, then we are more likely to infer an internal disposition for that behaviour. For example, if a person walks into a bank with a gun drawn, then there are likely to be very few outcomes from that behaviour (and most involving a violent outcome), and therefore we are likely to infer that the person has a violent, or criminal, disposition. However, if a person walks into a supermarket with a ten-pound note in their hand, there are a whole range of reasons for this behaviour, and therefore we are less likely to make an internal attribution.

3 IS THE BEHAVIOUR SOCIALLY DESIRABLE OR NOT SOCIALLY DESIRABLE?

If a person's behaviour is deemed to be socially desirable, then it tells us little about their internal disposition as their actions are likely to be driven by societal norms. For example, if we see a person going into a polling station to vote on general election day, then we wouldn't necessarily draw any inferences about their behaviour as voting is generally seen as the right thing that we should all do. However, if we saw the same person go into the polling station and deliberately 'spoil' their ballot paper, then as this behaviour is fairly unusual and not necessarily socially desirable, we are more likely to attribute their behaviour to an internal disposition, for example perhaps they have 'anarchic' tendencies.

'Given an inference that assigns an attribute to account for an act, the correspondence of that inference increases as the judged value of that attribute departs from the judge's conception of the average person's standing.'
(Jones & Harris, 1967, p. 2)

Other sources of information have also been put forward as being influential in leading to people making correspondent inferences, and these include behaviour that is high in *hedonic relevance* (the person's behaviour has important consequences for us as an individual) and behaviour that seems to be 'out-of-role' (the person's behaviour is not typical for the role that we perceive them in e.g. nurse, policeman, banker).

Whilst a number of studies have provided evidence to support aspects of this theory (see Case study below), it has tended to wane in popularity due to a number of limitations. For example, it suggests that inferences are made on the assumption of intentionality (i.e. the behaviour of the individual being observed was carried out deliberately), but there are cases where unintentional behaviours (e.g. carelessness) can lead to definite inferences. Also, the theory tends to concentrate a little too much on internal dispositions being the cause of behaviour, as opposed to external causes. The next theory of attribution specifically aims to address such problems.

Case study: The attribution of attitudes

Jones & Harris (1967) conducted an experiment to 'attempt to determine if people can make valid judgements of another's personality and attitudes on the basis of very limited information' (p. 4). Participants were asked to read a 200-word essay, allegedly written by a student regarding their views on Fidel Castro (remember this was the 1960s when Castro's Cuba was seen as undesirable by much of the western world). There were four conditions in the experiment – the essay was either 'for' or 'against' Castro, and the writer was either given a free choice of which view to take, or forced to write a specific viewpoint. Having read the essay, participants were asked to make a number of judgements about the writer's personality and dispositions. The crucial issue was when participants were asked a number of questions about the writer's attitude to Castro.

In both conditions where the essay was 'anti-Castro', participants judged the writer as having negative attitudes towards Castro. In the pro-Castro condition, where the writer was given a choice of which view to take, the participants judged the writer as holding 'pro-Castro' attitudes, in line with correspondent inference theory. However, surprisingly, in the pro-Castro condition, where the writer was forced to write the pro-Castro essay, participants also judged the writer as holding pro-Castro attitudes, thus showing that participants were making attributions based on internal dispositions, even though there were external 'situational' causes for the writer's behaviour.

Kelley's (1967) co-variation model

According to Kelley's **co-variation model,** in order to attribute a cause to an observed behaviour, people look for which factors co-vary most closely with an observed behaviour; they look to see if the suspected cause of the behaviour is always present when the behaviour is present and is absent when the behaviour is absent. Whilst behaviour could have multiple causes, the cause which co-varies (correlates) the closest with the behaviour is more likely to be attributed as the reason for the behaviour. We are acting like rational thinkers and making objective observations about behaviour in order to arrive at a conclusion for why the behaviour occurred (think back to the idea of Heider's naïve scientists).

Key idea: Co-variation model

An attempt to show how, using three sources of information, people attribute the cause of an individual's target behaviour with the factor that co-varies most closely with the behaviour.

The co-variation model suggests that, in order to determine whether the cause of the behaviour should be attributed to internal (dispositions) or external (situational) factors, people use three types of information:

1 **Consistency information:** Does the behaviour always occur in the presence of the potential cause (high consistency) or only sometimes (low consistency)?

2 **Distinctiveness information:** Is the behaviour only seen when the potential cause is present (high distinctiveness) or is it seen at any other times too (low distinctiveness)?

3 **Consensus information:** Does everyone carry out the behaviour in the presence of the potential cause (high consensus) or is it only the target individual who exhibits this behaviour (low consensus)?

For example, we notice that whenever Emily watches the film *Casablanca*, she always cries at the end. As keen observers of human nature, we want to understand why Emily does this. According to Kelley's co-variation model, we need to ask three questions. First, does Emily always cry at the end of *Casablanca* (high consistency) or only sometimes (low consistency)? Second, does Emily only cry at the end of *Casablanca* (high distinctiveness) or does she cry at the end of lots of other films too (low distinctiveness)? Finally, does everyone cry at the end of *Casablanca* (high consensus), or is it mainly Emily who does this (low consensus)?

If all three pieces of information are at the 'high' end, then we attribute Emily's crying as being due to her watching *Casablanca* (an external cause). However, if the consistency information is high, but the distinctiveness and consensus information are 'low', then we are more likely to attribute Emily's behaviour to the fact that she is a very sentimental person (an internal cause). Other combinations of the eight possible outcomes from the three pieces of information can lead to slightly modified attributions for the cause of the behaviour (see Table 4.1)

Kelley's model certainly seems to present a clear way to make an attribution for an individual's action, providing we have all of the necessary information to hand and enough time to process the data in order to arrive at our rational conclusion; and there is evidence to support the claims made by the model. However, to get all of the information needed for an attribution could require multiple observations – for example, we would need to observe not only Emily watching *Casablanca* (several times) and watching a number of other films too, but we would also

Table 4.1: The effect of consistency, distinctiveness and consensus on attributions.

Consistency	Distinctiveness	Consensus	Attribution
High	High	High	Emily's behaviour can be attributed to an external cause (i.e. the film *Casablanca*)
High	Low	Low	Emily's behaviour can be attributed to an internal cause (e.g. Emily is highly sentimental)
High	High	Low	Emily's behaviour can be attributed to a combination of the film *Casablanca* and an aspect of her personality/the situation
Low	High	Low	Emily's behaviour can be attributed to something about the experience of watching *Casablanca*.

need to observe many other people watching *Casablanca*. Kelley did seem to acknowledge that people often make attributions quickly and with less than the ideal amount of information, so he proposed the idea of 'causal schema' whereby people, based on their previous experiences, are able to 'fill in' the missing knowledge that they need.

However, this is not the only shortcoming of the model. For example, research has shown that when making attributions, whilst they tend to use consistency and distinctiveness information, people tend to underuse consensus information. Similarly, just because they have access to all three types of information will not mean that it will all be used. Finally, if we did make attributions based on co-variations (correlations) then we would be violating one of the basic scientific principles, namely correlations are not causes.

The overall assumptions of both Kelley's model and Jones and Davis' model is that people are rational observers able to make sometimes quite complex computations in order to arrive at a logical conclusion (and whilst some people are, most people aren't); but in reality we know that people take short-cuts to make decisions (see Chapter 4), and we also know that they can make biased judgements. Indeed, a number of biases have been put forward to account for why the attributions that we make are not always the correct ones, and three common ones are covered below.

Biases in attributions

1 THE FUNDAMENTAL ATTRIBUTION ERROR

When we observe the behaviour of an individual, we have a tendency to attribute it to an internal (dispositional) cause as opposed to an external (situational) cause – despite the fact that there might be clear evidence of an external cause for the behaviour (see Case study above: the writers of the pro-Castro piece in the 'forced choice' condition were judged to be 'pro-Castro' in their beliefs (internal causation) despite there being an external reason for their beliefs i.e. they were told to write a pro-Castro piece).

It is thought that the reason for this bias is due to perceptual salience; that is, the most striking thing about a situation is the person in it – therefore an internal attribution becomes a much easier explanation for the behaviour. People generally tend to take the easy option, especially when the alternative would require a more difficult and complex thought process to reach a judgement. Additionally, it might not always be easy to spot when subtle external forces are in operation. Until relatively recently, this bias was thought to be universal, although now it is believed that culture may play a part, with western (individualistic) cultures more likely to fall foul of the bias than eastern (collectivistic) cultures.

2 ACTOR-OBSERVER EFFECT

This bias suggests that we have a tendency to attribute the behaviour of another individual to internal causes, but when we display similar behaviour ourselves then we are more likely to attribute it to an external cause. For example, if we see a person shouting at another, then we attribute their behaviour as being indicative of an aggressive individual; however, if we shout at another person, we are likely to attribute the cause of our behaviour being due to the stressful situation in which we found ourselves.

There maybe two explanations for this effect. First, when attributing behaviour to another we focus on them as being the most important part of the scene; our focus is drawn to the person and not the background. However, when we come to explain our own behaviour, we don't normally picture ourselves as part of the scene in which our behaviour unfolds and therefore we only see the 'background'; thus we attribute our behaviour to the situation. The second explanation suggests that as we have a wealth of information about how we act in many different situations, we can understand how our actions might be influenced by our environment. However, when we look at the behaviour of another, we only have a limited amount of information about them, and hence we are more likely to assume that their actions are due to their personality (an internal cause).

3 SELF-SERVING BIASES

Sometimes when we make attributions about our own behaviour, we do it in a way so as to feel good about ourselves (or to avoid feeling bad), and this may mean we distort reality somewhat. If we have done something well, we attribute it to an internal cause (e.g. I scored the goal because I am a good footballer), but if something has gone wrong, then we attribute it to external sources (e.g. I missed the goal because the uneven pitch caused me to lose my footing at the crucial moment – and not because I am a bad footballer).

We do this for attributions about group behaviour too – if the group we belong to does something good, then it is due to something about the group (e.g. if I am the prime minister, I assume that our latest policy was such a success due to the brilliant minds in 'the cabinet'); but if the group does something wrong, then external factors are to blame (e.g. the latest policy was a failure because of unforeseeable changes in Europe).

Spotlight: Practical applications of attributions

Whilst attribution theory can seem quite a dry and complex topic, there are a number of very practical applications for which it can be used. At the very least, if we understand the processes we use to make judgements about others (and ourselves), and the biases that we may fall foul of, then it may help us to be more understanding of the points of view of others. In a more practical setting, such as mental health, where some symptoms of depression and schizophrenia relate to the attributions patients make about themselves (e.g. 'everything I do goes wrong') and others (e.g. 'everyone is talking about me and wants to cause me harm'), knowledge of this subject can allow practitioners to correct faulty causal attributions of their patients to facilitate the road to recovery. Similarly, in negotiations between hostile factions (e.g. Arabs and Israelis), understanding cultural differences in attributions may help to facilitate the brokerage of peace.

Summary

This chapter has provided an introduction to the topic of attributions. It has looked at why we have a need to understand the actions of others and how we go about reaching this understanding. Starting with Heider, and working through the two influential, but perhaps flawed, theories of Jones and Davis (1965) and Kelley (1967), we have begun to understand how people might assign causes to the behaviour of others (and groups) and themselves. Several biases in attribution have also been highlighted to explain why some of our judgements of others may not be as objective and accurate as we might like. However, this is just the beginning and there is much more to discover in the realm of attributions.

Food for thought

The next time you observe someone and reach a decision about them (perhaps when you meet a fellow student for the first time, or when you watch an interview with a celebrity on the television), take ten minutes later in the day to try to understand why you made the attributions about them that you did (e.g. did you think they were 'genuine' or perhaps 'arrogant'). Did you use all of the information available to you, or just some of it? How could the information presented in this chapter have helped you to reach a different attribution?

Dig deeper

Choi, I., Nisbett, R. E. & Norenzayan, A. (1999). 'Causal attribution across cultures: Variation and universality'. *Psychological Bulletin*, **125(1)**, 47–63.

Fincham, F. D. (2002). 'Attributions in close relationships: From Balkanization to integration'. In Fletcher, G. & Clark, M.S. (Eds.) (2002). *Blackwell Handbook of Social Psychology: Interpersonal processes*. Wiley-Blackwell.

Forsterling, F. (2001). *Attribution: An Introduction to Theories, Research and Applications*. Psychology Press

Hewstone, M. (1989). *Causal Attribution: From Cognitive Processes to Collective Beliefs*. Oxford: Blackwell.

Fact-check

1 Which of the following is not an idea on which Heider based his naïve scientist approach to why people make attributions?

   a If our behaviour has a reason behind it, then another individual's behaviour must also have a cause

   b We look for both internal and external causes for another's behaviour

   c We look for stable traits in others in order to bring predictability to our world

   d We have an innate need to understand scientifically the behaviour of others

2 'Beth is happy person because she is always smiling' is what type of attribution?

   a A defining attribution

   b An internal attribution

   c An external attribution

   d A co-varying attribution

3 Which of the following is not a source of information used by people according to correspondent inference theory?

   a Does the behaviour always occur in a given situation?

   b Is the behaviour freely chosen?

   c Is the behaviour socially desirable?

   d Does the behaviour lead to a specific effect?

4 In the Jones & Harris (1967) study looking at participants' judgements of the writer's attitudes regarding Fidel Castro, the results in which of the four conditions seemed to violate social inference theory?

   a For Castro; Free choice

   b For Castro; Forced choice

   c Against Castro; Free choice

   d Against Castro; Forced Choice

5 Which of the following is not a source of information used in Kelley's model to attribute a cause to a behaviour?
   a Distinctiveness
   b Consensus
   c Representativeness
   d Consistency

6 According to Kelley's co-variation model, if we observe a behaviour by another individual that only, and always, occurs in the presence of an object, then this behaviour is high in:
   a Distinctiveness
   b Representativeness
   c Consensus
   d Consistency

7 The co-variation model claims that if the information we have about another's behaviour is high in consistency, consensus and distinctiveness, then the cause of the behaviour is probably due to:
   a The situation in which the individual finds themselves
   b The individual's personality
   c A combination of the individual's situation and personality
   d None of the above

8 Which bias claims that we tend to make an attribution that makes us feel good about ourselves?
   a Fundamental attribution error
   b Actor-observer effect
   c Self-serving bias
   d The correspondence bias

9 Jane decides that her fellow teacher Geoff is an angry person because he shouts a lot, but when she shouts a lot, she claims it is because of her unruly students. This attribution bias is referred to as:
   a Fundamental attribution error
   b Actor-observer effect
   c Self-serving bias
   d The correspondence bias

10 In his time at Chess club, Peter has met a fellow player called Norman. Peter has noticed that in discussion about previous famous chess players, Norman always says he likes Bobby Fischer (despite everyone else saying that they dislike Fischer), both when he is at Chess club and at other places too, and he doesn't seem to have any other favourite chess players. Which of the following 'chess' attributions can we make about Norman?

   a None with any degree of certainty

   b Norman has a 'chess' personality

   c Norman only likes Bobby Fischer when in a 'chess environment'

   d Whether Norman likes Bobby Fischer is dependent on both his personality and the situation that he finds himself in.

Social cognition

We come into contact with many thousands of people, objects and situations in our lifetime, and, to our credit, we deal with most of them quite successfully. We make decisions about what is important for us to pay attention to, and what we can safely ignore. The topic of social cognition looks at how we do this, and why occasionally we might not use the information optimally.

When presented with information, whether it is in the form of meeting a person for the first time, or finding ourselves in a novel situation, such as attending a club or society, there are two main ways that we process it – quickly or slowly. The quick method tends to use minimal effort, 'rules of thumbs' (referred to as heuristics – see later in this chapter), and sometimes unconscious (automatic) processes to deal with the information as rapidly and as efficiently as possible. When people do this, the term **cognitive miser** can be applied: our time is precious to us and we don't want to spend more time than necessary on any given problem, especially if we have a limited cognitive capacity (for whatever reason). Decisions reached by 'cognitive misers' tend to be 'good enough' for most of the time. They are prone to biases in their thinking and decision making.

Key idea: Cognitive miser

An individual who employs a short-cut to make a decision due to a limited processing capacity.

The slow method is used when we decide that the situation or person with which we are confronted merits a more careful, logical and systematic analysis to ensure that any decisions we make are good ones. When people do this, the term **naïve scientist** can be applied (see also Chapter 3): we feel that we will gain the most from a more controlled and conscious (intentional) processing of the facts before making a decision. The assumption is made that such an individual is a rational decision maker with ample time and motivation to consider all of the facts of any situation they encounter, allowing them to reach a considered conclusion. They are less likely to be prone to biases in their thinking.

Key idea: Naïve scientist

An individual who employs a careful, logical and systematic approach when making a decision.

If presented with the same 'facts' about a person, the cognitive miser and naïve scientist could reach two different conclusions. The cognitive miser is more likely to engage in stereotyping (see Spotlight below) and utilize heuristics (see section on cognitive heuristics below), whereas the naive scientist is more likely to carefully engage with the facts of the situation to reach a more considered conclusion.

Regardless of the type of processing, people have the goal of understanding their environment, and to do this, they engage in social categorization.

Social categorization

In order to make sense of our surroundings and of other people, we attempt to understand them by trying to figure out the things to which they are similar (the categories to which they belong) and dissimilar. This can apply to objects, attitudes, opinions, concepts, people and events, and it is referred to as categorization.

Spotlight: Cognitive misers vs. naïve scientists

When driving along a road, if they see a car in front of them engage in some risky manoeuvring, a cognitive miser may make the assumption that the driver is a man; if they get stuck behind a slow driver, they may assume that the driver is elderly; if they see a car trying to park less than successfully, they may assume that the driver is a woman. These are common stereotypes of drivers. Naïve scientists (assuming they are a passenger and not a driver, thus giving them more time and cognitive capacity to process information) may identify other possible causes for the behaviour, such as the driver is unfamiliar with the road, and hence they may reach a different conclusion about the identity of the driver.

The way in which we define a category does not have a precise boundary, but instead is a little more 'fuzzy'. We think of things in terms of being more or less typical of a category. For example, if we take the category 'Pet', then a dog is more typical and a snake is less typical, but both can fall under the category of 'Pet'. The more prototypical something is of a category, the quicker we are to categorize it, and thus the more representative it is of that category.

Key idea: Social categorization

The act of classifying things, such as objects or people, as belonging to specific groups (or categories).

We are more likely to bring a category member to mind if it is more prototypical of the category (see Spotlight below). However, this can sometimes lead to an error in our thought processes.

Spotlight: Exploring prototypicality

For the following categories, write down the first three things that come into your mind:

1 Type of Fruit
2 Type of Transport
3 Type of Sport

It is likely that your answers include apple, banana, oranges (prototypes), rather than kiwi fruit, lychee or date; train, car, plane rather than balloon, hovercraft or cable car; football, tennis, cricket, rather than sumo wrestling, lacrosse or fencing. Of course, your personal circumstances may affect your categorization process, therefore if you are a lychee-loving sumo wrestler, then your answers to the exercise above may not be typical.

The way in which the content of categories is created is usually by some form of social learning (e.g. we are taught categories at school, by our parents or other role models) or exposure (e.g. we learn first-hand), but there is a danger that this can lead to stereotyping – the prototypes can become stereotypes. In many cases this won't be too much of a problem: for example, if someone says they are a pet lover, you will likely make the assumption that they own a cat or a dog. However, negative stereotyping is all too common, one type of which is called an **illusory correlation**.

An illusory correlation claims that two variables are related to one another even though there is no link. An example of this would be where people believe that members of certain races or social groupings are more likely to commit a crime despite no real evidence existing to support this notion.

A typical experiment to highlight the illusory correlation goes as follows: information is given to participants about two groups: group A is the majority and group B is the minority (if it helps, think of group A as representing males and group B as representing females), and twice as much information is given about group A as about group B; in both groups, twice as much positive information is given compared to negative information. Although there is no link between the group and the proportion of positive or negative information provided, when participants are presented with the information about the two groups, they are more likely to attribute negative behaviours to group B. Therefore, despite there being no real difference between the two groups, we are more likely to attribute a link in one group (an illusory correlation), but not the other, where no link actually exists.

Key idea: Illusory correlation

The assumption that two things are linked when in fact no such link exists.

'Illusory correlation refers to an erroneous inference a person makes about the relationship between two categories of events.'
(Hamilton & Gifford, 1976, p. 406)

So, in the example above, we know little information about the members of group B, but there is distinctiveness about the negative information; for group A, the same amount of negative information exists but it is almost diluted by the amount of other positive information. The negative information is seen as more representative of group B than it is of group A.

WHY DO WE CATEGORIZE?

It might be asked that if categorization can be bad, then why do we categorize? The short answer is that there are more good reasons to categorize than there are bad reasons, for example:

▶ It saves us time and cognitive processing in as much as it frees up cognitive resources for more important tasks.

▶ It makes things clearer/simpler and focuses our perception of the world.

▶ It gives us meaning and understanding.

▶ It helps us to make predictions about things (e.g. objects and social behaviour).

▶ It can help us to understand ourselves in relation to others.

WHEN DO WE CATEGORIZE?

Typically we categorize for many of the same reasons outlined above; that is, when time and cognitive load are limited, and when we need a rapid and straightforward impression of something. However, categorization can sometimes be invoked unconsciously by the features of something that we come across first (temporal primacy), when there are obvious differences between things or people (perceptual salience) and when some categories, such as race and gender, are so common (chronic accessibility).

CONSEQUENCES OF CATEGORIZATION

When we categorize, it can lead to a biased perception of information whereby we rely on certain stereotype-consistent information (see Spotlight below). One study found that if participants were told that a woman was a librarian then they were more likely to recall that she wore glasses; however, if they were told that she was a waitress then they were more likely to recall that she was drinking beer. Categorization can influence both our perception and what we remember, leading us to evaluate potentially the same information differently. It is not a large leap to see how social categorization can lead to prejudice (see Chapter 13).

Spotlight: Stereotyping

If you are invited to a party and told that you will meet a primary school teacher, you will be making assumptions about them before you have even been introduced. This is referred to as stereotyping, and will involve drawing on prototypes from categories. For example, you will likely assume that they will be female and quite young. Similarly, if you were told that you will be introduced to an engineer, you might assume you will meet a middle-aged man, who is quite practical.

Making such judgements, which are made almost without thinking, will in all likelihood allow you to deal with the situation more efficiently when it happens. However, there will be times when you are in for a shock as these types of short-cut can let you down.

If we should find ourselves categorized as part of a group to which a negative stereotype has been attached, then in all likelihood our performance at a task may be affected; this is referred to as a 'stereotype threat'. The reason for our poorer performance may simply be that we are worried about conforming to the negative stereotype. For example, it is an oft-cited 'fact' that girls are not as good at maths as boys, or that African-Americans are less intelligent than white Americans. In the latter case, it may be possible to induce the stereotype threat simply by asking a candidate to state their race at the beginning of a test. Research has certainly shown that if a person is made aware of a negative stereotype of the group to which they belong, it is more likely that their subsequent performance on a task will be impaired.

Cognitive heuristics

Given that most of the time we act as 'cognitive misers', we tend to make speedy and automatic (intuitive) decisions, thus engaging in non-systematic processing. We find that we can make adequate judgements about people and situations without spending a vast amount of time and effort: of course, these judgements may not be the best that we can make (because they can result in biased decisions and errors in judgements at times), but generally they will suffice and we are happy enough with this state of affairs. In summary, people have a tendency to reduce complex situations to simple ones by using 'rules of thumb' or heuristics. There are a number of common heuristics that we use.

THE REPRESENTATIVENESS HEURISTIC

This process involves using 'prototypical features' to classify a person or a situation. For example, if you walk in to a classroom or a lecture hall, and there is someone standing at the front, then you will assume that this person is the teacher or lecturer.

Case study: Daniel Kahneman and Amos Tversky

Daniel Kahneman and Amos Tversky (1972) are two researchers synonymous with cognitive biases and heuristics. In one experiment, they gave the following description of a man called 'Thomas' to their participants: 'short, slim and a lover of poetry'. They then asked them to decide whether Thomas was an Ivy League Classics Professor or a Truck Driver. Which would you choose? If you're anything like Kahneman and Tversky's participants, you probably said 'Professor' because the description sounds more like a typical professor than a typical lorry driver. However, given that there are only a very small number of Ivy League Classic Professors, and probably many thousands of lorry drivers, statistically speaking, Thomas is more likely to be a lorry driver. However, making the choice of 'professor' is an example of the representativeness heuristic.

This heuristic is a quick and easy way to classify people and situations, although it is prone to errors. For example, *the base rate fallacy* is such an error; this is when we ignore statistical information in favour of 'representativeness'. If for example we toss a coin five times and get the sequence 'H-H-H-H-H', when asked whether the next flip will be a 'H' or a 'T', most people will, assuming the coin is fair (i.e. not a coin with two heads and no tail!), plump for a 'T' (to represent a fair coin), even though statistically speaking there is an equal probability of either a 'H' or a 'T'.

Kahneman and Tversky explained the representativeness heuristic as:

> 'A person who follows this heuristic evaluates the probability of an uncertain event, or a sample, by the degree to which it is (i) similar in essential properties to its parent population and (ii) reflects the salient features of the process by which it is generated.' (p. 431)

Key idea: Representativeness heuristic

A mental short-cut used to assign a novel event to a category based on its similarity to an existing general category.

THE AVAILABILITY HEURISTIC

This short-cut relies on the speed with which we can bring to mind some pertinent information. For example, if we see in various media outlets (e.g. television, newspapers, etc.) pictures of the latest millionaire lottery winner, we are more likely to believe that we have a better chance of winning the lottery jackpot (hence the reason that lottery organizers like winners to agree to publicity photos). The availability heuristic is all about how easy it is to think of examples of a situation or event.

Key idea: Availability heuristic

A mental short-cut which uses events that come to mind more easily as a starting point for a decision.

THE ANCHORING/ADJUSTMENT HEURISTIC

This heuristic shows us how we develop a 'standard' (which is usually quite arbitrary) upon which we base future decisions. For example, read the following statement aloud:

'There are not too many situations to which we give too much consideration.'

Now choose a number between 0 and 10 and say it out loud.

The chances are that you chose a lower number than if you hadn't read the statement above. This is due to the prevalent use of the words 'too' and 'to' (homophones for 'two' which is a low number) in the sentence. And who knows, you may even have chosen the number 'two' itself. Other studies have shown that our estimation of the chances that it will rain today can be influenced by a random spin of a number wheel (e.g. where the numbers 1 to 100 are arranged around the circumference); for example, if the wheel generates the number 76, then our estimates of rain tend to be higher than if it generates the number 24 (wherein our estimates of rain tend to be lower). Much of the time, we don't even realize we are being influenced.

Key idea: Anchoring heuristic

A mental short-cut whereby an individual uses an arbitrary starting point to reach a final conclusion

Why do we fall prey to judgemental heuristics?

A number of explanations have been put forward as to why we might unconsciously utilize these short-cuts, and thus become susceptible to possible errors of judgement. For example, with regard to the 'representativeness heuristic', it may simply be too much effort (e.g. time and thinking power) to engage in the necessary cognitive processing required to reach a good decision. We may fail to factor in the sample size (e.g. a higher sample size will give us more confidence in our decision: hence an example of one lottery winner probably shouldn't make us rush out to buy a lottery ticket) or the source of the information (which may affect the predictive value: for example, publicity generated by lottery organizers probably isn't a good source on which to base our decision to play the lottery). Overall, we probably prefer the simple solution (whereby we are being a 'cognitive miser') to the more effortful one.

We may fall prey to the 'availability heuristic' because of the ease with which we can retrieve exemplars of a category. For example, a study by Schwarz et al. (1991) asked participants to recall either 6 or 12 examples of when they had been 'assertive'. They were then asked to rate whether or not they were an assertive person. In which condition do you think that participants were most likely to rate themselves as being higher in assertiveness? If you said the '12' condition, your answer is understandable but wrong: the people in the '6' condition rated themselves as the most assertive.

Why? Well it's due to the availability heuristic. It's probably easier to think of 6 examples of your own assertive behaviour than 12, therefore participants were likely to think they were more assertive because they could bring examples of the category ('assertiveness') more easily to mind; those in the 12 condition found the task harder and therefore concluded that they can't have been that assertive if they couldn't generate sufficient examples. Thus the ease in which we can bring information to mind can cause us to fall foul of the availability heuristic.

A further reason that we may be susceptible to heuristics may be due to our personality. For example, people scoring high in a personality trait called 'need for cognition' (NFC: the degree to which a person is likely to engage voluntarily in 'effortful thought') are less susceptible to biases caused by reliance on heuristics, because they are more inclined to think harder about a situation than those scoring low on 'NFC'.

There is certainly evidence to suggest that we can be primed to think, feel or behave in a certain way without us even knowing it (see Case study below). However, it is not always the case that priming will lead to stereotype activation and its attendant behaviour, as internal mechanisms can prevent it. For example, if a person is driven to be 'fair minded', then they are much more likely to process evidence more carefully and thus avoid stereotyping. Similarly, priming people to be creative can actually disrupt stereotyping.

Case study: Behavioural responses can be influenced by the activation of schemas

A study by Bargh et al. (1996) had participants engage in a word task whereby they were given several sets of words to rearrange into a meaningful sentence. In the control condition, participants were given neutral words to rearrange, but in the experimental condition, some of the words were related to old age (e.g. 'lonely', 'wise', 'grey'). Upon completion of the word rearrangement tasks, both sets of participants were asked to take their results down the corridor to a second experimenter. Unbeknownst to the participants, they were covertly timed as to how long it took them to walk down the corridor.

The results suggested that the participants in the 'old age' condition took about a second longer to make the walk than those in the control condition. The researchers suggested that this was because the 'old age' words acted as a prime which in turn activated an 'elderly' category (or schema) within the participants' memory; in turn, this schema caused the participants to behave in an appropriately stereotypical way i.e. they walked more slowly. It should, however, be pointed out that not everyone is in agreement about the findings of this study, but they are nevertheless intriguing.

This priming effect has been found in other areas too. For example, one study showed participants a picture of a professor before they took a general knowledge test (participants in the control condition were shown no such picture). It was found that those participants shown the picture of the professor were more successful on the test than those who weren't. The researchers argued that these participants had been 'primed' for intelligence.

Can we quash stereotypes once they are activated?

Despite our best efforts, there will be times when we may feel that we are in danger of stereotyping, and this raises the question as to whether it is possible to stop them affecting our judgement. There are a number of factors that come into play here:

1 Are we actually aware of the potential stereotyping threat?

2 Do we have the cognitive capacity available to 'fight' the threat, e.g. do we have time, or are we up against a deadline?

3 Are we motivated NOT to stereotype, or don't we really care?

If the answer is 'Yes' to all three factors, then it may be possible to avoid stereotyping.

Summary

People are required to process a tremendous amount of information on a daily basis, and for the most part they are able to use this information effectively, usually in a rough and ready way by using a number of different strategies. One strategy is social categorization, and this helps us to understand our environment. However, other strategies (heuristics), whilst they may lead us to acceptable decisions most of the time, do leave us susceptible to biases and stereotyping. Studying social cognition can help us understand such processes.

Food for thought

On the next occasion that you meet someone for the first time, try to put aside ten minutes later in the day and write down honestly what your first impressions of them were. Then try to explain your judgements in light of the content of this chapter.

Dig deeper

Fiske, S. T. & Taylor, S. E. (2013) *Social Cognition. From Brains to Culture*. Second Edition. Sage.

Hamilton, D. L. & Gifford, R. K. (1976) 'Illusory correlation in interpersonal perception: A cognitive basis of stereotypic judgments'. *Journal of Experimental Social Psychology*, **12**, 392–407.

Tversky, A. & Kahneman, D. (1974) 'Judgment under uncertainty: heuristics and biases'. *Science*, **185**, 1124–1131.

Wheeler, S. C. & Petty, R. E. (2001) 'The effects of stereotype activation on behaviour: A review of possible mechanisms'. *Psychological Bulletin*, **127(6)**, 797–826.

Fact-check

1 The belief that two variables are related to one another, even though there is no link, is referred to as:
  a Stereotyping
  b Prototypicality
  c Illusory correlation
  d Social categorization

2 A decision made that is likely to be good enough most of the time is characteristic of:
  a A fuzzy thinker
  b A cognitive miser
  c A naive scientist
  d A stereotypical thinker

3 A careful, logical and systematic analysis is more characteristic of:
  a A fuzzy thinker
  b A cognitive miser
  c A naive scientist
  d A stereotypical thinker

4 Which of the following is not a reason why we categorize?
  a It helps us make predictions about things
  b It saves us time and cognitive processing
  c It gives us meaning and understanding
  d All of the above
  e None of the above

5 A 'rule of thumb' employed to make a quick decision is more commonly known as:
  a Stereotyping
  b Cognitive heuristic
  c Social categorization
  d Prototypicality

6 You toss a coin five times in front of your friend, and it lands with a sequence of H-T-T-T-T. You ask your friend to predict what side it will land on next, and they say 'Heads'. This is an example of which bias?

a The base-rate fallacy

b The availability heuristic

c Anchoring

d None of the above

7 Reading recent stories in a newspaper about house burglaries makes you start to think that your house is more likely to be burgled than perhaps it was a year ago. This is an example of:

a The base-rate fallacy

b The availability heuristic

c The adjustment heuristic

d The representativeness heuristic

8 You tell a stranger who you met for the first time today that you work at a university. Then you ask them to guess what your job is: either a cleaner or a professor of psychology. They guess professor. They have just employed which heuristic?

a The availability heuristic

b The adjustment heuristic

c The representativeness heuristic

d None of the above

9 Which of the following has not been put forward as a reason for why we fall prey to the various judgemental heuristics?

a It requires too much effort to engage in the necessary cognitive processing required to reach a good decision

b It is due to the ease with which individuals are able to retrieve exemplars of a category

c It is because humans are generally too self-reflective

d It is because of certain personality traits that some individuals possess

10 Which of the following is not a factor in determining whether or not an individual is able to quash the activation of a stereotype?

a Awareness of a potential stereotyping threat

b Available cognitive capacity

c High levels of the personality trait 'need for cognition'

d The extent to which the individual is motivated not to stereotype

5

Interpersonal attraction: liking and loving

As the Blues Brothers (amongst others) famously sang: 'Everybody needs somebody to love.' and the topic of this chapter is all about the psychological aspects of how we make friends, fall in love, and all too frequently split up with partners. There can be no doubt that we do need others, as various chapters in this book have shown and will show, but how do we come to find that other person?

Why are relationships important?

According to the 'belongingness' hypothesis, humans have a fundamental need to socialize and form relationships with others (see Spotlight below). Failure to do so can lead to long-term problems, such as increased levels of stress, a decrease in levels of happiness and long-term health problems (although such findings do tend to be correlational in nature). There are many reasons which could contribute towards this need for affiliation, and these include the need for positive experiences (being in the company of people we like), the need for emotional support (seeking guidance and sympathy), and the need for comparison (to compare ourselves and our situation to those of others).

Spotlight: The 'need-to-belong'

According to Baumeister and Leary (1995), humans have a very basic motivation to belong; that is, they need to form a number of interpersonal relationships of good quality which are of a lasting and positive nature. They reviewed a number of strands of evidence and concluded:

> 'Again and again, we found evidence of a basic desire to form social attachments. People form social bonds readily, even under seemingly adverse conditions. People who have anything in common, who share common (even unpleasant) experiences, or who are simply exposed to each other frequently, tend to form friendships or other attachments. (p. 520)

Factors affecting friendship formation and liking

Having determined that we need to form relationships with others, we now need to look at how we do this and what factors might affect the success or failure of such relationship formation. One of the earliest studies to investigate this issue was by Leon Festinger and his colleagues; they discovered that proximity is a key determinant in how and why friendships form (see below). However, many other factors have also been found to play an important role in this process.

PROXIMITY

Generally speaking, this is one of the most important factors to determine whether or not we form a friendship with another person. The more we encounter someone, the greater the chance of a relationship forming. For example, if you regularly sit next to someone in a lecture, or in church, or work in the same room as them, then this physical proximity will likely lead to some form of friendship formation. Such proximity can also contribute to deeper relationships such as love. Also, proximity can overcome dissimilarity too: older studies have found that, in less tolerant times, those of different race formed friendships (despite societal forces suggesting that they shouldn't) simply by living next door to one another. Of course, there will be situations where proximity can be a bad thing – for example, when our neighbours do things that annoy or anger us, and also when we simply get bored of a person (perhaps they tell us the same jokes every time we see them).

Key idea: Proximity

The degree to which an individual is close to (in distance), or comes into contact with, another person.

A strong reason why proximity is an important predictor of friendship formation is familiarity: we like things that are familiar to us – we are conditioned through evolutionary forces to be suspicious of strangers and unfamiliar situations. Generally speaking, we like things that are predictable (but perhaps not too predictable – the old adage goes that 'familiarity breeds contempt'). The more familiar we are with someone, the less effort it takes us to interact with them, and the more likely we are to continue to interact with them – which in turn brings us back to the predictability factor.

SIMILARITY

In addition to proximity, similarity is also a strong predictor as to why we form friendships with people. Again, there is truth in the proverb that says that 'Birds of a feather flock together' – very rarely do 'opposites attract'! Many studies have manipulated experimental situations, through the use of questionnaires, to suggest to participants that they are either very similar or very different to other people in the experiment (even though no such similarity or difference actually exists): results conclude that we like people who we perceive to be similar to us more than we like people who we think are dissimilar to us.

Whilst such experimental studies produce findings that might be considered artificial, more naturalistic field studies also suggest that similarity is a strong predictor. For example, researchers have studied naturally occurring friendships (for example, between schoolchildren) and have found that the more similarity present (for instance, in terms of factors such as age, religion, family circumstances, academic capability, attitudes, values, interests, etc.), the stronger the friendship; this could be measured in terms of ratings of 'best friends'. Unfortunately, it is not only positive similarities that predict liking and friendship formation – similarity in antisocial traits, such as aggression, can also lead to relationship formation.

In terms of romantic relationships, the **'matching hypothesis'** predicts that individuals tend to choose potential partners based on the social desirability of appearance. For instance, in one study researchers used pictures of couples, either dating or newly-wed, and asked people to rate the individuals on a numerical scale (separately) for attractiveness. They found that there was a very strong similarity in the independent ratings of physical attractiveness for the couples; that is '6s' tended to marry '6s', but rarely did '4s' marry '8s'! Other studies have confirmed that whilst we might choose a very physically attractive partner for a one-off date (in our dreams, perhaps), when it comes to a long-term relationship, we are much more likely to choose someone of a comparable level of attractiveness to ourselves. Whilst this is a robust finding, as with most rules, there are exceptions. For example, individuals with very low levels of self-esteem tend to avoid people who they think are similar to them.

Key idea: The 'matching hypothesis'

Individuals are more likely to form relationships with other people who are of a similar level of physical attractiveness to themselves.

There are also many other factors which can affect whether or not we like, and thus form a friendship with, another person. For example, we tend to like people who express a liking for us ('reciprocal liking'), and we like even more the people who start off disliking us but who then come to like us. There is also a tendency to like those people who we perceive as competent, whether it is in terms of intelligence or social skills, and dislike those who are incompetent. Of course, if someone is too competent, this might actually prevent liking.

Other personal characteristics that have been found to be related to liking and friendship formation include personality and self-disclosure. For example, individuals are attracted to other individuals who exhibit personality traits such as kindness and warmth. Also, the degree to which individuals are prepared to 'open up' about themselves (referred to as self-disclosure) was also found to be a good predictor of long-term relationship formation. However, too little or too much self-disclosure may be a barrier, and there have also been found to be some gender differences with respect to self-disclosure: women tend to be greater self-disclosers than men.

Case study: A study of friendship formation in a housing complex

Festinger, Schachter and Back (1950) studied the relationship formation of married students living in the Westgate housing complex (a former navy barracks converted for the use of married couples who were students at the Massachusetts Institute of Technology); the housing complex consisted of a number of different buildings, some comprising flats on two different floors. The people who moved in to this housing complex had very little prior acquaintance with one another and this allowed Festinger and his colleagues to observe how and when relationships formed between the residents. One of the interesting things about this study was that there was already a high degree of similarity between the residents – they were all veteran married engineering students. This enabled the research to tease out what other factors might affect friendship formation beyond similarity of background.

A number of interesting findings emerged from the study. Friendships were about ten times more likely to form between those who lived in the same building than those who didn't. Those who lived on the same floor were more likely to form friendships than those who lived on different floors. Also, those who lived closer to the staircases between floors, and hence were encountered more often, were the most popular people with whom friendships formed. Overall, Festinger found that those who we come into contact with more frequently are the people with whom we are more likely to form friendships.

Theories of relationship formation and maintenance

There are many theories which look beyond individual factors when attempting to explain why friendships form and relationships thrive (or fail). These include social exchange theory and equity theory.

Social exchange theory views relationships in terms of rewards and costs. If the benefits outweigh the costs of staying in a friendship, a romantic relationship or even a marriage, then the relationship is likely to endure. According to this theory, the most enduring and fulfilling relationship is likely to be one in which the rewards are relatively high whilst the costs are comparatively low.

Key idea: Social exchange theory

The weighing up of costs and benefits before making a decision that will maximize benefits and minimize costs

However, it is not always straightforward to define simply what constitutes a reward and what constitutes a cost. In their most basic form, rewards can be anything that makes a person feel happy, or that a person defines as being valuable to them – these can range from compliments to physical gifts. Costs can be anything that an individual finds undesirable – these can range from having to do household chores to fierce arguments or physical abuse. Rewards and costs will vary from person to person and from relationship to relationship, for instance, rewards in a friendship may not be seen as such in a romantic relationship. Romantic relationships are likely to last much longer if the rewards are higher.

Of course, the success of a relationship may not simply be down to rewards outweighing costs, but the availability, or lack of, alternative relationships may also play a part. If no other form of relationship is available, then individuals may be able to endure higher costs within a relationship. We may also be able to endure high costs if we compare it to what we have been used to in the past and find that it is actually better. Thus this 'comparison level' will have an effect on our decision to stay in, or leave, a relationship.

Additionally, the amount of effort that we put into a relationship may also have an effect on whether or not we continue with it. The more we have previously invested, the less likely we are to leave it. It may therefore be easier to break a friendship, or end a romantic relationship, sooner rather than later. In short, the more commitment that an individual has already made, the more they are likely to endure in a relationship before ending it.

Whilst social exchange theory can offer an insight into why relationships endure or not, there are limitations with research in this area in that it tends to be conducted mainly on short-term student relationships as opposed to marriages, for example. Similarly, the effect of the personality of individuals within the relationship has not been well researched. This theory also suggests that individuals act as rational accountants when it comes to their relationship – which quite clearly is not always the case! Finally, social exchange theory has more *explanatory power* than it does *predictability power*: that is, we can use it to explain *why* a relationship endures or ends, but not always successfully *when* it might end.

EQUITY THEORY

Equity theory is similar in many ways to social exchange theory but hinges more on using the 'equity' between what people put into a relationship with what they get out of it to predict whether or not a relationship will endure. Thus if an individual puts more into a relationship than the other person, then they would expect to get more out of the relationship than the other person. Equity is therefore not the same as equality. By looking at an individual's input to, and output from, a relationship, it should be possible to predict whether or not a relationship will endure or end.

Key idea: Equity theory

A relationship is only considered fair by an individual if what they get out of it approximately equals what they put into it.

If, for example, John contributes too much to his relationship compared to what he is getting out of it, then it is likely that John will look to end the relationship. However, it is equally likely, according to this theory, that John will look to end the relationship if he is getting more out of it than he is putting in. The reasons for both scenarios might be slightly different (e.g. anger or frustration vs. embarrassment or shame), but the end result will probably be the same.

Research has measured, through the use of questionnaires such as the 'Hatfield Global Measure', whether or not relationships are equitable, over-benefitted or under-benefitted. The more a relationship moves away from equity, the greater the psychological distress felt by an individual, therefore the less happy the relationship will be, and the more likely the relationship will end.

There seem to be gender differences in matters of equity within a relationship. Women are typically more distressed by being over-benefitted whereas men are more distressed at being under-benefitted. There are also individuals who worry less about equity than others, and in these instances equity theory can lose its explanatory power as to whether or not a relationship will endure.

Both social exchange theory and equity theory take a very calculating view about relationships. They assume that there is no space for unconditional love in a relationship, which many researchers believe does actually exist: and if it does, then these two theories do begin to weaken a little in terms of their validity.

Love

As friendships progress, there is a chance that they will turn from liking into loving. Whilst instinctively we might know the difference between liking and loving (though on occasion our instincts may well lead us into some fairly embarrassing situations), the two concepts are surprisingly difficult to define.

One of the first researchers to try to determine the exact nature of love was Zick Rubin. He attempted to measure love definitively through the use of his 'Love scale' (he also devised a 'Liking scale' in an attempt to draw a distinction between the two). Participants in his study were dating couples who were asked to complete his two scales with regard to their romantic partner and a close friend (see Spotlight below).

Whilst some researchers argue that it is impossible to measure love, Rubin's scale does tend to have some face validity. For example, in an experimental situation, those who scored highly on the love scale were more likely to have greater eye contact with their partners than those who didn't; they were more likely to say that they were in love; and they were much more likely to still be in the relationship six months later.

Spotlight: Defining and measuring liking and love

According to Zick Rubin (1970), a researcher who developed scales for measuring liking and love, love is:

'... an attitude held by a person toward a particular other person, involving predispositions to think, feel, and behave in certain ways toward that other person' (p. 265).

Questions on his liking scale include:

▶ 'This person is one of the most likeable people I know.'
▶ 'I have great confidence in this person's good judgements.'

Questions on his loving scale include:

▶ 'I feel I can confide in this person about virtually anything.'
▶ 'I would do almost anything for this person.'

The questions were answered on a 1 (not at all) to 10 (totally) scale.

THEORIES OF LOVING

Other researchers have attempted to develop more encompassing theories of love which deal with different types in different situations. Two of the main theories are **Sternberg's 'triangle of love'** and **Lee's 'colours of love' typology.**

STERNBERG'S TRIANGLE OF LOVE

According to Sternberg (1986), love has three components:

1 **Intimacy:** this is an emotional component, and adjectives associated with it include *closeness* and *warmth*.

2 **Passion:** this is a motivational component, and is commonly associated with sexual desire and physical attraction.

3 **Commitment:** this is a cognitive component and is associated with a resolve to maintain the relationship be it in the short-term or the long-term.

Which combination of these three components are present, along with the strength of these components (high/low), allows us to determine the kind, and amount, of love that an individual is experiencing. At one end of the scale, if none of the three components are present, no love will be experienced; however if all three are present then Sternberg's model predicts that the individual will experience 'consummate love' (see Case study below for Sternberg's eight kinds of love).

Key idea: Sternberg's triangle of love

Three central components of love (intimacy, passion and commitment) combine to give seven further distinct kinds of love.

The model suggests that the more components that are present, then the more enduring the love. Consummate love is the strongest type of love, but also (perhaps regrettably) the rarest. Sternberg also suggested that each of the components differed from one another in terms of stability (intimacy and commitment are more stable than passion), controllability (commitment is more controllable than passion), and experiential salience (the extent to which we are consciously aware of how we feel: passion has more experiential salience than commitment).

Case study: Sternberg's eight kinds of love

Type of Love	Intimacy	Passion	Commitment
No love	✗	✗	✗
Liking	✓	✗	✗
Romantic love	✓	✓	✗
Companionate love	✓	✗	✓
Fatuous love	✗	✓	✓
Infatuation	✗	✓	✗
Empty love	✗	✗	✓
Consummate love	✓	✓	✓

✓ = Strength of component is high

✗ = Strength of component is low/absent

Sternberg's model is good to the extent to which it identifies multiple types of love and offers predictions about each type; it probably chimes true with the experiences that most of us have had throughout our life, thus giving it good 'face validity'. It also has good practical applications in that it could be used in relationship counselling by identifying which type of love each partner is showing and how changes can be made to bring them closer together. However, the model is not without its critics who claim that some of the components, for example commitment, are not clearly defined.

LEE'S COLOURS OF LOVE

Lee's 'colours of love' typology relies on an analogy to colour mixing, whereby there are three primary colours, and if we mix them we get secondary colours. This approach to love classification claims that there are three primary styles of loving:

1 **Eros** (romantic love): powerful physical attraction combined with a strong emotional experience.

2 **Ludus** (game-playing love): a fun, strategic relationship, with low commitment, and usually short-lived.

3 **Storge** (companionate love): characterized by a slow build-up of comfortable intimacy and gradual self-disclosure.

These in turn, when combined, give us three secondary styles of love:

4 **Mania** (Eros + Ludus): described as possessive/obsessive love.

5 **Pragma** (Storge + Ludus): described as realistic/practical love.

6 **Agape** (Eros + Storge): described as altruistic/selfless love.

Key idea: Lee's 'colours of love'

A colour analogy whereby three primary styles of loving (Eros, Ludus and Storge) combine to give three secondary styles of love (Mania, Pragma and Agape).

There are certainly similarities with Sternberg's types of love, though just fewer of them. For example, Eros would equate to romantic love, and Storge to compassionate love, though the names for Lee's types of love are a little less accessible and descriptive. Research, however, does tend to suggest that these are indeed distinct types of love. It has also found that different styles of love are preferred across genders, with men showing more preference for ludic and erotic love, whereas women were more storgic and pragmatic in their love style.

The breakdown of relationships

Inevitably many relationships hit the rocks, and researchers have attempted to map out the processes involved in such relationship decline. One attempt by Steve Duck has modelled the processes involved in relationship breakdown.

According to *Duck's model of relationship dissolution* (e.g. 1982), it is a process that occurs over a period of time, and goes through a number of different phases; there were four in the original model but a subsequent revision added a fifth phase.

1 **Intrapsychic phase (partner focus):** this phase is characterized by one or both partners reaching a point where they start to experience dissatisfaction with the behaviour of the other. At this stage, they say nothing to the other, and it may be that the other is not aware of their dissatisfaction;

2 **Dyadic phase (relationship focus):** this phase is characterized by one or both partners reaching the point at which they think they would be justified in exiting the relationship. They will tell the partner of their decision and discussions will likely ensue covering important issues within the relationship (e.g. roles and commitments). These discussions will either fix or hasten the end of the relationship.

3 **Social phase (going public):** if attempts to fix the relationship fail, then it becomes necessary to make public the dissolution of the relationship. Each partner will attempt to gather support from others (e.g. friends and relatives) with regard to their version of events. Whilst there is still a possibility of the relationship being saved at this point, each partner will go public with their 'story' in an attempt to portray themselves in the best possible light.

4 **Grave-dressing phase (tidying up):** it is now no longer possible to save the relationship, and every attempt will be

made to leave the relationship with their reputation intact. Every attempt is made to ensure that as little blame as possible is attached to the individual for the break-up; it is incredibly unlikely that one of the couple will attempt to take responsibility for its demise.

5 **Resurrection phase:** this phase is about each partner preparing themselves for any future relationship. The focus will be on learning from the mistakes of the previous relationship and figuring out how to use this knowledge to ensure the success of future ones.

One of the positive points of this model is its practical applications; it can be used to identify ways in which relationships can be repaired during the different phases of breakdown. It is certainly difficult to gain empirical support for such models as this due to ethical reasons; for example, any attempt to study a dissolving relationship may in fact sabotage any attempts to save it, and similarly, attempting to investigate a relationship when problems appear may bring about an end to the relationship which otherwise may not have occurred. Much of the time, second-hand reports are relied on to construct such models, and such reports may suffer with accuracy problems thus affecting the validity of the model.

Summary

As if we didn't know it already, relationships are complex and difficult to study. What we do know is that we can't function successfully without them. The formation stages are characterized by frequent contact, but this proximity is tempered by other factors such as similarity and individual differences. Various models have attempted to explain the formation and maintenance of relationships, and when friendship blossoms into romance, researchers have characterized the different types of love that might ensue. Finally, even though it is a challenging task, researchers have also constructed models to account for how relationships end. The life cycle of a relationship is most certainly a fascinating process to observe.

Food for thought

If you were setting up a dating agency, how would you apply the information in this chapter to ensure that your clients had the best possible chance of meeting the 'person of their dreams'? Consider the ethics of applying the theories in such a way.

Dig deeper

Baumeister, R. F. & Leary, M. R. (1995). 'The Need to Belong: Desire for Interpersonal Attachment as a Fundamental Human Motivation'. *Psychological Bulletin*, **117(3)**, 497–529.

Feingold, A. (1988). 'Matching for attractiveness in romantic partners and same-sex friends: A meta-analysis and theoretical critique'. *Psychological Bulletin*, **104(2)**, 226–235.

Jackson-Dwyer, D. (2014). *Interpersonal Relationships*. London: Routledge.

Sternberg, K. (2013). *Psychology of Love 101*. Springer Publishing Co.

Sternberg, R. J. (1987). 'Liking versus loving: A comparative evaluation of theories'. *Psychological Bulletin*, **102(3)**, 331–345.

Fact-check

1 Which of the following factors contribute towards our need to affiliate with another person:
   a The need for positive experiences
   b Avoidance of long-term health problems
   c The need for emotional support
   d All of the above

2 According to Leon Festinger and his colleagues in their study of the Westgate Student housing complex, which of the following factors played the most important role in the formation of relationships?
   a Individual differences
   b Shared background
   c Proximity
   d Similarity

3 In the above study, it was found that friendships between people living in the same building were:
   a Very unlikely to occur
   b Twice as likely to occur
   c Four times more likely to occur
   d Ten times more likely to occur

4 In relation to friendship formation, the principle of 'Similarity' suggests that:
   a Fools seldom differ
   b Birds of a feather flock together
   c Opposites attract
   d A rolling stone gathers no moss

5 The 'matching hypothesis' states that we are more likely to form a relationship with:
   a Someone who is of a similar level of physical attractiveness as ourselves
   b Someone who shares our interests
   c Someone who has the same personality traits as ourselves
   d Someone who comes from the same background

6 The most enduring ┊ one in which the rew┊ are comparatively lo┊
   a Equity theory
   b Social exchange t
   c Sternberg's 'trian
   d Duck's model of r┊

7 Which of the following ┊ 'triangle of love' theory┊
   a Intimacy
   b Desire
   c Passion
   d Commitment

8 According to Sternberg's ┊ are present, then we shou┊
   a Romantic
   b Companionate
   c Fatuous
   d Infatuation

9 In Lee's 'colours of love' typ┊ love types of 'Eros' and 'Lud┊ secondary love?
   a Storge
   b Agape
   c Pragma
   d Mania

10 Duck's theory of relationship d┊ stage, one or both partners will┊ decide that they would be justifi┊ This is characteristic of which p┊
   a The Intrapsychic phase
   b The Dyadic phase
   c The Social phase
   d The Grave-dressing phase

6

Social influence: conformity and obedience

This chapter looks at the topic of social influence. It is an important topic given that hardly a day goes by (if ever) without someone trying to get us to do something – sometimes we want to do it, and sometimes we don't. Likewise, we try to get other people to do things that we want them to do, and which they might not want to do. Sometimes the influence is relatively harmless, e.g. trying to persuade a friend to see the film that you want to see and not the one they want to see; but sometimes it is far more sinister, e.g. when a soldier carries out an act of torture on a prisoner of war because he is told to do so by his commanding officer.

When asked to think about the topic of social influence, many people tend to produce sinister examples. However, we should not lose sight of the fact that **social influence** is usually a good and necessary thing in order to keep life functioning smoothly. For example, what would happen if one morning we woke up and decided that, just because everyone else stops at a red traffic light, and goes at a green light, today we are not going to do what everybody else is doing; today we will go on red and stop on green. In short, society needs a good degree of successful social influence on a daily basis.

Key idea: Social influence

An attempt by one or more people to modify the behaviour, perceptions, attitudes or beliefs of another individual or group.

For example, a boss might tell his employee that things have to be done a certain way; a cult leader might recruit followers by informing them that if they join his group they will be saved, but damnation will surely follow if they don't; a politician urges a group of undecided voters to back his party in an election.

Social psychologists study why people are influenced by others and the mechanisms responsible. They also investigate what factors might affect people's tendency to be influenced. Generally speaking, three types of social influence exist: conformity, obedience and compliance. This chapter will look at the first two and the next chapter will address the third.

Conformity

As has been suggested, doing something simply because everyone else is doing it is generally not a bad strategy – it is sometimes the best way to get on in life. Social psychologists refer to this type of behaviour as 'conformity' or 'majority influence'.

Key idea: Conformity

An individual will change their attitudes or behaviour in order to adhere to existing social norms.

One of the earliest studies in this area was conducted by Muzafer Sherif, and utilized the **autokinetic effect**. Participants were seated alone in a dark room, a light was switched on, and they were asked to report how far they perceived the light had moved. They did this a number of times before the session was completed, and an average was recorded as to the distance that they perceived the light had moved (although it had actually remained stationary the entire time).

Key idea: The autokinetic effect

An optical illusion occurring whereby a stationary light appears to move in a completely dark room.

They were asked to return at a later time when they were again seated in the dark room, but this time two other participants (who had also previously taken part in the solitary condition) were also seated in the room. The light was switched on a number of times and the three participants were asked to report aloud as to how far the light had moved. They took it in turns to answer first, second or third.

Given that it was a fairly ambiguous task based on a quirk of our optical system, Sherif was interested to find out whether each of the three participants would remain independent in their distance judgements (as found when they were tested alone) regardless of what the other two participants said, or whether they would allow themselves to be influenced by the judgements of the others.

The results of the study clearly showed that, over a series of trials in three sessions, the judgements of the three participants converged on a distance different from all of their original independent judgements. For example if, in the independent conditions, participant A judged the mean movement of the light to be 7 inches, participant B judged 1 inch and participant C 3 inches, then by the end, all three participants would likely agree on an average movement of about 2 inches.

These findings suggest that when we are asked to do something of which we are uncertain, we look to other people to help us complete the task; we allow ourselves to be influenced by them. This is referred to as **informational influence**.

Key idea: Informational influence

An individual will change their behaviour to fit in with what everyone else is doing because they are unsure of the correct way to act in a given situation.

However, this is not the only reason that we allow ourselves to conform to the actions of other people. We may sometimes go along with the majority for a quiet life, even though we know what they are doing is wrong. Solomon Asch, in a famous experiment (referred to as the 'Line Judgement Task'), showed this to be the case.

Participants in a group of seven were asked to make judgements about which line out of a choice of three matched a target line (see below). Unbeknownst to the real participants, the other six people in their group were confederates (see Chapter 1) of the experimenter who were instructed to give incorrect answers in 12 out of the 36 trials. The naïve (real) participant was always situated in seat 6, therefore five confederates gave their answers before them. In the 24 control trials, all was well and the participant simply gave the correct answer in line with everyone else. However, in the 12 experimental trials, the participant was confronted with five other people who were giving an obviously incorrect answer. Asch was interested to see what they would do: would they remain independent, or would they conform to the majority and give an answer that they knew to be incorrect?

The results of Asch's study showed that out of the 12 experimental trials, 28 per cent of participants gave eight or more incorrect answers, 37 per cent gave at least one incorrect answer, and only 25 per cent of participants did not conform at all (i.e. they gave the correct answer despite the disbelieving stares from the confederates).

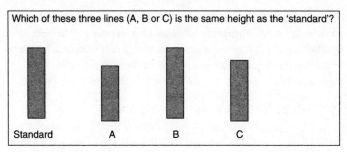

Which of these three lines (A, B or C) is the same height as the 'standard'?

Standard   A   B   C

Asch's line judgement task

Asch was understandably dismayed by his findings which indicated that supposedly intelligent people gave wrong answers just to avoid the social disapproval of others (this was confirmed through debriefing interviews with the participants after the experiment had concluded). Of course, another way of interpreting the results would be to laud the fact that 25 per cent of participants were able to remain resolute and resist majority pressure.

> 'That we have found the tendency to conformity in our society so strong that reasonably intelligent and well-meaning young people are willing to call white black is a matter of concern. It raises questions about our ways of education and about the values that guide our conduct.
>
> (Solomon Asch, 1955, p. 34

Overall, these findings suggest that when we are confronted with people who are obviously doing something wrong, or doing something that we disagree with, but who we want to impress (or who we don't want to upset or to disapprove of us), then we will allow ourselves to be influenced by them. This is referred to as **normative influence**.

RESISTING THE MAJORITY

Other research has investigated the circumstances needed to resist conformity pressures. One study using the Asch line judgement paradigm found that when a second person also gave the same answer (the correct answer) as the participant, then conformity rates dropped as low as 12.5 per cent. A further study found that when a second person gave a different answer to the majority (but not the correct answer) then conformity rates also fell. It seems that anything that breaks the monopoly of the majority can help an individual to resist.

Key idea: Normative influence

An individual will change their behaviour to fit in with what everyone else is doing to ensure that they are liked, or to avoid social disapproval, by the others.

Researchers have also looked for other factors which might suggest a person is more likely to conform. Findings suggest that a lower IQ, an authoritarian personality, and high levels of anxiety or feelings of inferiority, might lead to more conforming behaviour. However, other evidence suggests this is not the case, which leads to the conclusion that situational factors might also affect conformity. Similarly, an effect for gender was found in early research, with women showing more conformity than men. However, this was probably an artefact of the task type (which tended to be more male-oriented), as later research (which used more gender neutral tasks) found no effect of gender.

PERSUADING THE MAJORITY: MINORITY INFLUENCE

The question has also been raised as to whether it is possible for a minority to influence the majority. This idea is an important one which obviously has real-world implications; for example, in the political arena, could a minority party ever change enough minds in the electorate (the majority) to become a winner in an election. Equally, anyone who has ever seen the classic 1957 film *Twelve Angry Men* will wonder whether it would really be possible for one juror (e.g. Henry Fonda) to change the minds of the other eleven members of the jury. Minority influence can be important to promote creativity and change in society.

A number of theories have been put forward to explain how a minority could have an effect; for example 'conversion theory' and 'convergent-divergent theory'. To draw out the relevant elements from these different theories, we can say that in order for a minority to bring about change, they must:

1 Deliberately draw attention to themselves and promote an atmosphere of controlled conflict.

2 Be consistent in their message – express the same view over a period of time.

3 Be consistent in their group outlook – different members of the minority must agree with one another.

4 Not be too rigid – avoid being seen as dogmatic, but they should be more rigid on their core issues.

5 Not be too flexible – avoid being seen as inconsistent, but be prepared to be flexible on non-core issues (there is a fine line to be walked between achieving 4 and 5).

6 Show self-confidence – be firm and forceful when promoting their message.

In addition to the above points, any minority should seriously consider establishing their 'ingroup' credentials before espousing their minority views. For example, Tony Blair and his followers firmly established themselves as staunch Labour supporters before putting forward their slightly radical ideas of 'New Labour'. Had they not done this, but instead tried to change the party when still 'junior' members, they would likely have been marginalized, and the UK might now be quite a different place.

Having considered conformity, we now turn to another form of social influence where the two parties (the influencer and the target) are not on an equal footing i.e. one has more power than the other – namely **obedience**.

Obedience

Whether we like it or not, there are times when we simply need to obey a request from an authority figure – whether it is an edict from the Government to pay increased taxes, or a request from our boss to carry out a task. However, we would certainly like to think that we would only obey reasonable requests, and that we would know where we should draw the line.

Regrettably, there have been several well-documented cases throughout history where people have obviously not been able to draw the line, and for whatever reason, have carried out atrocities simply because they were told to do so by a superior (or leastways, that was their justification for their actions). Social psychologists have investigated the mechanisms behind obedience in the hope that they can prevent such events from reoccurring.

Key idea: Obedience

An individual will perform an action, or set of actions, in response to a direct order from a perceived authority figure.

Whilst Stanley Milgram is the name most commonly linked to obedience research in the 1960s and 1970s, there were certainly earlier studies in the area. For example, Landis in 1924 reported the results of a study where 71 per cent of participants obeyed an instruction to decapitate a live rat. They were handed a sharp knife and a live rat, and instructed by a man dressed in a white lab coat to cut off the rat's head: 15 out of 21 people did just this simply because they were told to do so by a supposed authority figure (i.e. the experimenter dressed in a white coat). There have certainly been other studies that have shown that people will obey a request more often if the person making the demand is dressed in a uniform of some kind.

STUDYING OBEDIENCE

However, it was Milgram who conducted possibly the most celebrated and infamous study in the field of obedience, and perhaps in all of social psychology. Milgram was interested in addressing the 'Germans are different' hypothesis to explain why some of the worst war crimes of the twentieth century were committed. German soldiers at the Nüremberg trials explained away their terrible actions by arguing that they were only following orders. Milgram was interested to test whether this could be true: was it something about the German people which accounted for these atrocities, or, given the same set of circumstances, would any ordinary person have done what they did.

> 'Obedience is as basic an element in the structure of social life as one can point to. Some system of authority is a requirement of all communal living ...'
>
> (Stanley Milgram, 1963, p. 371)

To try to answer this question, Milgram set up his basic experiment at Yale University. Under the guise of testing whether punishment affected learning, Milgram recruited participants (40 males between the ages of 20 and 50 from the surrounding area) and investigated whether they would deliver potentially lethal electric shocks to another person simply because they were told to do so by a man dressed in a white coat carrying a clipboard (a stereotypical authority figure).

Case study: Milgram's methodology

Participants were greeted by the experimenter (a man dressed in a white coat) and another man who was introduced as a fellow participant in the study (actually a confederate).The experimenter explained that the study required one of them to be the 'learner' and one the 'teacher'. The teacher would read out lists of paired words to the learner; the learner would then be given a key word and required to say out loud which word (from a list of four) was previously paired with it. Every time they gave an incorrect answer, an electric shock punishment would be administered by the teacher to see if it would help the learner to remember more or less effectively.

The assignment of who was the learner, and who the teacher, was supposedly a random process, but, through the use of trickery, it was always the confederate who became the learner. The confederate was seated in an experimental chamber and hooked up to a series of electrodes. The teacher was taken to a separate room which housed an electric shock generator linked to the electrodes – an imposing looking machine containing a series of 30 switches in 15 volt increments (from 15 volts to 450 volts). Each set of four switches was given a descriptive label, from 'Slight Shock' (15–60v), through 'Moderate Shock' (75–120v) to 'Danger: Severe Shock' (375–420v). The last two switches (435–450v) were simply labelled 'XXX'. The teacher was told to press the next switch in the sequence (starting with the 15v switch) each time an incorrect answer was given. To demonstrate that the machine was genuine, the teacher was given a 45v shock – actually the only real shock administered in the entire experiment.

The experiment then commenced, the word lists read out, and the punishment administered appropriately. If the teacher ever threatened to stop the experiment, or queried whether they should continue, the experimenter would deliver a series of four 'prods', such as: 'Please continue'; 'The experiment requires that you continue'. Only after the final prod was delivered and the teacher still expressed a desire to stop, or the maximum punishment (450v) delivered, was the experiment actually terminated. At this point, the maximum shock delivered was recorded and the participant was thoroughly debriefed. The participant was considered to be fully obedient if they had delivered all of the 30 shocks.

The results of Milgram's initial study were startling at the time and are still disturbing today. Despite asking a number of senior students and colleagues, before the experiment took place, to predict how many participants would deliver the top shock and thus be considered fully obedient (the mean estimate was that only 1.2 per cent would), no one was quite prepared for the outcome. Milgram found that 26 out of the 40 participants (65 per cent) delivered the 450v shock, despite obviously being very distressed at what they were doing. This was taken as evidence that perhaps the Germans weren't quite so different after all.

UNDERSTANDING MILGRAM'S INITIAL FINDINGS
Without a doubt, Milgram's findings courted controversy. Critics argued that the study was unethical, that the results were a one-off, that there were mitigating circumstances to explain the results, and that the findings were simply a product of their time.

To his credit, Milgram attempted to address the outcries of his detractors. For example, he showed how he systematically debriefed all of his participants (and in fact Milgram was one of the first researchers to do this), and contacted them at a later date to ensure they were suffering no ill effects (many of the participants actually thanked him for their experience). It was during these debriefings that he began to realize what was happening to his participants – namely they believed they were acting simply as an extension of the experimenter and not under their own volition; in effect, they were surrendering their autonomy. Thus Milgram developed the idea of an 'agentic shift' to explain why people obeyed an authority figure.

'The critical shift in functioning is reflected in an alteration of attitude. Specifically, the person entering an authority system no longer views himself as acting out of his own purposes but rather comes to see himself as an agent for executing the wishes of another person ... I shall term this the agentic state.'

(The Agentic Shift: Milgram, 1974, p. 133)

FURTHER EXPLANATIONS FOR OBEDIENT BEHAVIOUR

Milgram conducted an additional set of 18 'variations' based on his initial experiment to try to understand his findings further and to show that the results were certainly not an anomaly (and as we saw in Chapter 1, replication is essential to having confidence in our research findings). For example, some argued that it was only the prestigious surroundings of Yale University that caused people to obey the experimenter (referred to as 'situational effects'); to counter this, Milgram carried out a replication of his study in a suite of offices in a nearby city (Bridgeport) in order to dissociate the study from Yale. Whilst the levels of obedience did fall, it was still found that almost half of the participants (47.5 per cent) were still totally obedient.

Similarly when the experiment comprised female participants, obedience levels were identical (65 per cent), and when the personnel of the experiment were changed (i.e. the learner and the experimenter) to ensure that it wasn't their characteristics which caused the levels of obedience, lower but similar levels (50 per cent) were also found. Interestingly, there was a variation where the 'teachers' were allowed to set their own level of shock to administer to the learner (rather than deliver them in the set sequence). This variation was important to determine whether, if left to their own devices, participants would actually deliver the top shock, or whether it was the command of the experimenter that made them do it. Findings from this condition show that the mean level of shock was between the 45v and 60v level, which seems quite reasonable; however, one participant still decided that it was perfectly reasonable to administer the 450v shock!

With regard to the question of whether Milgram's findings were simply a product of their time, or whether some form of 'enlightenment effect' would moderate our behaviour in the present day, there have been a number of studies over the years that have replicated and added to his findings. Whilst ethical considerations make it quite tricky to investigate obedience in exactly the same way as Milgram, there have certainly been some ingenious attempts.

For example, an Australian study in the 1970s found that 13–14-year-old boys engaged in a behaviour that was likely to cause self-harm (as opposed to harming others as Milgram found) simply because an experimenter asked them to: 90 per cent turned a dial on a machine to a setting that was labelled as having a 20 per cent chance of permanently impairing their hearing. However, there are potentially confounding variables that might account for the findings of this study.

More recent studies in America have used a limited version of Milgram's paradigm (asking participants to deliver shocks up to 150v) to show that obedience levels are comparable to those found by Milgram over 35 years earlier. An even more inventive study, using a virtual environment, also found a worryingly high level of total obedience (32 per cent).

One pair of Dutch researchers argued that Milgram's paradigm lacked mundane realism (after all, when was the last time someone asked you to deliver an electric shock to another person?). Consequently, they developed an alternate methodology which they called 'administrative obedience'. Instead of an electric shock, participants were asked by an experimenter to deliver 'stress remarks' to a candidate (a confederate) taking a job application test; they were told that if the candidate failed the test they would not be offered the job. Despite this knowledge, almost 92 per cent of participants obeyed the experimenter and delivered 15 stress remarks which caused the candidate to fail.

As can be seen, obedience research is still being conducted, and is still delivering findings that are of some concern. It seems that ordinary people will carry out a number of dubious activities, simply because they are told to do so by a person who they perceive to have some kind of authority over them.

Summary

Whilst it is generally accepted that social influence is a necessity of day-to-day life, research has helped to understand why people are influenced by others. For example, we may conform to the behaviour of others because we are unsure of the correct way to act or simply because we want to be liked by them. Moreover, such conformity might be affected by a number of personal and situational factors. Occasionally, it might also be possible for the minority to influence the majority, but certain conditions need to be met. Similarly, research has helped us to understand some of the factors that might affect why people obey the request of an authority figure, even when the request may be to the detriment of others (or even ourselves). Worryingly, it seems that we might not yet have learned some important lessons from research conducted over forty years ago.

Food for thought

Imagine you are serving on a jury for a murder case. When the jury retires to consider their verdict, it quickly becomes clear to you that ten people believe the defendant is guilty, one person is unsure and only you believe the defendant is innocent. In light of the content of this chapter, list what forces you think would be at play in the jury room, and consider your strategy for convincing the other members of the jury that the defendant was innocent.

Dig deeper

Blass, T. (2007). *The Man who Shocked the World: The Life and Legacy of Stanley Milgram*. Basic Books.

Burger, J. M. (2009). 'Replicating Milgram: Would people still obey today?' *American Psychologist*, **64(1)**, 1–11.

Haslam, S. A. & Reicher, S. D. (2012). 'Contesting the "Nature" Of Conformity: What Milgram and Zimbardo's Studies Really Show'. *PLoS Biology*, 10(11)

Milgram, S. (1974) *Obedience to Authority*. Tavistock.

Zimbardo, P. (2008). *The Lucifer Effect: How Good People Turn Evil*. Rider.

Fact-check

1 What percentage of participants in Milgram's original study were totally obedient?
   a 50%
   b 55%
   c 65%
   d 70%

2 John goes to a restaurant with his friends. When it comes to ordering dessert, he is urged to have one because everyone else is having one. He initially says 'no' because he is not hungry, but because his friends start complaining that he is being unsociable, he changes his mind and orders a bowl of ice cream. This is an example of:
   a Compliance
   b Obedience
   c Normative influence
   d Informational influence

3 In his 'line judgement paradigm', Asch found that what percentage of his participants never gave a wrong answer despite the pressure of majority influence?
   a 13%
   b 25%
   c 37%
   d 49%

4 In the same experiment as question 3, what percentage of participants conformed to the majority decision at least once despite knowing that the answer they were giving was wrong?
   a 13%
   b 25%
   c 37%
   d 49%

5 The 'autokinetic effect' was used by which researcher to show that we sometimes change our decision in light of what other people say simply because we are unsure of how to act in an ambiguous situation?

  a Solomon Asch

  b John Darley

  c Stanley Milgram

  d Muzafer Sherif

6 Peter decides he wants to improve his chess-playing, so he joins an established chess club in his area. On the first night he goes along at 6:30pm, starts chatting to some people in the room and begins a game with one of them. Everything is going well. However, at 7pm, everyone suddenly stops playing, bows their heads and starts to recite over and over again: 'Chess is good, Chess is power ...'. After a few seconds, bizarrely Peter does the same. This is an example of:

  a Informational influence

  b Obedience

  c Normative influence

  d Compliance

7 Which of the following factors have been linked to increased conformity?

  a An authoritarian personality

  b A lower IQ

  c High levels of anxiety

  d All of the above

  e None of the above

8 Which of the following is not a good strategy for a minority to adopt in order to influence a majority?

  a Be consistent in their message

  b Generally keep a low profile

  c Walk a fine line between rigidity of position and flexibility of position

  d Ensure that all members of the minority agree with each other at all times

9 In one of his variations, how did Milgram show that sometimes situational elements might affect obedience levels?

 a He recruited female participants instead of using solely males

 b He allowed the 'teacher' to choose their own level of punishment to administer

 c He changed the clothes that the experimenter was wearing, from a white coat to a black coat

 d He moved the experiment from Yale University to the nearby city of Bridgeport

10 Which of the following is not a valid criticism of Milgram's experiments in general?

 a They really tell us nothing useful about the mechanisms involved in obedient behaviour

 b They violate the ethical principle of 'informed consent'

 c They lack mundane realism

 d All of the above are valid criticisms

 e None of the above are valid criticisms

7

Attitudes and persuasion

What do you think about the leader of your country? Should smoking be banned in all public places? Is global warming something you are concerned about? How do you feel about cricket or football? Would you buy a burger from a popular chain of fast-food outlets? Your answers to all of these questions reflect your attitudes.

Attitudes are important because they play a key role in how an individual views the world; therefore it is important to understand what an attitude is and how they are formed. To answer these questions, it is first necessary to measure them, and this is not always as easy as it might seem. Once we know what a person's attitudes are, the problem is then whether or not we can change them in terms of an individual's behaviour, either permanently (persuasion) or temporarily (compliance). This chapter aims to address these questions.

What is an attitude?

A number of definitions abound with regards to what an attitude is and isn't (see Spotlight below), but most contain a reference to some form of evaluative judgement, that is, do we favour something or not. In essence an attitude is how much we like or dislike something, and the 'something' (generally referred to as the *attitudinal object*) can be an object, a person or an idea. Attitudes are learned by an individual as opposed to them being innate.

Spotlight: Defining attitudes

Two definitions that seem to capture the essence of what an attitude is come from Eagly and Chaiken (1993):

> 'a psychological tendency that is expressed by evaluating a particular entity with some degree of favor or disfavor... psychological tendency refers to a state that is internal to the person, and evaluating refers to all classes of evaluative responding, whether overt or covert, cognitive, affective or behavioral' (p. 1)

and from Maio and Haddock (2010) who put it slightly more succinctly:

> 'an overall evaluation of an object that is based on cognitive, affective and behavioral information' (p. 4).

Differing aspects of an attitude

There are three aspects of attitudes in which social psychologists have taken an interest: content, structure and function.

It is generally agreed that **attitude content** can be split into three components – the ABC of attitudes:

1 Affective

2 Behavioural

3 Cognitive

Key idea: Attitude content

This refers to the affective, behavioural and cognitive components of an attitude.

The affective component refers to how we feel about something, and the emotions that it evokes. The behavioural component refers to how we act (or have acted) with regards to the object, and our experiences with it. The cognitive component refers to how we think about an object, the beliefs that we have with regard to it, and also the attributes we link with an object. For example, my attitude towards cricket is that I enjoy watching it as I find it quite soothing (*affective element*), I have played it in the past quite successfully (*behavioural element*) and believe it to be an intriguing game which not only requires physical skills but psychological ones too (*cognitive element*). This is an example of where all of the components of an attitude are in one direction, e.g. positive: this is referred to as the *valence* of an attitude.

However, some attitudes can be mixed. To take a simple example, I might think that having some knowledge of classical literature would make me a more rounded, better educated person (*positive cognitive*) but feel that life is too short to spend so much of my time on such a pursuit (*negative affective*) especially as when I have tried in the past to read such books they just send me to sleep (*negative behaviour*). If I went on to list many more positive aspects along with many more negative aspects of reading classical literature, this would represent an *ambivalent* attitude. This then leads us to consider the question of the **attitude structure**.

There seem to be two different views on the structure of attitudes:

1 One-dimensional view: this suggests that attitudes are measured on a continuum, one end of which denotes positivity and the other end denotes negativity. Completely positive or negative attitudes would seem to be accounted for by this view, as would situations where an attitude comprises many positive but one or two negative views (or vice versa).

2 Two-dimensional view: this suggest that attitudes should be plotted on a two-axis graph, where one dimension represents the amount of positive views with regard to the attitudinal object, and the other dimension represents the amount of negative views. Ambivalent attitudes seem better represented by this view.

Key idea: Attitude structure

This refers to the positive and negative dimensions of an attitude, and how they are distributed across the affective, behavioural and cognitive components.

The two-dimensional approach would seem to give a richer, more complete view of attitudes: for example, imagine an individual was asked to rate their attitude towards cricket on a nine-point scale (see attitude measurement below) where 1 indicated a negative view, 9 indicated a positive view and 5 was the mid-point: this would represent a one-dimensional view. If the individual circled the '5', what would we be able to infer about their view of cricket? It could indicate that they have never played or watched it, therefore they are using '5' to indicate that they have no positive or negative feeling; alternately, they might have lots of positive and negative views towards the game, and to represent this balance, they might choose '5' as a compromise position. A two-dimensional representation would give us a clearer view of which of the two positions was represented by the individual's attitude.

Whilst everyone has many attitudes, some are certainly held more strongly than others. *Attitude strength* can signal key information, such as how important an attitude is to an individual and the degree of certainty with which they hold a particular attitude. Certainly my attitude towards cricket is a lot stronger than my attitude towards classical literature. In general, it has been found that strong attitudes differ from weak attitudes on a number of dimensions:

▶ **Durability**: strong attitudes tend to be more temporally stable: they last longer (I've liked cricket since about the age of 15).

▶ **Resistant to change:** strong attitudes are less likely to crumble in the face of persuasive messages (no one has been able to persuade me that test match cricket is boring).

▶ **Influence:** individuals are likely to pay greater attention to information which is related to strong attitudes than they are to information related to weak attitudes (I'm more likely to read the cricket section of the sports pages than I am to read the horse racing section).

▶ **Behaviour:** strong attitudes tend to influence behaviour far more than weak attitudes (if I have the choice between watching cricket on television or reading a work of classic literature … well, I think you know the answer to that one!).

In order to understand why people hold different attitudes, it is necessary to understand the **attitude function**, and for most people they serve multiple purposes. According to Smith et al. (1956), attitudes have three primary functions:

1 **Object appraisal:** they help us to weigh up the positive and negative features of objects. This will help us to avoid harmful things and embrace the positive ones. It is generally considered to be the most important function of an attitude.

2 **Social adjustment:** they help us to identify others who we might like, and help us to avoid those we dislike.

3 **Externalization:** they protect us against things that might cause us some degree of internal conflict.

Others have proposed slightly different functions of attitudes, some of which bear a similarity to the three listed above, and some which add to them. For example, Katz (1960) argued that attitudes help us to express who we are and help to define us in terms of our self-concept; through the attitudes we hold, and share externally, others are able to learn about us. Some attempts have been made to measure the functions of attitudes more explicitly, such as the 'attitudes functions inventory' (Herek, 1987). However, some critics argue that such measurement tools are not accurate as individuals may not know themselves what functions their attitudes serve.

Key idea: Attitude function

This refers to the different purposes that an individual's attitudes serve.

Having looked at what an attitude is, and at the different aspects of attitudes, the next question to consider is how we might measure them.

Measuring attitudes

Attitudes are not tangible objects, instead they are buried somewhere inside an individual's head. This makes measuring them quite difficult (but that has never stopped social psychologists before). Generally speaking, there are two main ways of measuring attitudes:

1 **Explicit methods**: these ask direct questions about an attitude; an individual will be aware that this is happening.

2 **Implicit methods**: these tap into attitudes indirectly; an individual is usually unaware that their attitudes are being assessed.

Explicit methods typically use self-report questionnaires which ask an individual to report on their opinions about an attitudinal object. A typical questionnaire of this nature will use a 'Likert' scale, with some items being reverse scored, in order to assess an individual's attitude towards a particular attitudinal object, such as a political party or a brand of bread (see Spotlight below). This method is quite common, though limited in that the construction of questions ties a questionnaire to a specific object.

Other direct methods of measuring attitudes include the 'semantic differential approach', which has the advantage of being able to compare attitudes across topics. It simply uses a number of adjectives (such as good/bad; positive/negative) as anchor points on a scale. Individuals then mark a point on the scale to reflect their views of the attitudinal object. Using this method, it would be possible to compare an individual's attitude towards both cricket and classical literature more easily than using a Likert scale, which would require two specially constructed scales.

However, there are a number of problems with using direct methods of attitudinal measurement. For example, an individual might not actually be aware of what their attitude towards the object actually is. Additionally, great care must be taken with question development as slight differences in the way a question is worded can lead to different responses. However, the biggest issue is probably due to social desirability, which means that instead of giving responses that reflect their real opinions, an individual will more likely give a response that presents them in the best possible light (whilst this wouldn't necessarily be a problem with our cricket survey, it could well be a problem with more contentious issues such as immigration).

In an attempt to avoid some of the problems encountered with direct measures, a number of implicit (indirect) methods have been formulated. One such method is *evaluative priming*, and is based on the assumption that attitudes are associations between objects and evaluations, and the stronger the association, the more quickly it can be retrieved from memory. It also assumes that if an individual encounters the object, the evaluation will be triggered. To take such a test, an individual would be seated in front of a computer, and shown the name of the attitudinal object (referred to as the 'stimulus prime'). This is quickly replaced by an evaluative adjective (such as 'disappointing' or 'exciting'). The individual's task is to classify the adjective as quickly as possible as representing either a good or bad thing.

The speed with which the judgement is made is the key. In general, if we are trying to make sense of something, we find it easier to do so if we have recently seen something that is similar. Thus, if the individual is exposed to a stimulus prime that they like (e.g. cricket), they will be quicker at classifying a positive adjective (e.g. 'exciting') as good, but slower at classifying a negative adjective (e.g. 'disappointing') as bad. Similarly, if the stimulus prime was something they disliked (e.g. classical literature), they would be slower to classify a positive adjective, but quicker to classify a negative adjective.

Spotlight: Measuring attitudes directly

Questionnaires typically use a Likert scale to assess attitudes towards an object. For example, to measure attitudes towards cricket, researchers might construct a scale as follows:

The following questions are statements about the game of cricket. Please use a number from the following scale to reflect your personal opinion for each statement.

1 = Strongly disagree
2 = Disagree
3 = Uncertain
4 = Agree
5 = Strongly agree

1 Cricket is a game of skill.
2 Watching cricket helps me to relax.
3 Cricket holds no interest for me.
4 Cricket is a game of brute force and ignorance.

Each of the four questions would be answered using the 1–5 scale. Questions 1 and 2 reflect positive views towards cricket, and thus individuals giving low scores are reflecting a negative attitude; however, as questions 3 and 4 are reflecting negative attitudes, they would need to be *reverse scored* in order to provide a consistent view, thus anyone giving a '5' to question 3 or 4 (a negative attitude) would actually have their score changed to 1 (a score of 4 would be changed to 2). The scores from the four questions would then be added up to give an attitude score between 4 and 20; in this case, higher scores would reflect a more positive attitude towards cricket, and lower scores a more negative view.

However, using the semantic differential approach, attitudes towards cricket could be assessed by using a number of paired adjectives as follows:

Cricket

Bad :___:___:___:___:___:___:___:___: Good

Negative :___:___:___:___:___:___:___:___: Positive

Dull :___:___:___:___:___:___:___:___: Interesting

Using this method, attitudes towards other attitudinal objects (such as classical literature) could easily be measured and compared with one another.

Tests based on evaluative priming have been modified to test less desirable attitudes such as racism (imagine showing a picture of a white or black person as the stimulus prime, and then showing the word 'intelligent'). The 'implicit association test' (IAT) is another such indirect measure of attitudes, and has been used to measure prejudicial attitudes (see Chapter 13).

As well as direct and indirect methods, there has been some attempt to measure attitudes through an individual's physiological responses. For example, pupil dilation and galvanic skin response (essentially a skin sweat response) have both been linked with arousal, and the idea is that a strong arousal response would be a good indicator of the strength of an attitude. However, whilst there is some merit in this view, it is not always possible to determine the valence (positive or negative) of the attitude through such measures.

More recent research has used different types of brain scans (e.g. functional magnetic resonance imaging) to attempt to measure attitudes. However, these findings have not always produced good results; for example, voters were shown pictures of American presidential candidates, and according to the results of brain scans, Mitt Romney showed potential as a candidate, but Barack Obama showed neither positive nor negative signs. Add to this lack of predictive validity, the cost of individual brain scans (probably in the region of several hundred pounds a time), and it is easy to see why this method could be a non-starter.

Do attitudes predict behaviour?

The question of whether attitudes can predict behaviour is an interesting one. An early study by LaPierre (1934) served to illustrate this point. He was travelling across America with a young Chinese couple at a time when there was a strong anti-Asian prejudice, and was concerned about whether or not they would be able to find places to stay and eat. However, only once in over 250 establishments were they refused service which he found quite surprising. Upon the conclusion of his travels, LaPierre wrote to each of the establishments to ask whether or not they would be prepared to serve Chinese visitors; he found that only one establishment said that they would. Given his experiences on his travels, this was presented as evidence that individual attitudes were not good predictors of behaviour.

However, subsequent research, which has been conducted a little more rigorously than the study by LaPierre, suggests that the relationship between attitudes and behaviour may not be quite so simple. In fact, if the conditions are right, then attitudes can indeed predict behaviour, but this is contingent on a number of factors which include:

▶ **Strength of attitude:** stronger attitudes are much more likely to predict behaviour than weaker ones. However, on some occasions, a given behaviour can lead to the formation of a weak attitude (suggesting that the relationship between attitudes and behaviour is not always uni-directional).

▶ **Function of attitude:** attitudes used to express values are much more likely to predict behaviour.

▶ **Topic of attitude:** attitudinal topic can have an influence on behaviour. For example, research suggests that political attitudes are a better predictor of behaviour than attitudes towards blood donation.

▶ **Individual differences:** the personality of an individual has been found to affect the extent to which attitudes predict behaviour. For example, they are a better predictor for people scoring low in 'self-monitoring' than high scorers, but a better predictor for individuals scoring high in the trait of 'need for cognition' than lower scorers.

A number of different models have been formulated to help show how attitudes can predict behaviour, and probably the most well-known of which is Fishbein and Azjen's (1975) 'theory of reasoned action'. This model helps to explain the role that attitudes play in deliberate behaviour, and is based on the assumption that an individual's intention to act is the main determinant of their behaviour. Intention is influenced both by *attitude* (towards the behaviour) and *subjective norms*. An attitude in turn is affected by the anticipation that any behaviour will lead to a desired outcome, and also by the value that is attached to the desired outcome. Subjective norms refer to an individual's beliefs about how important others will view the behaviour. These norms are affected by an individual's beliefs about how they think others expect them to behave and how motivated the individual is to live up to these expectations.

There was much support for the model, but it quickly became clear that a third factor was also capable of influencing both an individual's intention to act and their behaviour – namely *perceived behavioural control*. This led to a revision of the theory, with the outcome being the 'theory of planned behaviour'. Perceived behaviour control refers to whether or not an individual is actually able to carry out the behaviour, regardless of their attitude and any subjective norms. For example, an individual might feel strongly about giving their old clothes to charity (*attitude*), and believe that others would approve of their behaviour (*subjective norm*), but unless they had some means actually to donate their clothes (such as a nearby charity shop and a means of getting there), the behaviour would not occur.

The model suggests that perceived behavioural control moderates behaviour in two ways: it impacts on an individual's intentions by assessing their confidence in their ability to perform the actions (i.e. do they have the resources needed to perform the behaviour?), and it impacts on an individual's behaviour by objectively assessing whether the action can realistically be performed (whilst an individual might believe they can perform an action, their perception might not be an accurate one).

Whilst the model certainly has the support of much empirical research, it is not without limitations: for example, it is not always clear as to which intention-affecting component exerts the greatest influence (or how this might change across situations), and it doesn't tackle the issue of how intentions get translated into action. Nevertheless, the model does give us an interesting insight into the attitude-behaviour question by suggesting both that attitudes are only one of a number of factors that might influence our behaviour, and that their effects are indirect ones.

Other models, such as the 'composite model' (Eagly & Chaiken, 1993, 1998) and the MODE model (Fazio, 1990) have also attempted to explain how attitudes influence behaviour: the former introduces a number of factors that might affect an individual's attitudes towards behaviour, most notably habits, whereas the latter looks at the role of attitudes in predicting both planned and spontaneous behaviour. However, having explored the relationship between attitudes and behaviour, the question must now be whether or not attitudes can be changed.

Changing attitudes – persuasion

Whether for good or bad, people try to change the attitudes of others: the Government might want to change the population's attitudes towards smoking, overeating or saving; advertising companies might attempt to change consumer behaviour by getting them to buy a new brand as opposed to an established brand; our close relations might want to change our attitudes towards other family members. Whilst, technically speaking, attitude change is different from persuasion, the two terms are often used interchangeably, with the latter term being more recognized by most people (see Spotlight below for a definition of persuasion). There has been a great deal of research looking at how persuasion works, with the perhaps idealistic belief that if we could change people's attitudes (such as reducing prejudice and crime), then the world would be a better place (though some advertising companies would undoubtedly be much richer).

Two of the most popular models of persuasion put forward the idea that there are two ways in which an individual can be persuaded. Petty and Cacioppo's (1986) '*elaboration likelihood model*' (ELM) suggests that there are two routes to persuasion: the *central route* and the *peripheral route*. The former involves the individual paying careful attention to the message being presented; they will reflect on the ideas and assess the evidence supporting the message. The latter involves the individual using cues that aren't related directly to the message. For instance, if we are watching a political debate on television, using the central route would suggest that we are paying particular attention to the words used by the candidate and whether their ideas seem rational and evidence-based. Using the peripheral route, we may pay more attention to the clothes they are wearing, how attractive we think they are, and how confident they look and sound. Which route we use can depend on many factors, such as:

▶ **How motivated we are to attend to the message**: high motivation tends to lead us down the central route, whereas low motivation tends to suggest we will use the peripheral route. Thus when we watch a party political broadcast on behalf of the Labour party, we are more likely to use the central route if we are a Labour supporter and more likely to use the peripheral route if we support a different political party.

▶ **Our capability to process the message**: if we feel that we can understand the ideas being put forward in the message and can generally make sense of it, then we are more likely to use the central route; otherwise we will rely more on the peripheral route.

▶ **Distraction**: the more distracted we are, the more likely we are to use the peripheral route; the more focused we are, the more likely we are to use the central route.

▶ **Time constraints**: if we have plenty of time, we will use the central route, but a lack of time could lead us down the peripheral route.

▶ **Individual differences**: our personality traits may lead us more predominantly down one route than the other; for example, those high in 'Need for Cognition' will be more likely to use the central route.

There are certainly other factors that might also affect how we process a message (e.g. our mood). Petty and Cacioppo don't rule out the possibility that an individual might use both routes to process a message, but instead suggest that one will be used more predominantly than the other, depending on many of the factors listed above. Research supports this model and also suggests that a message is more likely to be longer lasting if it is processed by the central route.

An alternative dual-route model of Persuasion has been put forward by Chaiken and Eagly (e.g 1980). Their 'heuristic systematic model' (HSM) is similar to the ELM in many ways. For example, it suggests that an individual has two modes of processing a message: *systematic processing* and *heuristic processing*. The first mode is analogous to the central route of the ELM and the second mode is similar to the peripheral route. The HSM also suggests that messages are likely to be processed simultaneously by both modes and affected by many of the same factors as the ELM. However, the major difference put forward by the HSM is what the authors call *the sufficiency principle*; they suggest that an individual will attempt to gather as much information as they need to make a decision (e.g. which candidate to vote for, which brand of washing powder to buy) but no more than is strictly necessary; an individual will balance the two modes of processing in order to get the information that they think they need.

Both models have been shown to be useful in explaining how an individual will react to a persuasive message. However, critics suggest that there is very limited evidence of simultaneous processing of a message in the way that both models claim there will be. An alternative to the dual-processing models is the uni model of persuasion put forward by Kruglanski, which claims that there is simply one route to persuasion. The model suggests that there isn't a qualitative difference between the two types of processing proposed by the dual-route models, just a quantitative one – the messages themselves dictate how much processing is needed by an individual, with longer messages needing more attention paid to them than shorter ones. Whilst this model has the advantage of being simpler than the other two, there is much evidence to suggest that many messages are processed in distinctly different ways, thus favouring the explanatory power of the dual-route models.

COMPLIANCE – SHORT-TERM BEHAVIOUR CHANGE
Changing behaviour based on more strongly-held attitudes tends to be a long-term process that can require a sustained

effort. However, there are some occasions when a temporary change in behaviour is required which is not driven by an attitude; for example, you know that your friend has a strict policy (attitude) on not buying raffle tickets, but just on this one occasion you want them to make an exception to their rule. This is also something that 'compliance professionals' try to do: you may have gone into a shop just to look at new televisions and had no intention to buy one – but the salesperson might have had other ideas (after all, their livelihood probably depends on it). Getting another person to agree to a request, which ends in a short-term change to their behaviour, is referred to as **compliance**.

Key idea: Compliance

A superficial change in behaviour due to a direct request from another person or group.

There are a number of strategies that can be used to bolster the chances of compliance in another person, and these include the use of:

1 Reciprocity

2 Commitment/consistency

3 Liking

4 Scarcity

The principle of *reciprocity* suggests that if I do something for you, then you will feel obliged to do something for me at a later time: the feeling of being 'in debt' to another is a hard one to shake and we will take the first opportunity to balance the ledger. Therefore, if you want your friend to buy a raffle ticket, try making them a cup of coffee (or a beverage of their choice), and then a little while later ask them to buy a raffle ticket – the first behaviour should greatly enhance the chances of compliance with your request. Reciprocity does not just work with giving something, but also with taking away something aversive, as research into the 'door-in-the-face' technique shows (see Case study below).

The use of *commitment and consistency* as a compliance technique relies on the idea that people like to be seen as consistent and reliable. One such tactic to use this strategy is the 'foot-in-the-door' technique. This involves subjecting an individual to a small, but reasonable request which will activate feelings of consistency and reliability. Following this initial request with a larger, but related request, can force the individual to comply with it in order to maintain their feeling of consistency and reliability. A classic study found that individuals who were asked to erect a large and obtrusive 'Reduce your speed' sign in their back garden were much more likely to comply with the request when they had first been asked (and agreed) to put a small 'Reduce your speed' poster in their window some days before.

Liking another person is generally a good way of increasing compliance. In general, we are much more likely to say 'yes' to a request if it comes from a person who we know and like. However, more recent research on the concept of 'fleeting attractiveness' suggests that even making a tenuous connection with someone can increase compliance levels. One piece of research found that participants who simply sat in a room with a person without any communication (whilst completing an experiment) were much more likely to accede to a request from them (49 per cent of the time) after the experiment was concluded, than if they were approached by them as a stranger (26 per cent). In the same set of experiments, if the situation was staged so that the participant believed that they shared the same date of birth with the person, then their compliance levels rose even more dramatically (62 per cent). The implications of such research suggests that building up even the most fragile of relationships with the target of your request can increase compliance levels dramatically (look out for such behaviour from salespeople in the future!).

Case study: Reciprocity and compliance – the door-in-the-face technique

Robert Cialdini and his colleagues (1975) investigated how compliance levels could be affected by the door-in-the-face technique, whereby a large, unrealistic request (which is unlikely to be acted upon) is followed by a more reasonable request. They set up a situation in which a class of students were asked to volunteer to chaperone a group of juveniles from a local detention centre on a trip to a nearby zoo; they were told it would require two hours of their time and would be unpaid. In this condition, only about 17 per cent of students volunteered. In a second condition, students were first asked to volunteer for a programme to act as counsellors at the local juvenile detention centre, which would require them to act as a big brother or sister to one of the detainees for about two hours a week over the next two years.

When no one volunteered for this opportunity (as no one ever did), the large request was followed up with the smaller zoo request (as outlined previously). In this condition, 50 per cent of students volunteered to act as a chaperone (compared to the 17 per cent in the initial condition). They speculated that this was because the researchers were seen to do the students a favour (i.e. they moderated the size of their request), and many students felt obliged to reciprocate in some way.

The threat of *scarcity* has also been found to increase compliance. If we find out that there is something that we can't have, we are likely to want it even more. Cast your mind back to shops that have advertised closing down sales, or 20 per cent discounts for one day only. Such events are designed to modify our behaviour. One study found that when recruiters at a student fair, who were looking to fill positions at their company, were given a choice of interviewing students who had either already got a job offer from another company (thus a scarce commodity), or students with no such job offers, they were more likely to go for the former group.

These four strategies represent very effective ways for increasing compliance levels, and thus bringing about a temporary change in the behaviour of another. It will come as no surprise that such strategies are used regularly and creatively both by compliance professionals (such as salespersons) and con artists.

Summary

Attitudes play an important role in our lives, and this chapter has shown what an attitude is, of what it is comprised and how social psychologists have attempted to measure them. It has also become clear that our attitudes do predict our behaviour in many situations. Additionally, evidence from the persuasion literature has shown that it is possible to change our attitudes based on the way in which persuasive messages are processed; research in the field of compliance has also illustrated that it is perhaps possible to by-pass our attitudes and effect a short-term change in our behaviour.

Food for thought

When you are next watching adverts on television, try to identify what component(s) of your attitudes they are targeting, and how they are attempting to modify your attitudes (your beliefs about the product, how you feel about the product, and whether or not you will buy the product). Are they hoping for a long-term change in your attitudes or just a short-term change in your behaviour?

Dig deeper

Brock, T. C. & Green, M. C. (Eds.) (2005). *Persuasion: Psychological Insights and Perspectives*. Second Edition. Sage.

Cialdini, R. B. (2013) *Influence: Science and Practice*. Fifth Edition. Pearson.

Eagly, A. H. & Chaiken, S. (1993) *The Psychology of Attitudes*. Harcourt Brace Jovanovich.

Gass, R. H. & Seiter, J. S. (2011). *Persuasion: Social Influence and Compliance Gaining*. Fourth Edition. Pearson.

Maio, G. R. & Haddock, G. (2010) *The Psychology of Attitudes and Attitude Change*. Sage.

Fact-check

1 With regard to the content of an attitude, which of the following is one of its components?
   a Affective
   b Cognitive
   c Behavioural
   d None of them are
   e All of them are

2 Generally, an attitude towards an object will be either positive or negative. This is referred to as an attitude's:
   a Strength
   b Function
   c Valence
   d Structure

3 In terms of their structure, ambivalent attitudes are best represented by which of the following views?
   a One-dimensional
   b Two-dimensional
   c Three-dimensional
   d Four-dimensional

4 Which of the following is not a dimension on which strong attitudes differ from weak attitudes?
   a Resistance to change
   b Durability
   c Openness
   d Influence

5 Which of the following functions of an attitude is generally considered to be the most important?
   a Object appraisal
   b Social adjustment
   c Externalization
   d They are all equally important

6 Which of the following methods is not an explicit measure of attitudes?
   a Self-report questionnaire
   b Evaluative priming
   c Semantic differential approach
   d All of the above are
   e None of the above are

7 Which of the following is not a factor when considering the extent to which attitudes can predict behaviour?
   a Attitude strength
   b Attitude function
   c Attitude topic
   d Attitude valence

8 Which of the following components appeared in the 'theory of planned behaviour' but not in the 'theory of reasoned action'?
   a Attitude
   b Subjective norms
   c Perceived behavioural control
   d They all appeared in the 'theory of reasoned action'

9 The 'central route of processing' is a component of which model of persuasion?
   a The theory of reasoned action
   b The heuristic systematic model
   c The uni model
   d The elaboration likelihood model

10 The 'foot-in-the-door' compliance technique is based on which of the following strategies?
   a Commitment/consistency
   b Reciprocity
   c Liking
   d Scarcity

8

Prosocial behaviour

There are many stories in the media that tell of tales of courage and compassion; the rescue services at the Twin Towers on 9/11, soldiers in Afghanistan putting their own lives at risk to save those of their comrades, or an individual who jumps down on to tracks at an underground station to save a child from an onrushing tube train. Regrettably we also come across astonishing tales of people's lack of humanity, such as the case in New York in 2010 where Hugo Tale-Yax lay on the pavement in a pool of blood for over an hour, having been fatally wounded going to the aid of a woman who was being attacked. Many people passed by him without offering aid (some even took photographs), and by the time someone did eventually stop to help, it was too late. Social psychologists have striven to understand both types of behaviour.

Defining and studying prosocial behaviour

Generally, there seem to be three types of behaviour aimed at helping others, though the definitions do seem to vary from source to source. According to Bierhoff (2002), these three types of behaviour are defined as:

▶ **Helping behaviour:** This is characterized as an intentional act which is carried out to benefit an individual. This covers all forms of interpersonal support and it is not necessarily voluntary. For example, an assistant in a shop can help a customer, but they do this because they are paid to do so, not necessarily because they choose to do so. This form of behaviour can also be antisocial: for example, an individual can help another person in order to make them look incompetent.

▶ **Prosocial behaviour:** This type of behaviour is purely voluntary and is valued positively by society (and therefore may be culturally determined). It has positive consequences, contributes to the physical and/or psychological well-being of an individual, and is not motivated by professional obligation.

▶ **Altruism:** There is some debate about whether pure altruism actually exists as this type of behaviour puts the emphasis on the needs of another without any consideration of benefit to the helper. This would be exemplified by the parable of the Good Samaritan, or perhaps by the act of heroism by an individual at an underground station outlined above. However, it is difficult to define such an action as purely altruistic as it may have been carried out in order to alleviate anticipated personal distress.

'... the broad range of actions intended to benefit one or more people other than oneself – behaviors such as helping, comforting, sharing and cooperation'... Altruism is motivation to increase another person's welfare ... Prosocial behaviour need not be motivated by altruism; altruistic motivation need not produce prosocial behaviour.

(C. Daniel Batson, 1998, p. 282)

One of the challenges faced by researchers is to capture and understand the diversity of prosocial behaviour. For example, there are many different dimensions to helping, and these can include:

- ▶ Planned vs. spontaneous

- ▶ Serious vs. non-serious

- ▶ Direct vs. indirect

Planned helping might include a regular monthly donation from your wages to a charity, whereas *spontaneous* helping could include giving directions to a motorist who stopped you in the street whilst you were out walking. Helping in a *serious* situation could include going to the aid of victims of a car crash, whereas *non-serious* intervention might be characterized by helping to pick up dropped groceries from a basket. *Direct* helping would be exemplified by assisting in an immediate fashion, such as rushing over to a person who has collapsed in the street, whereas *indirect* helping would, in such a situation, be characterized by calling the emergency services. A good theory should be able to explain why we help in all of these different types of situation.

Similarly, a question has also been raised regarding how often prosocial behaviour actually occurs in daily life and whether simple lab experiments (of which social psychologists are very fond) can actually capture the richness and diversity of the helpfulness of individuals. For example, helping behaviour can actually increase over time, and if an experiment only looks to capture whether an individual helps within a given time frame (e.g. a ten-minute experiment), then it might not capture delayed helping. Likewise, the amount of helping is rarely measured – it is normally only captured in a yes/no format without any contextualization. For example, a child or adult who donates to a charity collection is said to have shown some form of prosocial behaviour, but the helping might be viewed differently if the donation represents either a substantial, or negligible, amount of their individual wealth.

For a complete understanding of how and why individuals help (or not), researchers must attempt to capture the full gamut of behaviours.

Approaches to explain why people help

There are two broad approaches to explaining prosocial behaviour: the *biological approach* (nature) and the *learning approach* (nurture). The former suggests that we are predisposed to help (it's in our genes) whereas the latter suggests that we are taught whether, and how, we should help.

According to the biological approach, genes that further our chances of survival should be passed on, and those that don't should disappear. The survival of our genetic lineage is all important, and this has implications for the field of prosocial behaviour. If the biological approach is to play a major role in explaining why people do or don't help, there should be evidence to suggest that individuals only help others when it promotes (or at least doesn't adversely harm) their gene survival. There is some evidence to suggest this is the case. For instance, Burnstein and colleagues administered a questionnaire asking people about their likely helping behaviour towards family and strangers, in emergency (e.g. a house fire) and non-emergency (e.g. helping with the shopping) situations. They found that whilst there was a broad range of helping in non-emergency situations which didn't seem to discriminate between those who were genetically related and those who weren't, when it came to a life-or-death emergency situation, helping was prioritized towards genetic relatives.

Key idea: Biological approach to helping behaviour

The assumption than an individual is genetically predisposed to help others (nature).

A further study, which capitalized on a real-life situation where there was a fire at a holiday resort hotel, found a similar occurrence. Survivors were interviewed about their behaviour when they found out that the building was on fire. Those who reported re-entering the burning hotel said that they went in search of family members, and not friends or strangers. This supports the idea that helping is intended to promote gene survival.

However, whilst there is some evidence to support this broad explanation for why people help, the biological explanation for helping behaviour is quite a limited one. Firstly, the evidence used to support it tends to be based on hypothetical questionnaires or anecdotal evidence which is subject to biases, such as social desirability. Secondly, according to this perspective, altruistic behaviour should have disappeared (effectively been bred out of the species) as it serves no purpose if the goal is to promote gene survival. It cannot readily explain why people sacrifice their own lives for those of strangers.

A more plausible approach to explaining helping behaviour is offered by the **learning approach**. Individuals help others because they learn that it is the right thing to do. They learn it from those that they trust (e.g. parents) or those that they like and respect. Similarly, there are rules (norms) of civilized society which help to explain when, and whether, we should help another: evidence suggests we learn these norms early on in life.

Key idea: Learning approach to helping behaviour

The assumption that an individual learns how, and when, to help others from various sources (nurture).

The *norm of reciprocity* (and we come across this very powerful norm many times in social psychology) suggests that there is the assumption that if we help others, then, if we need their aid in the future, there is an increased likelihood that they will help us. This would explain helping behaviour given to a stranger with whom it is possible that we will interact in the future.

The *norm of equity* suggests that we should give benefits (help) roughly in proportion to those benefits that we receive from others. We quickly learn that if somebody only gives back a fraction of what they receive, then we should be guarded about what we give them in the future. This norm is important in regards to interpersonal relationships (see Chapter 5).

The *norm of social responsibility* claims that we should simply help other people because they need it, and because it is the right thing to do. This would explain why we give to charities where there is no expectation that we will get anything back.

Norms are a useful explanation for why we might help others. However, they are not without their problems. For example, they are good as explanatory tools (e.g. John gave money to a homeless person because they needed it) but not as predictive tools (e.g. we can't use them to tell us *when* (or if) John will give money to a homeless person). They can also be a little circular in their explanatory power (e.g. John gives money to a homeless person. Why? Because of the norm of social responsibility. How do we know the norm of social responsibility exists? Because people like John give money to homeless people). Finally, as explanatory tools they can contradict one another: the norm of social responsibility predicts that John will give money to a homeless person, but the norm of reciprocity predicts that he won't (as he can't reasonably expect that person to help him in the future).

Broadly speaking, the learning approach says that we will help others because we learn that it is the right thing to do, and there are a number of ways that this happens:

▶ **Giving instructions**: children are told to be helpful by their parents.

▶ **Reinforcement**: rewarded behaviour is more likely to be repeated, therefore if we are rewarded for helping, we are more likely to do it in the future.

▶ **Modelling**: we see other people helping (usually those who we like or respect, but not always), and therefore we are more likely to help ourselves.

Evidence suggests that modelling, based on Bandura's **social learning theory**, is a very powerful tool to increase learning.

Studies show that children watching television programmes with prosocial content are more likely to engage in helping behaviour than children who don't. Modelling has also been found to be effective with adults too (see Case study below). Numerous pieces of research have shown that if an individual sees others behaving helpfully, whether on TV, in computer games, or in pictures, then they are more likely to be helpful themselves. Interestingly, we'll come across social learning theory again in Chapter 9, when we look at explanations for why people behave aggressively.

Key idea: Social learning theory

Bandura's theory that suggests we learn behaviour from appropriate 'models', such as parents or respected others.

Case study: The helpful motorist

Bryan and Test (1967) carried out a simple piece of research. Motorists passed a car with a flat tyre and a woman standing by it. In one condition, the woman was alone and in the other she was still standing by the car but another motorist had stopped and was giving her help. Further down the road, the motorist encountered (coincidentally!) another car with a flat tyre. Results of the study found that those motorists exposed to prosocial behaviour (as modelled by the motorist who had stopped to help) were 50 per cent more likely to stop and help than those who had not been so exposed.

The search for explanations for why people help or don't help stemmed from the Kitty Genovese incident reported in the New York newspapers in 1964. Kitty was a 28-year-old bar manager who was fatally stabbed as she returned home from her job in the early hours of one morning. As she walked from her car to her apartment, a man grabbed her and she screamed. Lights went on in the nearby apartments, the man stabbed her, she screamed and slumped to the ground. It seemed that the lights drove off her attacker but no help was forthcoming. According to media reports, her assailant returned twice more to attack her and still no help came. When someone finally did call the police, she was dead. The headlines were unkind to the 38 people who reportedly heard her cry for help but did nothing: the incident was labelled as 'bystander apathy' and spawned a whole strand of research to try to explain it (though subsequent reports of this incident suggest this version of events might not be entirely accurate – see Manning et al., 2007).

The cognitive model of helping behaviour

Latane and Darley (1968) proposed a *cognitive model* to explain why people do, or do not, help in an emergency situation (such as the Kitty Genovese incident). They suggested that there were five questions that needed to be answered before an individual would decide to help. At each stage, if the answer was 'no', then no help would be forthcoming: only five positive responses would lead to helping behaviour. The stages are:

1 NOTICE THE EVENT

Failure to notice an emergency situation will obviously result in no help being given. To test which factors might be important in explaining whether or not a situation might be noticed, Darley and Batson (1973) conducted a study using students at a theological seminary. Half of the students were asked to think about the parable of the Good Samaritan (*helping oriented*), and half were asked to think about professional problems facing the priesthood (*task oriented*). Students were then told that they had to report to another building to give a presentation on their topic, but they were told that either: (i) they had plenty of time to do so (no time pressure); (ii) they had just enough time to do so; or (iii) they were running late (maximum time pressure). En route to the building, it was arranged so that the students would pass someone (a confederate) slumped in an alleyway, head down and eyes closed, coughing and groaning.

The researchers were interested to see who would stop and who would carry on. The obvious expectation was that those who were preparing to talk about the parable of the Good Samaritan would be most likely to stop to help. However, this was not the case. It transpired that the best predictor of helping behaviour was the amount of time pressure the participants were under: those with plenty of time to spare were more likely to stop than the others. Those in the maximum time pressure situation seemed not even to notice the confederate. Therefore, time pressure, rather than frame of mind, seems to be a good indicator of whether or not we will even notice an emergency situation.

2 INTERPRET THE EVENT AS AN EMERGENCY

Assuming that the incident is noticed, it must be interpreted as an emergency. Whilst there are times when a situation is a clear-cut emergency, there are many more times where a situation is ambiguous: for example, is the person slumped on the pavement simply drunk or are they seriously ill; is that steam coming out of the vent or smoke from a fire? In an ambiguous situation, we have a tendency to look to others to help us define it; if they appear not to be concerned, then we are more likely to conclude that the situation is a non-emergency. This is referred to as **pluralistic ignorance**. If, however, a person is on their own, they are much more likely to double-check as they have no frame of reference. This conclusion has been supported by the findings from many experiments.

Key idea: Pluralistic ignorance

The phenomenon whereby bystanders assume that nothing is wrong in an emergency situation because no one else appears to be concerned.

3 ASSUME RESPONSIBILITY

Having decided that the situation is one that warrants some form of helping behaviour, the individual must decide whether or not it is their responsibility to intervene. Again, it seems that the more people there are present, the less likely the individual is to help. This is referred to as **diffusion of responsibility**; the sense of responsibility felt by any one individual will decrease as the number of witnesses increases.

This rule can be mitigated by a number of factors. For example, an individual's sense of competence: if they feel that they are uniquely qualified to help, e.g. they are a medical doctor and they witness an accident where someone is injured, then they are more likely to help. Similarly, if the individual notices that other witnesses appear to be more qualified to help, e.g. they are dressed in nurses' uniforms, they will be less likely to help. Finally, more recent research suggests that, whilst the probability of receiving help decreases as the number of bystanders increases, this effect may only be found for non-dangerous emergencies: where the emergency is severe, help is likely to be received regardless of more than one bystander being present (Fischer et al., 2006).

Key idea: Diffusion of responsibility

The more witnesses there are to an emergency situation, the less likely any one individual will be to offer help.

4 KNOW THE APPROPRIATE FORM OF ASSISTANCE

Having accepted responsibility for helping, if the individual does not know the appropriate form of assistance to give, then they are unlikely to intervene directly. Thus if they feel that a person who has collapsed on a hot day is in need of CPR, but they don't know how to administer it, then they are less likely to help; but if they feel that the person has heatstroke, and can be helped by being given a drink, then they may feel more able to do this, and therefore they will intervene.

5 IMPLEMENT THE DECISION TO HELP

The final stage requires actual intervention. It may be that the previous four stages have been passed successfully, but there are still barriers to intervention. For example, it could be an inherently dangerous situation and to help might risk their own lives, or they may simply feel afraid of appearing foolish if they do the wrong thing.

Case study: The smoke-filled room experiment

Latane and Darley (1970) asked individuals to volunteer to fill in a questionnaire measuring 'attitudes to urban life'. When they reported for the study, the participants were taken to a room to complete the survey. They were either alone in the room, with two other strangers or with two confederates. After a short time, smoke was pumped into the room, and the reactions of the participants observed.

When they were alone, within two minutes, 50 per cent had left the room to seek help; after six minutes, 75 per cent had left the room. When they were with two other strangers, after two minutes, only 12 per cent had left the room, and after six minutes the figure had only increased to 36 per cent. When they were in the room with two stooges, who had been instructed to pretend that nothing was amiss, only 10 per cent eventually left the room to seek help, despite at one point the smoke being so dense that it was unlikely they could clearly see the questionnaire!

Latane and Darley concluded that the presence of others inhibits people from responding to an emergency situation, especially if they seem to be unconcerned by the unfolding events. These types of experiments (see also Latane and Rodin's (1969) 'Lady in Distress' study) can perhaps start to give us an insight into bystander apathy.

Overall, the model has an intuitive feel to it, and can account for both emergency and non-emergency situations; there is also some good evidence to support it. However, it is perhaps a little far-fetched to believe that there is any conscious attempt by an individual to address the five questions before deciding to intervene. Additionally, the model is a little too linear, and also doesn't take into account the emotional reactions of the individual who is contemplating offering help. Nevertheless, it provides a good first step in understanding the cognitive processes that may be involved in determining whether or not an individual will offer help in an emergency situation.

The bystander-calculus model

Another model, which attempts to address the shortcomings of the cognitive model, is the bystander-calculus model (Piliavin et al., 1981). This suggests that bystanders, who perceive a person in trouble and in need of assistance, work through three stages:

1 **Physiological arousal**: when exposed to a potential emergency situation, an individual experiences a change in their physiology (e.g. their heart rate). Initially, there is a decrease in physiological signs (an *orienting response*) as they try to figure out what is happening. Then, as they prepare to act (or not), their physiological signs increase (a *defence reaction*). In general, the greater the arousal, the more likely it is that the individual will act.

2 **Labelling the arousal**: exactly how the individual will act depends on how they label their arousal. The arousal does not trigger a specific emotion, instead it is left to the individual to decide whether they are feeling *personal distress* (they are more likely to leave the scene without helping) or empathic concern (they are more likely to intervene with helping behaviour).

3 **Evaluating the consequences** (via a reward-cost matrix): however, before intervention is assured, the costs and benefits are weighed to decide if, and what type of, helping will be offered (see Spotlight below).

This model has the advantage of considering the emotions of the potential helper, but still has a slightly mechanical feel to it.

Spotlight: Weighing the costs of intervening

According to stage 3 of Piliavin et al.'s bystander-calculus model, an individual will weigh up the costs of helping (high/low) and the costs of not helping (high/low) before making a decision to intervene or not. This is illustrated in the table below:

	COST OF HELPING	
COST OF NOT HELPING	**Low**	**High**
High	Directly help	Indirect intervention or seek to lower cost for not helping
Low	Depends on personal norms	May ignore; May deny the problem; May leave the scene

Only one situation dictates automatic helping. All of the others may depend on personality characteristics, time and other factors. The predictions are general, and do not appear to account for the most extreme situations.

Other theories have also been used to explain helping behaviour. For example, *social exchange theory* suggests that whether or not an individual helps is based on self-interest. Rewards and costs are weighed (albeit implicitly rather than consciously), and only if the latter outweigh the former will help be offered. Rewards and costs will vary from individual to individual, for example the costs of jumping into a river to save a drowning person will be prohibitively high to a non-swimmer but negligible to an Olympic-class swimmer; a normally helpful person will be unlikely to help if they find themselves under unbearable time pressures. This theory, popular in the area of interpersonal attraction (see Chapter 5), bears a resemblance to stage 3 of the bystander-intervention model, but has been criticized by some as being inappropriate for the discussion of prosocial behaviour as it certainly doesn't allow for the existence of altruism.

Other theories have concentrated more on the impact of where the emergency takes place. For instance, Milgram's 'urban overload hypothesis' proposes that the location of an incident can determine whether or not helping behaviour will be offered. Initial findings suggested that more help was given in rural areas as opposed to urban areas. For example, one study conducted in Australia suggested that a man limping down a street, who then falls over and reveals a bandaged but bleeding shin, was helped approximately 50 per cent of the time in a small town, but only

15 per cent of the time in a city. This finding was repeated for a number of different types of helping behaviour (e.g. helping a lost child or giving directions to a stranger) in a number of different countries (though not all – see Case study below).

Milgram put forward his theory which suggested that people living in cities are continually being bombarded with stimulation and that they keep to themselves in order to avoid being overloaded by it. Consequently they are unlikely to help as much as those living in less stimulating environments (such as towns or villages), although a slight modification to the theory suggests that it is the population density which affects helping rather than its actual size: the greater the density, the less likely help will be offered.

Case study: Cultural differences in helping behaviour

Levine (2001) reports on the amount of help given in different cities throughout the world. In one situation, a supposedly blind man (actually a confederate) was about to make his way out on to a busy road at a pedestrian crossing. In Rio (Brazil), 100 per cent of the time he was offered help before putting his life at risk. However, he fared less well in other cities: passers-by in New York (USA) and Rome (Italy) only helped about 75 per cent of the time, and those in Shanghai (China) only helped a little better than 60 per cent of the time. Overall, using a composite score of helping in three different types of situation, Rio and San Jose (Costa Rica) rated as the top two most helpful places in the world, with New York and Kuala Lampur (Malaysia) ranking as the bottom two (22nd and 23rd).

Finally, the 'empathy-altruism model' proposes a slightly more upbeat explanation for helping behaviour. Proposed by Batson (1991), this model suggests that if we can put ourselves into the metaphorical shoes of a person who is in need of help, and experience what they might be feeling, then we are more likely to help. In short, if we can feel empathy for the person in need, then we will exhibit altruistic behaviour. However, the model goes on to suggest that if we don't feel empathy for the person, then we may still help but only if it is in our self-interest to do so (i.e. the rewards outweigh the costs). This theory has its merits in that it suggests that altruism can exist, however it is very difficult to determine the exact nature of the motives underlying some potentially very complex behaviour: that is to say, do people experiencing empathy help purely out of concern for the person in need or do they do it to alleviate their own growing personal distress?

Most of the previous explanations are situational in nature and don't consider the core attributes of the individual who is proposing to help. This potentially crucial factor should not be ignored.

Individual differences in helping behaviour

It is generally agreed that any type of behaviour, prosocial or otherwise, is a product of both the situation in which an individual finds themselves and the individual's personal characteristics. To this end, a number of researchers have attempted to determine whether or not there are personality traits linked to helping behaviour. Early research found no personality variables that reliably predicted helping behaviour, although positive relationships were found between helping and:

▶ the belief that one's fate lies within one's control;

▶ mature moral judgement;

▶ the need for social approval;

▶ the tendency to take responsibility for the welfare of others.

More recent research reported by Bierhoff (2002), using retrospective interviews with rescuers of Jews during the Second World War, suggested that helpers score more highly on personality characteristics such as social responsibility and internal locus of control, that they placed much more emphasis on an adherence to ethical rules, and they attached much more importance to personal responsibility. Other research has also shown that individuals scoring highly in characteristics such as empathy and agreeableness are more likely to help compared to low scorers. There is also the possibility that unlikely traits, such as Machiavellianism, will, under a specific set of circumstances, lead to more prosocial behaviour.

As well as personality, gender has also been found to mediate helping behaviour. Certainly within western cultures, help offered tends to coincide with cultural norms for genders. The male role is seen to be a more heroic and chivalrous one, and consequently men are seen to help in more heroic and chivalrous ways compared to women. For instance, 91 per cent of individuals who received the Carnegie medal (awarded to individuals in America for risking their lives to save a stranger) were men; though this could of course be due more to physical attributes than to gender. The norm for females is one that places more emphasis on nurturing and caring, and typical helping interventions by women are likely to involve longer term commitment and nurturance, usually directed towards friends rather than strangers; they are much more likely to do volunteer work in communities than men.

> '... research on prosocial behaviour yields patterns of gender specialization that are well known in daily life. Although it is incorrect to claim that there is a more helpful sex, a persistent pattern emerges of female emotionally supportive and sensitive behaviour, especially in close relationships, and male agentic behaviour, often directed to strangers and to the support of social collectives.'
>
> (Alice Eagly, 2009, p. 653)

A final personal characteristic that might affect prosocial behaviour is mood. There can be no doubting that being in a good mood makes us more likely to help others, and there is much research to back this notion (the 'feel good, do good' effect). A good mood, induced in a variety of ways such as performing well on a test, receiving a gift or simply thinking happy thoughts, has led to an increase in helping behaviours, such as contributing money to charity or donating blood.

Being in a bad mood, however, does not necessarily lead to a decrease in helping behaviour. Feeling guilty, for example, has been found to lead to an increase in prosocial behaviour. A field study found that churchgoers were more likely to donate money to charity before attending Confession than after! More controlled experiments, whereby guilt was induced by leading the participant to believe that they had broken a passer-by's camera (they were asked by the passer-by to take a picture and given their camera), found that when there was an opportunity to help a person in distress at a later juncture, guilty participants were more likely to intervene than participants who had not been subjected to the guilt manipulation.

Applying the research

Given the assumption that the world would be a better place if we were all more helpful people, some thought has been given as to how we might put the theories underlying prosocial behaviour into practice. For example, could we increase the likelihood of people donating blood or reporting shoplifting activity?

There is some evidence that just listening to a lecture on this subject can help to increase prosocial behaviour. During the break in one of my lectures on this topic, a student told me that they had just been out to buy a snack and had been given too much change; instead of keeping it as they would have done normally, they returned the surplus to the cashier (I didn't know whether to be proud or shocked). A more controlled example of this effect was found when students were randomly assigned to listen to a lecture either on Latane and Darley's bystander intervention research, or on an unrelated topic. Two weeks later, the students participated in what they believed to be a sociology study. As they were being led to a room by an experimenter, they passed a student lying slumped against a wall. The experimenter didn't appear to be concerned and just carried on walking. Results found that 43 per cent of students who had listened to the prosocial lecture previously stopped to check on the student compared to 25 per cent who hadn't. It would appear that simply knowing something about factors affecting prosocial behaviour (in this case, pluralistic ignorance) may increase helping behaviour.

Similarly, many of the other ideas that have been encountered in this chapter can also be used to increase helping behaviour. Imagine that you own a shop and find that you are prone to shoplifters stealing your stock. Using Latane and Darley's cognitive theory, you decide to put up a number of signs telling your customers what constitutes shoplifting and how they can report it if they see it: this would help to overcome any ambiguity that might be felt by witnesses to a shoplifting event (and if you offered a reward, even better). Likewise, imagine that you wish to increase blood donation, and you are recruiting on a University campus or on the high street. Using the learning approach (specifically Bandura's social learning theory), you might have confederates modelling the behaviour that you want others to emulate – namely, you would have your stooges pretend to sign up to donate blood, with the theory being that if people see others signing up to help, then they too will be more likely to sign up.

Summary

Prosocial behaviour is a complex topic – just defining what is and is not helpful or prosocial can be tricky – and researchers certainly have a number of hurdles to jump through to understand this type of behaviour fully. Nevertheless, a number of theories have been advanced to try to explain if, and when, people will help when the situation requires it. Whether or not such behaviour is learned or innate is also a matter for debate, as is the exact contribution made by the situation and the person's individual characteristics. However, there can be no doubting that the applications of this research are of great importance to society as a whole.

Food for thought

Imagine you are the co-ordinator for a local conservation organization and you realize that the band of volunteers is diminishing. How would you use the information in this chapter to recruit more helpers? Or, as the chief constable of a regional police force, how would you use the information to orchestrate a campaign to help achieve local community safety by getting people to report suspicious activity in their area?

Dig deeper

Bierhoff, H. (2002) *Prosocial Behaviour*. Psychology Press.

Eagly, A. H. (2009) 'The His and Hers of Prosocial Behavior: An Examination of the Social Psychology of Gender'. *American Psychologist*, **64(8)**, 644–658.

Fischer, P., Greitemeyer, T., Pollozek, F. & Frey, D. (2006) 'The Unresponsive Bystander: Are Bystanders More Responsive in Dangerous Emergencies?' *European Journal of Social Psychology*, **36**, 267–278.

Manning, R., Levine, M. & Collins, A. (2007) 'The Kitty Genovese murder and the social psychology of helping: the parable of the 38 witnesses'. *American Psychologist*, **62**, 555–562.

Fact-check

1 A shop assistant helps a customer to choose which television to buy. According to Bierhoff, this is referred to as:
  a Helping behaviour
  b Prosocial behaviour
  c Altruistic behaviour
  d None of the above

2 Which of the following is not a dimension on which helping behaviour should be studied?
  a Planned vs. spontaneous
  b Direct vs. indirect
  c Serious vs. non-serious
  d None of them are valid dimensions for study
  e They are all valid dimensions for study

3 According to Burnstein's study looking at a biological explanation for helping, which of the following is not true?
  a In a non-emergency situation, people will help the elderly as a priority
  b In an emergency situation, people will help children above all others
  c In a non-emergency situation, there is no differentiation between helping relatives and non-relatives
  d In an emergency situation, priority will be given to helping those who are related to the helper

4 John helps Jack because he has been helped by him in the past. This behaviour can be explained by:
  a The norm of social responsibility
  b The norm of equity
  c The norm of reciprocity
  d The norm of fair return

5 According to the learning approach, we learn to help by seeing people we like and respect helping others. This is referred to as:
  a Giving instruction
  b Taking instruction
  c Reinforcement
  d Modelling

6 Which of the following is not a stage in Latane & Darley's cognitive model of helping behaviour?
   a Notice the event
   b Interpret the event as an emergency
   c Diffusion of responsibility
   d Know the appropriate form of assistance

7 The 'smoke filled room experiment' provides evidence for which concept highlighted in Latane & Darley's cognitive model?
   a Diffusion of responsibility
   b Cognitive dissonance
   c Physiological arousal
   d Pluralistic ignorance

8 According to Piliavin et al.'s Bystander-Calculus model of helping behaviour, which of the following four sets of circumstances will lead to direct helping?
   a Lost cost of helping and high cost of not helping
   b High cost of helping and high cost of not helping
   c High cost of helping and low cost of not helping
   d Low cost of not helping and low cost of helping

9 Levine (2001) surveyed a number of international cities with regards to their helping behaviour. Which country's city ranked lowest?
   a Brazil
   b USA
   c Malaysia
   d Italy

10 Which of the following is not true with regards to individual differences in helping behaviour?
   a Machiavellianism has been linked with helping behaviour
   b Men help more often than women
   c A good mood promotes more helping behaviour
   d They are all true
   e None of them are true

9

Aggression

According to a report in the *Times* newspaper in 2005, an off-duty policeman was queuing for tickets outside a cinema when he spotted a brawl involving about forty teenage girls. Being a dutiful individual, he attempted to break up the fight but, instead of resolving the situation, he ended up being set upon first by one girl who punched him in the face and then by some of the others. Many passers-by watched what was happening but none went to his aid. This incident draws a nice link between the previous, and the current, chapter. Why did no one go to the aid of the policeman (hopefully you now have some ideas about how to explain this), and why did the girl(s) attack him in the first place?

This chapter attempts to supply a definition which encapsulates all of the various forms of aggression, and outlines the difficulties of actually measuring aggression. It looks at the two major theoretical positions – biological (nature) and social (nurture) – which attempt to explain aggression, before moving on to look at how individual differences and situational variables might account for aggressive behaviour.

Defining and measuring aggression

It is difficult to arrive at a comprehensive definition of aggression in all its various forms. For example, it would need to include verbal and physical behaviour, direct action leading to aggression and a failure to act which results in aggression, direct and indirect aggression, overt and covert aggression, aggression that is unprovoked and that which is retaliative, physical aggression and psychological aggression, and so on and so forth. On top of that, there are also cross-cultural issues to consider, such that what might be seen as acceptable behaviour in one culture may be seen as taboo in another: for example, a faction of Australian aborigines see violence as ordinary and necessary, but Western cultures would view it as anti-social and probably illegal (see Spotlight below).

Spotlight: Defining aggression

An early attempt to define aggression comes from Baron (1977) who states that it is 'any form of behaviour directed toward the goal of harming or injuring another living being who is motivated to avoid such treatment'.

A good definition should probably incorporate *intent*, the *expectancy* that an action will cause harm, that *avoidance* of aggression from the victim's point of view is preferable, and that any such behaviour is a *violation of social norms*.

It is generally accepted that there are two type of aggression:

1 **Hostile aggression:** In this form, aggression is usually provoked by pain or upset, and is very emotional. Often it is performed as an end in itself. It might be illustrated by a boyfriend who punches his girlfriend after she yells at him.
2 **Instrumental aggression:** This type of aggression is usually more calculated and has a specific aim. For example, the actions of an assassin, a boxing match or perhaps an act of terrorism.

Key idea: Hostile aggression

Behaviour with the intention of inflicting pain or harm to another, usually involving emotion.

Key idea: Instrumental aggression

Aggressive behaviour with some aim other than inflicting pain, usually as a means to an end.

On top of the difficulty of defining aggression comes the problem of measuring it objectively. Early studies used simple verbal measures. After enduring some form of provocation, participants were asked to rate another person on various characteristics, with the assumption being that negative ratings would be presumed to show aggressive behaviour (as a result of the provocation). This type of measure comes with at least two problems: there is a lack of consequences attached to the aggressive behaviour (very rarely the case in the real world); and there is the problem of social desirability, in that participants may not reveal the full extent of their feelings, or they will perhaps tailor their responses to those that they believe the experimenter is looking for.

An alternative technique was pioneered by Buss (1961) when he created the aggression machine. Essentially an electric shock generator (which of course delivered no such thing due to ethical reasons – though just having participants *believe* that they were delivering electric shocks to another person raises ethical questions), the machine was used to gauge the number, duration and intensity of shocks that one person would deliver to a target who had provoked them in some way.

Other experimental methods for measuring aggression include:

▶ **The teacher-learner paradigm:** used by Milgram in his obedience studies(see Chapter 6), whereby the learner is given some form of aversive stimuli (electric shocks in the early days, but replaced by loud noises and other less controversial methods in more recent studies) by the teacher (the real participant) when they fail at a task. The level of aversive stimuli administered is taken as a measure of aggression;

▶ **Essay evaluation:** participants are asked to write an essay and told that it will be evaluated by another participant (a confederate) who will judge it by the number of electric shocks (later replaced by other measures such as level of negative verbal feedback) they administer to the real participant. Later, the participant gets to do the same to the confederate, and aggression is measured by the number of shocks (or verbal feedback) delivered.

▶ **Competitive reaction time:** participants are informed that they are taking part in a competitive reaction time task against an opponent. Whoever wins each trial gets to set the level of aversive stimuli delivered to their opponent (typically an electric shock, but later substituted with a loud noise, or the simple deduction of points from the opponent's total which will decrease the level of reward they are able to claim). The real participant always wins the first trial, and a measure is taken of their 'unprovoked' level of aggression. Their responses after their opponent has delivered shocks to them are then taken as a measure of their aggression;

▶ **The hot sauce paradigm:** avoids using electric shocks and instead measures the amount of hot spicy sauce that a participant puts on the food of a confederate who has provoked them, and who they know dislikes this type of sauce. The quantity of sauce administered is taken as a measure of the participant's aggression. Other studies have given the participant a choice of sauces which differ in their levels of hotness, in order to measure both the quantity and quality of aggressiveness after a participant plays a violent or non-violent video game. This method is perhaps more ethically acceptable than the others mentioned previously.

Whilst these methods may indeed measure aggression, there are other explanations: the participant may genuinely want to help the learner and thus their responses are actually prosocial and not aggressive; they may simply be complying with the cover story of the experiment; or the shock responses may be measuring some form of power or competitiveness.

There are also methodological limitations to these studies: for example, they are measuring aggressiveness where there is no fear of retaliation from the recipient of the aggression (perhaps not realistic in everyday life). Similarly, some methodologies force the participant into an aggressive response, when they might not want to deliver one, or would prefer to use a non-aggressive response. It has also been questioned as to whether these artificial situations generate responses that equate to aggression found in the real-world (external validity).

An alternative, non-experimental, method for measuring aggression is to use observational techniques, whereby aggressive behaviour is observed in naturalistic settings, either as it unfolds in real time (*naturalistic observation*) or in a more systematic, but unobtrusive way (*field experiments*). Naturalistic observation could involve observing aggressive incidents at a football match or in a school playground; these observations in turn could lead to ideas to be tested in a more formal setting. Field experiments devise some kind of intervention in a real-world setting and then measure resulting aggression: for example, Baron (1976) investigated aggressive behaviour at a traffic light by manipulating the amount of time a confederate took to drive off after the traffic light turned green and measuring the number of times that other drivers honked their hooters (taken as aggressive behaviour). Whilst these types of studies are more likely to be free of social desirability responses, and thus more of an indication of aggression in a naturalistic environment, they suffer from a lack of control whereby other extraneous variables might intervene to compromise the aims of the studies (for example, the individual dispositions of the car drivers in Baron's study, an issue that would normally be controlled for by the random allocation of participants to conditions in experimental studies, but which is simply not possible in field studies).

Having looked at some of the issues to be resolved when studying aggression systematically, it is now possible to look at two general approaches – biological explanations (nature) vs. learning explanations (nurture) – which have attempted to account for why people behave aggressively.

Biological explanations for aggression

This approach takes the form of 'instinct theories' of aggression which explain why humans have an innate need to aggress. According to Freud, aggression is inevitable, and his early psychodynamic theory suggested that it was a reaction to frustration experienced in pursuit of pleasure and the satisfaction of the libido. He later modified his idea to allege that, alongside the desire for self-preservation, referred to as **Eros** (the life instinct), there was a second instinct more focused on destruction, referred to as **Thanatos** (the death instinct). He claimed that this destructive aggressive energy needed to be continually turned away from the individual towards the outside, in order to prevent self-destruction: aggressive behaviour thus serves as an outlet when Eros and Thanatos are in conflict. This is sometimes referred to as a hydraulic model – aggression is a way of dissipating the build-up of pressure. From Freud's model we get the idea of *catharsis*, whereby hostility and aggression are diffused in a non-destructive way.

Key idea: Eros and Thanatos

According to psychodynamic theory, to protect Eros (the life instinct) within an individual, the destructive energies of Thanatos (the death instinct) must be continually deflected away, and this manifests outwardly as aggression.

Another biological theory of aggression, similar to Freud's theory in as much that it is a hydraulic model, comes from Lorenz, who believed that aggression has a species serving function. Lorenz claimed that aggression is an innate behavioural disposition which derives from the idea of natural selection, and increases the species' chance of survival. The potential for conflict leads to geographical dispersion which has the effect of ensuring that members of the same species have sufficient resources to survive and flourish. Applying an animal model to humans, he claimed that hierarchies developed and fights between rivals ensured selection of the strongest and healthiest to lead. Ultimately, aggression builds up and needs to be released in a socially acceptable way (hence it is referred to as a hydraulic model). In animals this is done through threat displays and the ritualization of aggression; very rarely do fights lead to permanent injury or death due to their use of appeasement gestures. It is questionable whether this model can really be applied to humans, who have developed weapons that can kill from a distance.

These two models, whilst having an intuitive feel to them, do face some difficulties when it comes to being accepted by the scientific community. For example, Freud's theory is basically untestable – how does one measure Eros and Thanatos? Lorenz's theory, based on the animal model, and the false assumption that animals don't kill one another, is seen as oversimplifying the complexity of human behaviour. Both theories would suggest that if aggression was instinctual or biologically determined, then all societies should be equally aggressive, and this seems not to be the case.

Social learning explanations for aggression

A more accepted view of aggression is that it is a learned behaviour. As with prosocial behaviour, two of the main ways in which aggression is learned is through imitation and reinforcement. The former suggests that if children (and adults) see a 'model' (e.g. a parent or a respected other) behaving in a certain way then the behaviour, in this case aggression, is most likely to be replicated. For example, children seeing their footballing heroes engaging in fist fights on the football pitch are more likely to repeat the behaviour the next time the opportunity arises when they play football.

Reinforcement suggests that behaviours which are rewarded are repeated and those which are not rewarded will not be repeated. For example, a child (or adult) who acts aggressively to get something they desire, and who gets to keep it with no adverse effects, is more likely to repeat the behaviour; those who are punished for their actions (e.g. sent off on the football pitch) are less likely to repeat the behaviour in the future. One of the key studies to support these concepts comes from Bandura and his Bobo doll studies (see Case study below).

Case study: Bandura and the Bobo doll

Albert Bandura carried out a number of studies using a large inflatable (Bobo) doll to show that aggression is learned through imitation and reinforcement. In one study, four five-year-old children were taken into a room that contained a number of toys which included the Bobo doll. In the non-aggressive condition, they saw an adult playing with the toys but ignore the Bobo doll; in the aggressive condition, they saw the adult perform physical (sitting on it and punching it) and verbal (the adult said things like 'Pow') aggression against the doll. The children were then taken to another room where they experienced mild frustration (they weren't able to play with the toys in the room). Finally they were taken to another room where there were more toys and a scaled-down version of the doll. Observations were made of the children and it was found that those who observed the aggressive adult were more aggressive (they imitated specific aggressive acts that they had seen) towards the doll than those who had observed the passive adult and, overall, boys were more aggressive than girls. This showed the role of imitation as a cause of aggression.

Another variation of the study showed that when children were shown a film of the adult model being either rewarded, reprimanded, or neither, for kicking and punching the Bobo doll, children in all three groups were again more likely to be aggressive (compared to a control group); but those who saw the adult model being rewarded for their aggressive behaviour were even more likely to be aggressive towards the doll. This showed the role of reinforcement as a cause of aggression.

A final variation of the study had children in one of four conditions: the children went into a room directly to play with the doll (control condition); the children viewed a video of an adult model kicking and punching the Bobo doll (video condition); the children viewed this behaviour directly (live condition); or the children saw the adult model dressed in a cat costume and the room in which they abused the Bobo doll was made-up to look like a cartoon (cartoon condition). It was found that children performed the most aggressive acts when they viewed the model's aggressive behaviour live, and the least aggressive acts in the control condition; the video condition was second in terms of aggressive acts and the cartoon condition third. This tends to suggest that TV violence (and cartoons) doesn't affect a child's aggressive behaviour nearly as much as perhaps was thought – certainly compared to seeing it firsthand.

Of course, just because an individual sees an act doesn't mean that they will always repeat it; it is likely that learning also takes place as to when imitation is appropriate. Critics of Bandura's research have argued that the behaviour seen in his studies is not actually aggression because it is not carried out against another person. They also argue that just because the children imitated the aggressive behaviour in the lab doesn't mean that they would imitate the behaviour in the real world.

Another social theory that attempts to explain aggressive acts is the **frustration-aggression hypothesis** put forward by Dollard at al. (1939). This is built on the premise that we feel frustration when we are blocked from achieving a goal. The strength of our frustration is determined by a number of factors such as how many times we are blocked, whether the blocking is total or partial, and how strong our desire is to achieve the goal in the first place. The frustration-aggression hypothesis in its simple form has two basic premises:

1 Frustration always leads to some type of aggression.

2 Aggression always comes from some form of frustration.

A basic experiment to demonstrate this would be to prevent (or not) an adult or a child from getting something they desired, and then measuring their aggression. Those who were frustrated show more aggression than those who were not.

Key idea: Frustration-aggression hypothesis

The idea that all frustration leads to aggression and all aggression is caused by some form of frustration.

Some other variables that have been shown to exacerbate the frustration-aggression phenomenon include:

▶ when the interruption of a goal is unexpected;

▶ when the interruption of a goal is seen as illegitimate;

▶ when the goal is closer to being achieved.

However, many critics have claimed that the frustration-aggression explanation is far too simplistic. For example, there are other responses to frustration, such as crying, apathy, or running away (personally I tend to eat chocolate if I'm frustrated!); aggression isn't always a consequence of frustration. Additionally, if aggression does result from frustration, it is not always straightforward to predict the target of the aggression. For example, if you've had a bad day at the office you are more likely to go home and (metaphorically) kick the cat than you are to kick your boss (although you may be sorely tempted!).

To circumvent some of these criticisms, the theory was modified to suggest that frustration is only one of a number of possible stimuli for aggression. However, aggression was still seen as a 'dominant response tendency' following frustration. A number of researchers investigated further as to which specific external stimuli might lead to aggression.

Berkowitz formulated the idea of the '**weapons effect**' whereby the presence of weapons (in all their different forms, e.g. guns, knives, clubs, etc.) are more likely to cause aggression than when they are not present. This led to the coining of the phrase that 'the finger might pull the trigger, but the trigger can also pull the finger'. Many studies show that more aggression is displayed when weapons are present (e.g. shotgun and pistol) than when neutral items are displayed (e.g. badminton racquet). However, these experiments have been criticized as they tend to use male students more often than not, and there are studies that have not replicated the effect. It may be that it isn't the mere presence of the weapons that causes aggression, but instead how individuals interpret the weapons usage.

Key idea: The weapons effect

The notion that the mere presence of a weapon is more likely to increase the incidence of aggression.

A further social explanation suggests that arousal can lead to the triggering of aggressive tendencies. Whilst Berkowitz suggests that a very specific form of arousal – namely anger – can lead to aggression, Zillman proposed the *excitation-transfer model* which used the idea that any form of arousal can have the potential to make us more aggressive. We could, for example, have experienced any event which caused us to become aroused, whether it was through feelings of love, excitement, fear, or the like; however, when we remove ourselves from the event, some residual arousal (excitation) remains. According to this model, the lingering arousal can be carried over (transferred) to another (anger-eliciting) situation, and if we experience frustration or annoyance, then the remaining arousal may cause us to behave more extremely in the situation than if we had not been previously aroused. However, it is important that the attribution for the lingering arousal is not able to be linked to the previous event, but is instead misattributed to the current event which therefore strengthens the aggressive response.

The model has been supported empirically and can be used to explain aggression in a number of real-world situations, such as violence at football matches. For example, the model would suggest that the sheer excitement of watching your team play, or perhaps the disappointment at seeing them lose, may cause you to be aroused. If, at a later time, you then encounter some opposition supporters who then irritate you in some way, the remaining arousal from the previous event (watching your team) might cause you to be more aggressive towards them than if you had encountered them when you were experiencing no residual arousal (perhaps on a non-match day). Some recent research does lend credence to this theory as an explanation for football-related violence, but it does also suggest that the level of identification with your team will play a mitigating role: high identifiers will be more likely to aggress whereas low identifiers are more likely to simply feel sad and avoid any potentially violent situations.

Mediating factors in aggression

In addition to the set theories that attempt to explain aggression, there are many other factors that have been shown to play a mediating role in whether or not aggression occurs. These include individual characteristics such as personality or gender, and environmental factors such as alcohol, temperature and, of course, the media.

Personality characteristics such as a 'Type A' personality have been found to be linked to higher levels of aggression. Type A personalities are highly motivated, assertive and competitive compared to more controlled and laid back Type B personalities. Similarly, those individuals who score highly in measures of trait anger, irritability, emotional susceptibility, or who show a hostile attributional style, are more likely to show higher levels of aggression than individuals who show increased levels of self-control or perspective taking. The belief that there is a link between low self-esteem and aggression has been shown to be more complex than was first believed: it may be that low self-esteem leads to aggression through experiencing shame and humiliation, but many types of aggression require some form of risk-taking that wouldn't be characteristic of individuals with low self-esteem. Similarly, high self-esteem doesn't necessarily making an individual immune to being aggressive (see also Chapter 2).

The obvious *gender differences* with regards to aggression would suggest that males are more aggressive than females, and there is much evidence to support this common sense view. For example, one review of a number of studies showed that men evidenced far higher levels of aggression (both physical and verbal) compared to women in early adulthood, and the largest gender difference seems to occur between the ages of 18–30 (young adults). However, divergence in aggression levels start very early in life, and by pre-school there is a marked difference in levels of personal aggression between boys and girls, though some research claims that the difference may start to appear in toddlerhood. Boys generally show physical aggression and girls are more likely to show indirect aggression.

There have been a number of explanations proposed to account for gender differences in aggression. For example, in childhood, the quicker maturation of girls in infancy may lead to higher levels of self-regulation, or the greater prevalence of rough-and-tumble play by boys, which spills over into aggression, quickly helps to normalize the acceptance of aggressive behaviour. Equally, gender role norms, whereby boys are expected to be more aggressive, and girls are expected to refrain from such behaviour, may have an effect on the development and frequency of aggression.

In adulthood, explanations for gender differences in aggression have included *hormonal differences* (e.g. testosterone), an *evolutionary perspective* and *socialization pressures*. Whilst there is some evidence for a link between an increase in testosterone in males and the greater likelihood of aggression, overall the link is quite weak and tends to rely more on animal studies. Strong evidence would show a variation in male aggression as levels of testosterone fluctuated within the individual and this type of evidence has not been found in a number of studies that have looked for it.

The evolutionary perspective argues that in order to procure a prime female mate, males are required to show more aggression to do so. Evidence from experimental studies (as well as crime statistics) to support this idea has shown that it is primarily young males who show higher levels of physical aggression. Linked to this perspective is the idea that male aggression also occurs to demonstrate their status and power, and to protect it when it is under threat. Accordingly, research shows that males whose status is under threat are far more likely to show aggression than those whose status is not under threat; however, such studies tend to be correlational and not causal in nature. Females, on the other hand, tend to show more indirect aggression than men. The evolutionary perspective suggests that this is because it carries less risk of harm to self than physical aggression, and females cannot afford to jeopardize their traditional nurturing role in bringing up offspring.

Finally, gender differences in aggression can be explained by socialization. It is likely that males learn that it is acceptable for them to be aggressive ('boys will be boys') whereas females learn that it is not acceptable to be aggressive ('it is very unladylike'). The stereotypes will be reinforced by parental reinforcement, such as praise for boys who stand up for themselves and girls who avoid aggressive situations. They are also reinforced by the toys that they are given and the role models to whom they are exposed on television and in real life (there are more aggressive male role models than female, and more nurturing female role models than male). Learning is a very powerful factor in explaining why males are likely to be more aggressive than females.

Whilst individual characteristics go a long way to explaining why aggression occurs, environmental factors should not be dismissed lightly. For instance, it is believed that increased *alcohol* consumption leads to higher levels of aggression, and this is indeed supported by many studies. However, other research has shown that there is no apparent link between the two. The most likely explanation for the apparent contradiction in research findings suggests that alcohol hinders our normal cognitive functioning, and changes the extent to which we allow situational and contextual cues to influence our behaviour. Thus when we are drunk, we might be more influenced by those around us chanting 'fight, fight, fight', than if we were sober in the same situation; in the former situation, we may find ourselves engaging in a brawl that we would have avoided when we were sober by simply ignoring the chants of those around us.

Overall, it seems that whilst a large body of evidence supports the idea that alcohol plays a strong role in aggressive behaviour, given that not all intoxicated individuals act aggressively, we should perhaps be cautious in concluding that it has an unmediated role in leading to aggressive behaviour.

Temperature has also been investigated as a factor in the occurrence of aggression. Many studies have shown that as temperature increases, so the likelihood of aggression also increases. Crime statistics suggest that more violence is perpetrated during hot weather. However, when the temperature gets too hot, violence decreases. Studies investigating the geographic effects seem to show that aggression is more prevalent in hotter regions (e.g. southern states of America) than in cooler regions (e.g. northern states of America). Of course, these kinds of findings are correlational and should be treated with caution, and other regional explanations for the increase in aggression may exist. Other research has looked at the temporal effect of temperature: that is, they have mapped aggression within a stable population over a longer period of time as temperature fluctuates. Findings here suggest that violent crimes peak in the summer months (hotter periods) rather than in winter months (cooler periods). Again, other explanations for this pattern of aggression are possible, such as aggression being due to a change in people's routines across the seasons rather than to temperature fluctuation. More controlled experimental research also suggests that an increase in temperature leads to more aggression, though, as previously mentioned, when the temperature was too high, aggression decreased. Overall, there is a strong link between increased temperature and aggression, which may have worrying implications for the future (see Spotlight below).

Spotlight: Aggression and global warming

Krahe (2013) suggests that maybe we should be concerned regarding the findings of links between temperature and aggression:

'The implications of studies that support the heat hypothesis are worrying in the face of global warming. If increases in temperature are systematically related to increases in violent crime, then the continuous rise in global temperature will represent a risk factor for the rise in violent crime.' (p. 113).

There are other environmental factors that have also been linked to an increase in aggression and these include noise, crowding and air pollution. However, no discussion of environmental factors would be complete without looking at the often-debated effect of media on violent behaviour.

The role of the media

Whether or not the media has an effect on aggressive behaviour has been discussed for many years. Generally, research has looked at the effect that violent TV programmes (and films) and computer games may have; however, other research also suggests further media effects, such as violent lyrics in songs, may also have an exacerbating effect.

For the media to have a significant effect on aggression it must first be shown that viewers are exposed to violent and aggressive content in television programmes and films; and research shows that this is indeed the case. In fact, one recent study suggested that UK audiences were exposed to 42.5 violent acts per hour, though it was restricted to just ten television programmes. It was also found that in many cases, violent actions were shown to have a beneficial effect (any readers of my age who were avid watchers of *The 'A' Team* television programme will know exactly what I mean). Similarly, violent content was found to be prevalent in video games and even in music videos (though this did vary considerably by genre: rap videos – 29 per cent; R&B – 9 per cent).

With regards to the effect of media violence, some cross-sectional studies suggest that individual self-report of watching programmes with violent content correlates positively to the ratings of others in terms of their aggressive behaviour. Experimental studies that used computer games with violent content found that violence that is rewarded with some form of positive consequence leads to the promotion of more aggressive thoughts and aggressive behaviour. A vast literature exists that has attempted to address this question, and the finding does tend to suggest that there is anywhere from a weak to a strong positive effect for media violence affecting aggressive tendencies (but the effect is definitely there). Generally, media violence has the greatest effect if it is shown to be either rewarded or to go unpunished, or to be justified in some way. Likewise, if the violence is perpetrated by a respected media figure (role model), then this is also more likely to lead to aggressive behaviour by the viewer. These tendencies have been found to have both short-term and long-term effects.

Of course, there are critics who suggest that the role of media violence is over-played, and evidence certainly exists that has shown very little (if any) effect of media violence on aggressive tendencies. They point to studies such as Bandura's (see Case study above), and add the common sense view that not everyone who is exposed to media violence necessarily becomes more aggressive (there was even a thought for a number of years that watching violence on TV had a cathartic effect – see 'Reducing aggression' below). There are certainly some moderator variables that can affect whether or not an individual is likely to become more aggressive in the face of media violence; these include personality variables such as trait aggression, past experience with media violence, the way in which the violence is presented, and passive vs. active exposure. Nevertheless, the preponderance of evidence does suggest that media violence leads to increased levels of aggression, and thus ways to reduce aggression in society would certainly be welcomed.

Reducing aggression

For many years it was thought that the controlled release of pent-up aggressive feelings was a successful way to reduce aggression. Thus it was believed that watching violence on TV or in films might dissipate aggressive tendencies. Similarly, participating in physical activity, such as taking up boxing classes, might help to release steam. Referred to as *catharsis*, this method of aggression reduction relied on biological theories, such as those of Freud and Lorenz (see above). However, this idea was quickly refuted and shown to be counterproductive. For example, one study showed that people who hit a punch bag believing that it reduced stress were later more likely to punish someone who had transgressed against them compared to individuals who had not used a punch bag. As Bushman (2002) remarked, 'venting to reduce anger is like using gasoline to put out a fire – it only feeds the flame'.

One of the main approaches to understanding aggression has also been used in its reduction. The *learning approach* suggests that we are more likely to aggress by watching others be aggressive (imitation) or by being rewarded, or at least not punished, for being aggressive. Consequently, these methods have been used reasonably successfully to reduce aggression.

The use of punishment in preventing aggression has been shown to be effective but it has a number of stipulations attached to it. These include:

▶ The punishment must be sufficiently adverse.

▶ The punishment must have a high probability of being imposed.

▶ Its effectiveness is increased if other, more attractive, behavioural alternatives are available.

▶ The offender must be rational enough to be able to calculate the costs of the punishment against the perceived rewards of the aggression.

▶ The punishment must follow immediately after the transgression in order for it to be perceived as being contingent upon the aggressive behaviour.

Only if these conditions are fulfilled is punishment likely to be effective. It is more likely that for many forms of aggression these conditions will not co-occur, and therefore a more effective intervention will be required.

One such intervention is observational learning. Built on the principle of Bandura's social learning theory, exposure to a non-violent role model has been found to be an effective way of reducing aggression. This will allow the observer to acquire an alternative behaviour to reduce aggression. It is, however, more likely that observation in combination with learning strategies for implementing the observed behaviour will be more effective than observation on its own.

Whilst learning theory has been shown to be an effective intervention for reducing aggression, other methods have also been shown to have an effect. At an individual level, these include anger management techniques, and training individuals to elicit behaviour incompatible with aggression (for example, studies found that using calming music helped to reduce frustration and stress levels on a stressful commute to work by car). At a societal level, these include the use of legislation, and the removal of violent stimuli from the environment (such as the restriction of access to firearms).

Summary

Aggressive behaviour is a complex topic to study, partly due to the myriad forms that it takes, and the requirement that psychologists investigate the topic in an ethical way. The most effective way of explaining aggressive behaviour has been found in the learning approach, with a number of social models attempting to explain the presence and prevalence of aggression. Many mediating factors, at both an individual and environmental level, have been shown to affect the occurrence of aggression, and the same theories used to explain aggression have also been shown to be the most effective at reducing it. There can be no doubt that violence in society is a worry, but by understanding its origins, and the factors involved in its sustenance, it may be possible to reduce its prevalence – though a complete eradication of aggression is an unlikely, and perhaps even an undesirable, outcome.

Food for thought

As the managing director of a football club, or perhaps the local chief constable, how would you use the theories outlined in this chapter to prevent aggressive behaviour by the football fans (for both home and away supporters) in and around your stadium? How would you measure (ethically) whether your efforts were having a significant effect?

Dig deeper

Anderson, C. A. et al. (2010). 'Violent video game effects on aggression, empathy, and prosocial behavior in Eastern and Western countries: A meta-analytic review'. *Psychological Bulletin*, **136(2)**, 151–173.

Krahe, B. (2013) *The Social Psychology of Aggression*. Second edition. Psychology Press.

Lorenz, K. (2002). *On Aggression*. Routledge.

Ritter, D. & Eslea, M. J. (2005) 'Hot sauce, toy guns, and graffiti: A critical account of current laboratory aggression paradigms'. *Aggressive Behavior*, **31**, 407–419.

Russell, G. W. (2008). *Aggression in the Sports World: A Social Psychological Perspective*. OUP USA.

Fact-check

1 Which of the following is not an element to be included in a good definition of aggression?
   a Intent
   b Expectancy
   c Singularity
   d Avoidance

2 A person shoots a politician because he believes that his ideas are dangerous to society. This is an example of which type of aggression?
   a Instrumental
   b Hostile
   c Ecological
   d Expected

3 The machine pioneered by Buss to measure aggression measured which of the following:
   a Duration of electric shock
   b Intensity of electric shock
   c The number of electric shocks
   d All of the above
   e None of the above

4 Which of the following methods for measuring aggression typically does not involve the deliverance of electric shocks?
   a The teacher-learner paradigm
   b The competitive reaction time task
   c The essay evaluation task
   d They all do
   e None of them do

5 Baron's study involving aggressive behaviour at a set of traffic lights was which kind of study?
   a A field experiment
   b A naturalistic observation
   c A cross-cultural study
   d None of the above

6 Which of the following theories is an example of a hydraulic explanation for aggression?
 a The frustration-aggression hypothesis
 b Freud's psychodynamic theory
 c Social learning theory
 d The excitation-transfer model

7 Which of the following is an example of a learning theory of aggression?
 a The frustration-aggression hypothesis
 b Social learning theory
 c The excitation-transfer model
 d They all are
 e None of them are

8 Bandura's Bobo doll experiments are used to support which of the following theories?
 a The frustration-aggression hypothesis
 b Freud's psychodynamic theory
 c Social learning theory
 d The excitation-transfer model

9 Which of the following traits has not been linked to increased levels of aggression?
 a Type 'A' personality
 b Type 'B' personality
 c Emotional susceptibility
 d Self-esteem

10 Which of the following stipulations is not true with regards to punishment being an effective method for reducing aggression?
 a The punishment must be reasonably adverse
 b The punishment must have a high probability of being imposed
 c Its effectiveness is increased if other, more attractive, behavioural alternatives are available
 d The offender must be rational enough to be able to calculate the costs of the punishment against the perceived rewards of the aggression

10

An introduction to groups

One line of thought goes that if the human race is to survive, then it will need to travel to the stars. If we are to do this, then the first stop is probably to establish a colony on Mars; this will involve sending a small group of astronauts on an essentially one-way journey which will take approximately 150–300 days (depending on orbital alignments, and other such factors). In order to do so, it will be vital to ensure that the group is stable, and able to function optimally in conditions of extreme isolation and hardship. In fact, experiments have already been conducted to study the functioning of groups in such conditions, from the Biosphere projects in the Arizona desert in the 1980s and 1990s (e.g. Biosphere 2, 1991), through to the Mars 500 experiments between 2007 and 2011. Knowing how groups work is one of the first steps to sending humans into space.

Space travel is just one of a multitude of reasons as to why we need to understand groups (see below). Given that the majority of important decisions affecting us all are made by groups (whether it be locally by a council, nationally by a Government, or internationally by the UN Security Council), it is important that we understand group processes to ensure that groups function as well as they possibly can. Whilst other chapters will look at group-specific topics such as decision making (Chapter 11) and intergroup conflict (Chapter 14), this chapter starts from first principles and attempts to address some basic group questions such as: what is a group?; why do we join groups?; what properties does a group have?; and how can a group affect the functioning of an individual?

> 'Small groups have always been a major focus of social psychological theory and research. The reasons for this abiding interest in groups are not difficult to identify. At a theoretical level, an understanding of groups is essential for almost every analysis of social behavior. Some of the most intriguing forms of social behavior, such as leadership, majority-minority relations, status and role differentiation, and socialization, are group phenomena. And small groups provide important contexts within which other forms of social behavior occur.'
>
> (Levine & Moreland, 1998, p. 415)

What is a group?

Psychologists have attempted to explain what a group is and isn't (see Spotlight below). For example, are three people standing at a bus stop a group? Or a number of psychology students sitting in a lecture theatre attending to their lecturer's every word? It prompts the seemingly philosophical question of 'when is a group not a group?'

Early theorists attempted to address the definition problem. According to Lewin, a group was defined by sharing a common fate, Sherif believed that a group had to have a formal or implicit social structure, and Bales thought that a group only existed if face-to-face interaction was possible (clearly before the Internet). These early definitions were good attempts, but are clearly inadequate given the current nature of society. This of course begs the question as to whether today's definitions will be adequate in 60 or 70 years' time.

Spotlight: Defining a group

According to Brown (1999): 'A group exists when two or more people define themselves as members of it, and when its existence is recognized by at least one other [who doesn't define themselves as belonging to the group].'

This definition is by no means perfect, after all it probably excludes secret societies, but it will suffice for general purpose use.

Johnson and Johnson (1987) offer a complex, but perhaps slightly more comprehensive, definition of a group:

1 A collection of individuals who are interacting
2 Two or more persons who perceive themselves as belonging to a group
3 A collection of individuals who are interdependent
4 Individuals who join together to achieve a goal
5 Individuals who are trying to satisfy some need
6 Their interactions are structured by a set of norms or goals
7 A set of individuals who influence each other.

In general, a group should have a degree of bonding, which, in the examples above, would mean that three people standing at a bus stop wouldn't be a group (they would generally be referred to as an 'aggregate'), but the students probably would be.

There is also another aspect of the group to address, and that is how being part of a group will affect our thoughts, feelings and behaviour. The *individualistic perspective* suggests that the people in the group will behave in more or less the same way as they would when by themselves. However, the *collectivistic perspective* suggests that a group is more than the sum of its parts, and when a group forms, the individuals may behave very differently. For example, if you were riding on the Manchester metro system, you would be unlikely to sing and shout if you were on your own; however, if you were wearing a Manchester United shirt, and were surrounded by other people wearing United shirts, then perhaps you would be much more likely to do so, especially if everyone else was shouting and singing.

Why do individuals join a group?

There are many reasons why individuals join groups. As we saw in Chapter 5, Baumeister and Leary's 'belongingness hypothesis' suggests that humans have a need to form interpersonal relationships, and this idea extends to needing to join groups. Generally, group membership affords advantages that might not otherwise be available, and it also offers security and protection; from an evolutionary perspective, being part of a group increases our chances of survival. In addition, being part of a group can tell us things about ourselves: it allows us to make comparisons with similar others to ensure that we are 'doing the right thing'; it helps to define ourselves and gives us our unique social identity; it can help to reduce uncertainty and can increase our self-esteem which will make us feel better about ourselves.

Forsyth (1996) suggests that, because not all groups offer all of the things we need, we may therefore need to belong to more than one group. He goes on to list further advantages of being part of a group:

▶ **Belonging**: groups promote contact, regulate our relations with others and typically increase the quality and duration of our social interactions.

▶ **Intimacy**: group membership can give us warm, supportive and loving relationships.

▶ **Generativity**: being part of a group can help to increase our productivity and to accomplish both personal and shared goals. For example, we might join a writers' circle to help us write more, or a chess club to improve our game. Groups can help us to complete tasks that we might find difficult to do on our own.

▶ **Support**: a group can help its members to cope with major and minor crises, and give them access to both emotional and tangible resources in times of need. It can offer encouragement, provide mutual assistance and share much needed resources.

▶ **Influence**: certain groups can offer an arena in which to exercise and apply social power and influence. They potentially provide the means by which we can influence far more people than we could on our own. For example, if a scientist has important findings to disseminate to the general public, then being a member of the Royal Society will give them far more influence in terms of publicizing their work.

▶ **Exploration**: other groups can provide information, exposure to new ideas and new experiences, instruction and opportunities for learning.

When we join groups, there are generally two possibilities: the first is that we are forming a group from scratch (for example, when we are a member of a jury, or perhaps decide to form a neighbourhood watch group to protect the homes in our locality), and the second is that we are joining a group that already exists (for example, when we apply for a job with a company or a corporation and get accepted). These two processes have been studied quite closely by social psychologists.

Forming a group

There are a number of theories that look at group formation, and they all tend to have similar stages. These include:

1 **Orientation**: potential group members begin to familiarize themselves with each other.

2 **Conflict**: the group members attempt to define group goals.

3 **Structure**: some semblance of organization for the group appears.

4 **Work**: the group begins to function and works towards achieving the task(s) for which it has been created.

5 **Dissolution**: the group disbands, either as a consequence of completing its task, or because it has encountered difficulties that it cannot resolve.

One of the more memorable theories of group formation was put forward by Tuckman in 1965 (see Case study below). Group formation theories have implications for how cohesive a group becomes, and this cohesion (see below) may in turn have an effect on the successful functioning of a group. It should also be noted that models of this nature specify the *usual order* for development of a group: however, not all groups will go through all stages, and not all groups will complete the cycle.

Key idea: Tuckman's group formation model

A five-stage model which proposes to explain how groups form initially, function and dissolve.

Tuckman's model of the stages of small group development has become 'the most predominantly referred to and most widely recognized in organizational literature' (Miller, D. (2003, p 122)).

Case study: Tuckman's model of group formation

Tuckman proposed a five-stage model that was based on a literature review of small group development. Critics have pointed out that the 'therapy-group setting' was perhaps overrepresented in his review and therefore its original framework was a limited one. However, as with all good theories, it has been somewhat hijacked and applied to a wider field. Whilst his model broadly parallels other models, the thing that sets Tuckman's slightly above the rest, and thus makes it easier to recall, is his memorable naming of the five stages:

1 Forming: At this stage the group is without norms (see below), but as the individuals begin a series of guarded interchanges with one another, the ice begins to break, and an information exchange between its potential members begins.

2 Storming: Tension begins to fade with regards to the newness of the group, but it starts to rise as the individuals start to define the goals and roles of the group. There may also be conflict as individuals vie for the role of group leader. Generally, conflict is commonplace, can help to clarify group goals, and may actually be a good thing as a catalyst for creating group cohesion.

3 **Norming:** The group starts to become unified and organized. Dissenters have either left the group or quietened down, and mutual trust and support amongst members begins to appear. The group becomes more cohesive and rules for group functioning (norms) emerge.

4 **Performing:** The group starts to produce. However, productivity is not always immediate and may require the group to mature. Many real-world examples show that it is only towards the end of a group's life (e.g. a climate change conference) that something is achieved. Of course, not all groups will reach this stage.

5 **Adjourning:** Entry into this stage can either be planned (as in the case of a jury when it has reached its verdict) or spontaneous (as in the case of an unsuccessful team). In the latter case, it could be a stressful event, and members may tend to blame one another for the group's failure. This stage was added as a revision to the model in 1977.

Joining an existing group

Moreland and Levine (1982) put forward an influential model with regard to the stages that an individual will go through when joining an existing group; this is referred to as the **group socialization model.** Initially, two processes dominate when searching for groups to join:

1 **Evaluation:** the individual will weigh up the costs and rewards of joining the group.

2 **Commitment:** the individual will consider the relationship requirements between themselves and groups that they may join.

The two processes are linked, and the model makes the assumption that the evaluation and commitment between the group and the individual will change over time. The commitment that an individual feels towards the group will increase as they put more into the group in the form of time, energy and personal resources. The downside to this increase in commitment is the additional costs which in turn has an effect on their evaluation of the group.

> **Key idea:** Moreland and Levine's group socialization model
>
> The model proposes to explain how an individual integrates into, and functions within, an existing group, and how the existing group facilitates, and reacts to, this integration.

The group socialization model proposes that there are five stages, and each stage involves a two-way process between the individual and the group; there is also a 'transition point' from one stage to the next to denote the changing relationship between them. To illustrate a real-world application of this theory, think of the two parties as the employee and the company.

1 INVESTIGATION STAGE

The employee is looking for a company to join (*reconnaissance*) and is likely applying to more than one; the company is looking for new employees (*recruitment*) and is investigating the value of a number of individuals. At this stage the individual is *a prospective member*. The transition point from this stage to the next is referred to as ENTRY.

2 SOCIALIZATION STAGE

Having become employed by the company, the employee is now a *new member*, and will attempt to accept the rules and values of the company (*assimilation*); the company in turn attempts to adapt to the needs of their new member (*accommodation*). At this stage, the commitment of both parties has increased compared to the first stage. The transition point from this stage is referred to as ACCEPTANCE, but can be delayed for a number of reasons such as tension between the new members and the existing members.

3 MAINTENANCE STAGE

Having entered this stage, the employee is now a *full member* and both they and the company have considerably increased their commitment to one another. This stage reflects the need of both parties to continually negotiate their roles; the employee may wish to be promoted or the company may wish the employee to carry out slightly different functions from when they originally joined. If the process runs smoothly, many individuals will stay in this phase until they leave the group (e.g. the employee retires). However, if the relationship deteriorates, then the transition point from this stage to the next is DIVERGENCE.

4 RESOCIALIZATION STAGE

If the employee starts to become dissatisfied with their role, or the company perceives that the employee is working against the group, the employee is downgraded to a *marginal member*. The commitment from both parties now starts to decrease. As with stage two (socialization), there now follows a process of negotiation where the company and the employee try to reach a satisfactory resolution to their problems (*accommodation and assimilation*). If this is successful, then the transition point is CONVERGENCE, and the employee re-enters the maintenance stage; if it is unsuccessful, then the transition point from this stage is EXIT, reflecting the employee resigning or being fired.

5 REMEMBRANCE STAGE

In this stage, both parties will review their shared experience; the employee will review what happened leading up to them exiting the company (*reminiscence*), and the company will also review what has happened and perhaps reflect on their recruitment process to see whether such events can be prevented in the future (*tradition*). There may still be a little connection between the two parties and commitment may not necessarily be non-existent.

The group socialization theory seems to have a feel of authenticity (face validity) about it and probably maps on to the experiences that many of us have had when joining existing groups. If the theory is a good one, then it should be able to be applied to a multitude of situations different to that of the employee and the company.

Having looked at the process of either forming or joining a group, we now turn our attention to three important properties of groups, namely cohesiveness, norms and roles.

Group cohesiveness

A number of attempts have been made to define the exact nature of cohesiveness. We seem to instinctively know when we are a part of a group that appears to function smoothly. An early attempt at a definition was put forward by Schachter and colleagues who claimed that cohesiveness was 'the cement that binds' a group together and for many years it was thought that the cement comprised interpersonal attraction: if you liked your fellow group members then the group would be a cohesive one. However, two obvious problems spring to mind with this idea:

1 Large groups, where individual members won't ever meet each other, can still be cohesive.

2 It is possible for a group to be cohesive even when some members dislike others.

A further study helped to shine some light on the definition problem. Groups were asked to design a new student dormitory, and were either given a detailed briefing about how to go about doing this (easy task) or no briefing at all (hard task). Additionally, the groups were manipulated so that individuals believed they either had similar, or dissimilar, values to the other members (thus varying interpersonal attraction). At the end of the task, cohesion within the groups was measured by asking the question: 'Would you wish to remain in the group for a further session?'. It was found that similarity of values had no effect on this measure, but a better predictor of cohesion was the task type: 85 per cent of individuals elected to stay in the group when the task had been an easy one. This suggested that interpersonal attraction didn't account for group cohesion, but the task facing a group did.

Key idea: Group cohesiveness

The way in which a group acts upon its members to bind them together in some form, both to each other and to the group as a whole.

More recent research by Carron and colleagues, mainly with sports groups, suggests that group cohesion has two dimensions:

1 An instrumental basis – that is, a group has a purpose

2 An affective basis – that is, the social bonds that develop between group members.

Together these two strands entwine to bring about cohesiveness. A number of assumptions follow from this research:

▶ There is more than one factor that might account for whether or not a group sticks together.

▶ All dimensions are not necessarily equally present across different groups to the same extent, or at the same time in a group's life.

▶ Any specific dimension does not have to be present in equal amounts in groups of a similar nature.

▶ A multi-dimensional model of cohesion does not mean that all dimensions are equally salient throughout the life cycle of a group. Thus a group, such as a Sunday morning football team, could initially be formed, and stay together, based purely on social reasons, but gradually as they become more successful, the basis for its cohesion could change from affective to instrumental (for instance, they start to win trophies).

It is also interesting to note that cohesion can also be affected by outside forces in the form of competition or threat. Therefore, we should accept that cohesiveness can be affected by both intra-group and inter-group processes.

A final factor to consider with regards to cohesiveness is task outcome. It perhaps goes without saying that the more cohesive a group, the more likely they are to be successful. However, there is also strand of research that suggests that direction of this causality may be reversed: in fact, the more successful a group is, the more cohesive it becomes. Similarly, research has questioned whether it is only success that leads to cohesiveness. Having myself been a member of a boys football team who were regularly thrashed by the opposition (only losing 20–0 was on occasion considered a triumph!), I can attest to the fact that we were a remarkably tight-knit group despite our losses. This does seem to go against the grain of research. However, one enlightening study suggests that cohesiveness can be affected by choice. If an individual chooses to join a group, which later turns out to be unsuccessful, then cohesiveness might not be affected; however, if the group membership is forced, then cohesiveness is much more likely to deteriorate.

Group norms

Groups need rules to function, and these rules are fairly idiosyncratic. However, norms have been found to have a profound effect on group members. For example, a famous study by Newcomb (The Bennington College study) found that group norms were able to override individual norms. Using the naturalistic setting of Bennington College – a liberal all-girl college that paradoxically recruited from conservative families – Newcomb found that even though girls entered the college in their first year with strong conservative attitudes, by the time they were in their final year, their attitudes had changed markedly. He measured this by taking advantage of a presidential election and recording the voting preferences of the pupils. Findings suggest that whilst almost two-thirds of first year students voted for the conservative candidate, thus retaining their personal values, third- and fourth-year students were much more likely to vote for the liberal candidates, thus being influenced by the norms of the college (and some even voted for the Communist party!). Follow-up studies of the girls after they left Bennington College suggested that they retained their new-found liberal values, and showed the enduring influence of **group norms** on the individual.

Key idea: Group norms

Idiosyncratic rules for a group which govern the way in which its members are expected to think and behave.

Whilst the Bennington College study isn't without its critics (for example, age may have been a factor in voting preference, and there was no random allocation of participants to different groups: see Chapter 1), other more tightly-controlled experimental findings have found the same outcome – the impact of group norms has a strong effect on the behaviour and attitudes of individuals.

Overall, norms serve an important function within groups by:

1 providing a frame of reference through which the world of the group is interpreted;

2 bringing order and predictability to life;

3 minimizing personal stress in novel or ambiguous situations;

4 helping to regulate social existence and co-ordinate the activities of the group members.

Norms are also very closely tied to group goals. Once the goal of a group is established, norms help to ensure that the goal is reached, and perhaps not exceeded. A study of workers on a factory production line, where the norm was to produce 50 units per hour, found that when a new and enthusiastic worker joined the line and began to produce 60 units per hour, the other workers very quickly applied strong pressure on the new member to adhere to the norm of the group (i.e. 50 units per hour). Failure to do so may have given the factory management an opportunity to change the workers' conditions of employment.

Norms also have a role in enhancing and/or maintaining the identity of a group. This can be done in a number of ways, such as prescribing the manner in which members act and even dress. A study of adolescent gang members found that the clothing they wore was a very strong indicator of their identity and was rigidly enforced throughout the group; failure to wear the prescribed clothing was met with sanctions from other group members. This identity-enhancing function of norms can be seen in a wide variety of groups, such as political parties (e.g. towing the party line to become a good Tory) and sports groups.

However, group norms are not always prescriptive. There is likely to be a range of acceptable behaviours available to members, especially where the norm is peripheral to group life – this is referred to as **'latitude of acceptance'**. For instance, in University life, students are generally allowed to wear whatever they want (a wide latitude of acceptance), but when it comes to submitting coursework, the deadlines are very strictly enforced (a very narrow latitude of acceptance). It has also been found that higher status members of a group (such as a leader) are able to get away with a little more than the group members, but where the issue is of key importance to group life, they are held to a very high standard and expected to be a model group member (e.g. backbench MPs may break the party rules and only suffer minor consequences, but if a high profile cabinet minister were to do so, they would likely be required to resign).

Key idea: Latitude of acceptance

The degree to which the behaviour of group members is able to deviate from the group norms (rules).

Group roles

Roles play an equally important part of group life, and are typically either *formal* or *informal*. The former has specific duties attached to it, with some form of consequences linked to the performance of the role e.g. worker in a factory, head teacher, police officer. The latter is an ambiguous role that has fewer consequences attached e.g. the 'organizer', or the 'listener', in a group of friends. Roles provide a number of benefits to a group as they help to:

▶ ensure a division of labour to reduce the likelihood of physical and cognitive overload of any one member (such as the leader);

▶ bring predictability and order to the group's existence so that any one member will know what is expected of themselves and other members in terms of their behaviour;

▶ form part of a member's self-definition within the group, which in turn contributes to their social identity (an important factor for the continued well-being of an individual).

Research suggests that roles are important in staving off potential problems. For example, when the role of an individual becomes overloaded, ambiguous or comes into conflict with other roles, it can lead to increased fatigue, increased anxiety, lowered job satisfaction and the development of mental illness.

Key idea: Group roles

The expected behaviour assigned to some, but not necessarily all, individuals within a group to facilitate the optimal functioning of both the individual and the group.

However, roles are not without their disadvantages. For example, if a role is defined too rigidly, a group may not be able to adapt to new situations, sometimes with disastrous consequences, such as the flight crew where all were aware of the adverse weather conditions but no one checked for ice on the wings because it wasn't in their role description. Similarly, a group becoming too predictable can make it more vulnerable to being targeted by enemy forces.

There are many roles that exist within a group, some more important than others. Chapter 12 will look at one such role, namely that of the leader, and address such questions as who is likely to become a leader, what do they do, and how this role can affect the functioning of a group.

Summary

Given the ubiquity and importance of groups in everyday life, it is important to understand what they are, how they form, how they function and the effect they have upon their individual members. Research into such areas as cohesiveness and norms has important implications for both the formation and optimal functioning of groups. Only through an in-depth understanding of groups can we ensure that future human endeavours are successful, whether they're earth-bound or in outer-space.

Food for thought

Think about a group that you have joined or formed, and attempt to assess the degree to which the processes outlined in this chapter actually applied. Equally, if you are about to join, or form, a group, think about the way in which you can make the process an easier one by applying the information outlined in this chapter.

Dig deeper

Baron, R. S. & Kerr, N. L. (2004) *Group Process, Group Decision, Group Action*. Open University Press.

Carron, A. V. & Brawley, L. R. (2000). 'Cohesion. Conceptual & Measurement Issues. *Small Group Research*, **31(1)**, 89–106.

Hogg, M. A. & Abrams, D. (1988) *Social Identifications. A Social Psychology of Intergroup Relations and Group Processes*. Routledge.

Fact-check

1 Which of the following would probably not be defined as a group?
   a Astronauts on the international space station
   b Sunbathers on a beach
   c Students in a lecture theatre
   d Supporters watching a game of football

2 What idea did Baumeister and Leary put forward to suggest why individuals need to join a group?
   a Social identity theory
   b The collectivistic perspective
   c Group generativity theory
   d The belongingness hypothesis

3 According to Tuckman's model of small group formation, at which stage is mutual trust and support amongst group members first likely to occur?
   a Forming
   b Storming
   c Norming
   d Performing

4 Moreland and Levine's group socialization model suggests that:
   a An individual will weigh up costs and rewards before joining a group
   b The evaluation and commitment between a group and an individual will change over time
   c The more resources that an individual invests in a group, the more their commitment will grow
   d All of the above

5 In the group socialization model, the transition point between being a new member and a full member is:
   a Entry
   b Acceptance
   c Convergence
   d Divergence

6 Based on Carron's work with sports groups, which of the following is not an assumption about cohesiveness?

a There is more than one factor that might account for whether or not a group sticks together

b All dimensions are equally present across different groups to the same extent, and at the same time, in a group's life

c Any specific dimension does not have to be present in equal amounts in groups of a similar nature

d A multi-dimensional model of cohesion does not mean that all dimensions are equally salient throughout the life cycle of a group

7 Newcomb's 'Bennington College study' investigated:

a Group norms

b Group cohesion

c Group formation

d Group socialization

8 Which of the following is not an important function of norms within a group?

a Providing a frame of reference through which the world of the group is interpreted

b Minimizing personal stress in novel or ambiguous situations

c Helping to regulate social existence and co-ordinate the activities of the group members

d All of the above

9 Peter works as a lawyer for a law firm, and he is required to wear a suit when meeting clients. Failure to do so would land him in hot water with his boss. This requirement has:

a A broad latitude of acceptance

b A medium latitude of acceptance

c A narrow latitude of acceptance

d None of the above

10 Which of the following would not be considered a formal role with respect to group membership?

a Head Teacher at a junior school

b Chief negotiator for a union

c The 'joker' in a group of friends

d They are all formal roles

11

Group processes

There are not too many of us who have never either worked in a group, or in front of a group. As a student, we may be required to work in a group to collect data, or to present the findings of our individual work in front of a group; as an employee, we may be tasked by our boss to work in a group to find a solution to a problem, and then to present our solution to him, or our colleagues, or the entire company. Having looked at the nuts and bolts of groups previously (Chapter 10), this chapter starts to look at the more intricate and applied workings of a group. It will cover the effects that a group has on an individual's performance, whether we can predict if a given task would be more effectively completed by an individual or a group, and whether working as a part of a group brings out the optimal performance in an individual. It will conclude by looking at whether groups always make better decisions than individuals.

Audience effects and social facilitation

It has been noted on many occasions that an individual carrying out a task alone performs very differently to when they have to carry out the same task in front of an audience. For example, we might practise our presentation the night before in front of a mirror and think that it went pretty well, but when we deliver it in front of our colleagues the next day, it might be a totally different story.

One of the first people to notice this so-called 'audience effect' was Norman Triplett, and he is sometimes credited with conducting the first social psychology experiment. Triplett was very interested in cycling and regularly studied magazines listing the race times of cyclists. He noted with interest that individuals always seemed to cycle faster when others were present (e.g. they were paced) than when they cycled alone. Triplett (1898) speculated that competition between people had the effect of energizing and improving performance on motor tasks. He decided to put this to the test and created a 'competition machine'; this was basically two fishing reels attached to a board. He then measured the time it took children to reel-in the fishing twine, either when they performed alone, or when they performed side by side with another individual (e.g. in competition). He found that the latter condition promoted faster times, and he concluded that competition energized performance. It should be noted that Triplett did not carry out any statistical analysis on his data (it was the 1890s after all) but merely reached his conclusions by looking at the trends in the data (in fact, a more recent analysis of his data using modern statistical techniques concluded that most of his findings were non-significant!).

However, this idea laid dormant for a number of years until Floyd Allport in the 1920s revived the idea and referred to it as **social facilitation**. He thought that this idea of performance enhancement would extend to circumstances beyond competition, and believed that the *mere presence* of others would suffice. A typical experiment to test this assumption would be to ask participants to write down as many associations as they could for a word printed at the top of an otherwise blank piece of paper. It was found that more than 90 per cent of participants were able to generate more word associations when they were performing the task in the presence of others than when they were performing it alone.

Key idea: Social facilitation

The idea that an individual's performance is affected by the presence of other people.

However, other research conducted using different, and sometimes more complex, tasks didn't always find the same results. It seemed that sometimes, as well as having an enhancing effect, performance could be adversely affected by the presence of others. This thorny issue remained a problem until the 1960s when a researcher named Robert Zajonc (his surname rhymes with 'science') came along with his 'drive theory of social facilitation'.

According to Zajonc's theory, the presence of others causes an instinctive arousal which motivates individuals to perform 'habitual behaviour patterns' (dominant responses). He claimed that this arousal acted as a 'drive', and, based on his theory, made two predictions:

1 The presence of others will facilitate (e.g. improve) performance when an individual's dominant response is the correct one.

2 The presence of others will impair (e.g. worsen) performance when an individual's dominant response is an incorrect one.

Using cockroaches (whose dominant response apparently is to seek shade by running in a straight line when a light is pointed at them), and an interesting piece of apparatus (a kind of stadium) that allowed other cockroaches to act as an audience, Zajonc found evidence to support his theory. When in front of an audience, an individual cockroach would perform its dominant response quicker than if alone; however, when required to perform a non-dominant response (in this case, to turn a corner to find the shade), it was performed slower when other cockroaches were present than when alone.

Zajonc concluded that the *mere presence* of an audience can facilitate or impair an individual's performance dependent on their dominant response. When our dominant response is the correct one, we are likely to perform it even better in front of others (for example, a well-practised saxophonist will perform their favourite piece even more brilliantly in front of an audience – all other things being equal); when our dominant response is an incorrect one, we are likely to perform worse in front of others. Generally, these findings have been replicated on humans in a number of different domains. For example, above average, or below average, pool players were asked to perform either alone or in front of four passive observers. Results found that, for the good players, performance increased from 69 per cent (alone) to 80 per cent (in front of others), whereas it decreased from 36 per cent (alone) to 25 per cent (in front of others) for the poorer players.

However, competing theories argue that 'mere presence' isn't enough. Cottrell (1972) advanced the *'evaluation apprehension theory'* which, whilst using the idea of Zajonc's drive, claimed that increased arousal is caused by fear of evaluation, and not simply the mere presence of others. Its premise is that we have an instinctive need to look good in front of others. Cottrell conducted a simple experiment where participants were asked to carry out a well-learned task in front of either an inattentive audience (they were blindfolded) or an attentive audience who were paying close attention to the participant's performance. A third condition had other people in the room (mere presence) but only because they were waiting to participate in a different experiment. Cottrell found that only when the audience was attentive was social facilitation found. However, other research has not supported this theory, and it's also hard to believe that the cockroaches in Zajonc's original experiment were worried about being evaluated by other cockroaches!

A third more convincing explanation for social facilitation is Baron's (1986) *'distraction-conflict theory'*. This theory claims that increased arousal is caused by attentional conflict between paying attention to the audience and also to the completion of the task. Together, these two distractions will lead to an impaired performance on difficult tasks, but on easier tasks, the drive is able to overcome the distractions and performance improves. In an experiment to test the theory, participants were asked to perform a hard or easy task either alone, alongside someone completing the same task (which is more likely to be distracting as there is the tendency to compare performance with the other), or alongside someone completing a different task (minimal distraction as they are not a relevant source of comparison). Results showed that the hard task was performed worse in the distraction condition, but the easy task was performed more successfully. Distraction-conflict theory has two main strengths: it can account for the findings from animal studies, such as Zajonc's cockroaches, and it can allow any form of distraction (e.g. noise) to produce social facilitation effects.

There are some general problems with 'drive' theories of social facilitation. For example, it's not clear as to what the 'drive' actually is. Zajonc's drive is a bit nebulous and hard to define (and measure), and therefore it is difficult to confirm or refute the existence of it as a mediating mechanism. Although physiological measures of arousal may access the 'drive', the absence of physiological arousal is no guarantee that the drive is not operating.

Having looked at the effect that a group (an audience) can have on an individual's performance, it is now time to look at what happens when a group tries to perform a task; that is, the task requires some form of interaction and co-ordination between individuals in the group. It is likely that the presence of all the group members will have an effect on one another in terms of their performance, and it is also likely that how well the group performs may also depend on the nature of the task itself. This leads to the question of whether it is possible to predict whether any given task can be performed better by a group than by an individual – which is a useful prediction to be able to make when trying to determine the best use of one's resources.

Steiner's task taxonomy

In order to make this prediction, Steiner (1972, 1976) produced a 'task taxonomy' to tackle this question. The taxonomy enables group tasks to be classified dependent on whether or not it is possible to divide up labour to complete a task, whether there is a predetermined standard for the task that needs to be met, and how the input of individuals contributes to the overall group performance. Each of the three dimensions is best represented by asking three questions:

1 Is the task divisible or unitary?

2 Is it a maximizing or optimizing task?

3 How are individual outputs related to group outputs?

A *divisible task* benefits from the division of labour, that is different people perform different tasks (such as producing a newspaper or building a house). A *unitary task* cannot be broken down into sub-tasks (such as pulling a rope).

A *maximizing task* is an open-ended task that stresses quantity, that is, an individual does as much as they can (such as selling raffle tickets for charity, or generating ideas). An *optimizing task* has a pre-determined standard that needs to be met, and the goal should neither be under-achieved or exceeded (such as being asked to recruit 50 participants for a study, or bake 12 cupcakes for a charity bake sale).

The final question regarding individual inputs can be broken down into five further types of task:

1 **Additive**: the output of the group is the *sum* of all individual inputs. For example, selling raffle tickets for charity or collecting data for a study. *The group performs better than the best individual member.*

2 **Compensatory**: the output of the group is the *average* of all the individuals' inputs. For example, a team time trial over an obstacle course. *The group performs better than many of its members.*

3 **Disjunctive**: the output of the group is that of *one selected* individual's input, and it's not always guaranteed to be the best one. For example, a group has to select one of its members to complete a task, answer a question or solve a problem. *The group performs equal to, or less than, the best member.*

4 **Conjunctive**: the output of the group is that of the slowest or least able individual. For example, in a team race, the team's time is that of their last member to cross the line. *The group performs equal to its worst member.*

5 **Discretionary**: the output of the group in relation to its members' input is not predicted by the features of the task. Instead, it is possible for the group to decide on the best way to complete the task.

Steiner's task taxonomy makes it possible to classify a task with reference to these three sets of parameters. For example, making a car is a divisible, optimizing, conjunctive task. It should therefore be possible to determine whether a specific task is more suitable for a group than an individual.

Another thing that Steiner predicted was that a group's actual output would never be equal to a group's potential output. He believed that this was due to some form of **process loss**. This could be due to problems in co-ordinating the behaviour of the various individuals (*co-ordination loss*) or due to psychological factors (*motivation loss*).

Key idea: Process loss

Deterioration in group performance, compared to individual performance, due to some form of interference between group members.

Ringelmann, in 1913, was one of the first people to investigate this phenomenon, which gave rise to the so-called **Ringelmann effect**. He asked young men to pull on a rope linked to a measuring device, and found that the more individuals there were pulling, the less the average force was exerted per person. A later experiment attempted to determine the exact nature of this process loss by using real groups and pseudo groups of differing sizes. The real groups had everyone attempting to pull a rope as hard as they could, whereas the only person pulling in the pseudo group was the first individual; the other individuals pretended to be pulling but were actually confederates. In this way, it was possible to distinguish how much of the Ringelmann effect was due to process loss (i.e. the problem of everyone pulling together at the same time) and how much was due to motivation loss (i.e. no need to pull as hard because others in the group would 'take up the slack'). This deterioration in performance due to motivation loss was christened '*social loafing*'.

Key idea: Ringelmann effect

The amount of force exerted by an individual decreased for each additional individual added to the group effort.

'Social loafing is the tendency for group members to expend less individual effort when working together than when working alone. In most studies of social loafing, this motivation loss is due not to a particular pattern of interaction among group members, but to the absence of interaction coupled with the belief that individual task contributions are pooled.'
(Levine & Moreland, 1998, p. 440)

Social loafing

Social loafing has been found to occur across a number of different experimental tasks. For instance, when participants were asked to clap, cheer and shout, the amount of noise generated by two people together fell by 29 per cent compared to the amount generated by one individual on their own. When there were four people in the group, the output was reduced by 49 per cent, and by 60 per cent when there were six in a group. Generally it has been found that after the group size increases beyond about eight, there is a levelling-off effect of the amount by which the group output is affected. It has also been found that social loafing may be a cultural effect (see Spotlight below).

Spotlight: Is social loafing a cultural phenomenon?

A study by Earley (1993) compared the group and individual outputs of participants (full-time managers) from the USA (an individualistic culture), Israel, and China (a collectivistic culture). They were asked to carry out a range of tasks, over the space of an hour, which approximated those carried out by managers (such as form completion and memo writing – bear in mind these were the days before e-mail existed). In the 'individual condition', participants were asked to put their name on each completed item and told that their individual completion rate would be calculated; in the 'group condition', they believed they were working as part of a team and were told to put each completed item in a team basket so that the team's output could be calculated at the end. It was found that participants with a more individualistic outlook (i.e. from the USA) completed more items when they believed they were performing as an individual compared to when they believed they were performing as a team member. Conversely, individuals with a more collectivistic outlook (i.e. from China) completed more items when they worked as part of a team than when they performed as an individual. These results lead to the conclusion that culture is a factor in social loafing.

A number of explanations have been put forward to explain social loafing. These include:

▶ **Output equity:** individuals loaf in groups because they expect other people to do the same. They loaf in order to maintain equity.

▶ **Evaluation apprehension:** the presence of others in a group allows a greater degree of anonymity for an individual.

They become less identifiable and if they are unmotivated to perform a task, it provides cover for an individual to hide. Performing alone would not provide such cover, thus the individual would be more apprehensive about being evaluated and they would be more likely to overcome their unmotivated state.

▶ **Matching to standard:** people loaf because they have no clear idea of the level of performance that is expected of them. They are therefore more likely to set themselves a lower threshold of achievement.

▶ **Social impact theory:** the number of other people in a group affects an individual's attitudes and behaviour. If there are two people in a group, the impact of being asked to do something can be diffused, hence the feeling that the level of effort required is reduced. The more people in a group, the less and less responsibility each individual might feel for the task. As a cynic once claimed: "Teamwork means never having to take all the blame!"

As social loafing can be damaging to the productivity of a group, a number of ways to reduce it have been suggested (see Spotlight below). Of course, social loafing is not an inevitable consequence of working in a group, and people may work harder as part of a team when they consider that a task is of great importance and where they feel that their colleagues may not be working quite as hard as they should. Also, where competition exists with another group, individuals are less likely to loaf; the presence of an 'outgroup', and potential intergroup competition, has the potential to transform a group's behaviour (see Chapter 14).

Despite the potential for social loafing, groups are formed on a daily basis to perform a number of tasks that individuals couldn't perform on their own. They are asked to make decisions that have the potential to transform the lives of many others. With this is in mind, psychologists have studied closely how groups make such decisions.

Group decision making

It is not unreasonable to assume that if you put a bunch of clever people together, you will get a good decision from them; even if you put a group of average people together, for example, in the form of a jury, you might expect an average decision. However, this is not necessarily the case.

Spotlight: Reducing social loafing

Working in a group can lead to a 'drop-off' in the performance of an individual. Potentially, this can be reduced by:

▶ ensuring individuals work in small groups;
▶ taking care to assign individuals to tasks that they find interesting;
▶ making sure that the members of a group work with others they like or respect;
▶ explaining that contributions from each person are unique and important;
▶ ensuring that each individual's contribution can be identified;
▶ individuals expecting their co-workers to perform poorly;
▶ working with others from cultures where a group is valued more highly than an individual.

Some of these factors are controlled more easily than others, but the more that are employed, the less likely social loafing is to occur.

One of first people to recognize this formally was a researcher called Stoner (1961) who asked business students to make judgements about a number of hypothetical situations (known as 'choice dilemmas'). They were first asked to do this alone, then as part of a group formed at random, then on their own again. At each of these three stages, they were given the *same* choice dilemmas. For example, in one dilemma they were told that an engineer could stick with his current job which pays a modest but adequate salary, or he could consider changing to a new job which offered a potentially higher salary in the future but which had uncertain long-term security. The individual, or group, was asked to judge the lowest acceptable risk for them to advise the character in each dilemma to try the risky alternative.

Stoner found that the decisions made by the groups were nearly always riskier than the average of those made by individuals prior to group discussions. In addition, based on the post-group individual decisions, instead of returning to the levels of the pre-group decisions, most individuals continued to make riskier decisions. This led Stoner to conclude that this **'risky shift'** (as it became known) appeared to be internalized.

Key idea: The risky shift

The tendency for groups of individuals to make much riskier decisions than they would on their own.

Other researchers refined this work, and using the same 'choice dilemma' methodology, found that whilst there was a tendency for groups sometimes to make riskier decisions than they would as individuals, there was also the possibility that group decisions would be more cautious than individual decisions. They termed this phenomenon **'group polarization'**, and it is a fairly robust finding that has been noted in a wide variety of populations. Generally, the size of the group polarization shift correlates with the average individual starting position: if the individuals in the group were more extreme initially, then the group's decision became even more extreme.

These findings were not confined to the slightly artificial choice dilemmas. For example, Moscovici and Zavalloni (1969) asked French students to state their attitudes towards both General DeGaulle and America (at the time in France, DeGaulle was very popular, and America was very unpopular). When these individual students were randomly assigned to groups and asked to debate their attitudes again (on the same two topics), it was found that they became even more pro-DeGaulle and more anti-America.

> **Key idea:** Group polarization
>
> The tendency for groups of individuals to make more extreme
> decisions, both riskier and more cautious, than they would on
> their own.

However, these findings were not without their critics. For
example, it was pointed out that these randomly formed
groups were 'ad-hoc', were without any form of history
or possible future, and the decision was a hypothetical
one. Other research using existing groups found no such
polarization in their decisions.

Nevertheless, given that group polarization is a fairly frequently
occurring phenomenon, researchers set about determining why
it might happen. Three possible explanations have been put
forward.

1 POLARIZATION THROUGH COMPARISON

This explanation, referred to as 'social comparison theory',
and championed by Sanders and Baron (1977), claims that
polarization occurs because people wish to maintain a positive
self-image, and this is possible by ensuring that their beliefs on
important social values accord with those of others. Therefore,
the key to doing this is to understand the position of other group
members with regard to the social value in question. Initially,
each individual believes that their position is representative of the
feeling of the group, but when they discuss it with others, they are
more likely to see that their position is in fact a more moderate
one, and that others endorse the social value much more than
they do; therefore the individual will shift their position (polarize)
to present a more favourable image of themselves.

2 POLARIZATION THROUGH PERSUASION

The second theory claims that it is not the comparison with
others that is important, but instead, it is the content of the
discussion that is crucial. This 'persuasive arguments theory'
was championed by Burnstein and Vinokur (1977), and
assumes that any issue being deliberated is much more likely to
produce a preponderance of arguments in one direction than

another. Each individual does not automatically have access to all of the arguments, and only through discussion will they do so. Once all facts are discussed openly, individuals will shift their position (polarize) in the direction where the majority of the arguments lie.

3 POLARIZATION THROUGH INTERGROUP DIFFERENTIATION

The third theory claims that the important issue is not the content of the argument, but from whom the argument comes. They key process in this theory is social identification with a group. When a group discusses an issue, members are more likely to conform to the group's position to maintain a positive identity, and this position will be more pronounced if the issue being debated makes group identity more important. The group position becomes more extreme (polarizes) when they are not only trying to emphasize ingroup values, but where they are also trying to differentiate themselves from an 'outgroup'.

Each of these theories has their strengths and weaknesses. For example, group polarization was found to occur when individuals didn't know the true views of the others in the group but the strength of the argument was high, thus supporting the persuasive arguments view. However, this view assumes that new information always emerges in a group discussion, and other research has shown that this is certainly not always the case: groups tend to spend a lot of time discussing the information they already have rather than trying to discover new information. Similarly, intergroup differentiation theory works well to explain polarization when there is clearly an 'outgroup'; however, this isn't always the case (e.g. a jury). Brown (1999) concludes that the first two theories are more likely to hold sway when we don't know too much about our fellow group members and where the decision we have to make is a novel one, and the third theory is much more persuasive for existing groups.

Of course, just because a group's decision is more polarized than that of an individual, doesn't make the decision an incorrect one. However, there have been a number of occasions when a group's decision has turned out to be quite disastrous, and this prompted Irving Janis (1972) to put forward a theory to explain why groups sometimes make bad decisions: he called his theory 'groupthink'.

Groupthink

Using a series of case studies of American governmental decisions (see Case study below), Janis constructed a three-stage model of poor decision making. The stages are:

1 Antecedents

2 Symptoms

3 Consequences

Antecedents are conditions that exist prior to groupthink occurring. These include:

▶ Group cohesiveness

▶ Structural faults of the group, namely:

   ▷ Lack of impartial leadership

   ▷ Member homogeneity

   ▷ Group isolation

   ▷ Lack of procedural norms

▶ Stressful situational context

Cohesiveness refers to members all having similar views and opinions, and thus rejecting anyone with a deviant viewpoint. Janis conceived of cohesiveness as referring to interpersonal attraction as opposed to task cohesiveness (see Chapter 10).

The structural faults in the group referred to a directive leader making it clear about the decision that he wanted the group to make, the members of the group being far too similar in their outlook and background, being isolated from other groups and possible dissenting views, and a lack of a systematic procedure to make decisions. The stressful situational context may lead to urgency overriding accuracy and the need for the best possible decision to be made.

Case study: Irving Janis and groupthink

Janis based his original model (1972) and his revised model (1982) on a number of case studies involving foreign policy decisions by the American government that went wrong. These included:

▶ The Bay of Pigs (failed attempt to invade Cuba)
▶ The Korean war
▶ The Vietnam war
▶ Pearl Harbor
▶ Watergate

He also included case studies illustrating when correct decisions were made, showing how groupthink can be avoided. These included:

▶ The Cuban missile crisis
▶ The Marshall plan

The *symptoms* of groupthink include:

▶ **Overestimation of the group:** this includes an illusion of invulnerability whereby a tide of over-optimism can lead to extreme risk taking. It also includes an unquestioned belief in the morality of the group, and the tendency to ignore ethical and moral consequences of any possible decisions.

▶ **Closed-mindedness:** the group is far more likely to engage in a collective rationalization wherein they discount warnings or fail to consider other information that might have a bearing on their decision. It also indicates a simplistic tendency to stereotype outsiders, such as believing that enemy leaders are simply evil, or not capable of countering any actions decided upon by the group.

▶ **Pressures towards uniformity:** a tendency towards self-censorship whereby group members feel inclined to minimize, or rationalize away, any doubts that they might have. There is also an illusion of unanimity where the assumption is made that each individual agrees with the majority (group) view. Anyone daring to question the group's decision has pressure put on them to desist, and '*mindguards*' are appointed to protect the group from such dissenters.

The *consequences* of groupthink inevitably include defective decision-making and a high likelihood of a bad decision. These consequences come about due to an incomplete survey of possible alternative decisions, an incomplete survey of the objectives of the group, and a failure to examine the risks associated with the group's preferred course of action. Additionally, a failure to reappraise initially rejected alternatives, a selective bias in processing information pertaining to the decision, and a failure to draw up contingency plans, are also factors leading to the likelihood of a bad decision being made.

'Groupthink refers to a deterioration in mental efficiency, reality testing, and moral judgements that results from in-group pressures.'
(Janis, 1982, p. 9)

On the face of it, the groupthink model has an intuitive and pleasing feel to it. Subsequent high-profile decisions, such as the Challenger space shuttle disaster and possibly the decision to invade Iraq, have been flagged as being due to groupthink. Some experimental evidence, mainly testing antecedents such as cohesiveness, has also given credence to the model. Another advantage to the model is that it gives us clear guidance on how to avoid bad decision-making: simply reversing the symptoms and consequences provides a list of good practice for group decision making, such as appointing a 'Devil's advocate' to argue against any decision the group reaches (the opposite of a 'mindguard') and the employment of 'last chance meetings' to overcome a failure to reappraise initially rejected alternatives.

However, critics of groupthink have pointed out that any model based mainly on anecdotes and case studies does not have a strong foundation. Similarly, not all aspects of the model have been empirically well-tested (either alone or in combination), and there seems some doubt as to whether the model can be applied to the decisions of everyday groups, as opposed to governmental decisions. Additionally, there are areas of the model that lack clarity, such as exactly how many antecedents need to be present, and indeed which ones, in order for groupthink to occur. Nevertheless, despite these objections and reservations, the model remains a popular one.

Summary

It appears then that there is more to groups than meets the eye. Their effect on an individual can be a two-edged sword – if the individual is good at what they do, then their performance may be enhanced, but if not… then the individual had better beware. It also seems possible to predict when a group will be more suited to complete a task than an individual and this can help with resource planning. Similarly, if we are aware of the possible decline in an individual's performance within a group, and can understand why this might be so, it may be possible to plan in order to reduce or remove the effect.

When we take a group as a whole and look at how the individuals combine to make decisions, we see a distinct shift from how they might act as individuals: group decisions may become more polarized and the decisions reached may not be optimal ones. Understanding the effects of groups, and how they work, can have many practical applications for us as individuals on a daily basis (for example, students can use social facilitation effects to ensure that their exam performance is optimal) that we would ignore this research at our peril.

Food for thought

Imagine you are responsible for organizing the production of a pantomime (or any other kind of theatrical production or event) in your local community. How would you use the information in this chapter to ensure that everyone performed to their maximum potential (e.g. no social loafing, no stage fright, etc.)?

Dig deeper

Baron, R. S. & Kerr, N. L. (2004) *Group Process, Group Decision, Group Action*. Second Edition. Open University Press.

Brown, R. (1999) *Group Processess*. Second Edition. Wiley-Blackwell.

Forsyth, D. R. (2013) *Group Dynamics. International edition*. Wadsworth Publishing Co.

Janis, I. (1982) *Groupthink*. Houghton Mifflin

Fact-check

1 Who coined the term 'social facilitation'?
  a Floyd Allport
  b Norman Triplett
  c Robert Zajonc
  d James Steiner

2 Which of the following is not true with regards to Zajonc's explanation of social facilitation?
  a The presence of others causes an instinctive arousal which leads to a drive
  b The drive facilitates the performance of an individual when the dominant response is the correct one
  c The drive impairs the performance of an individual when the dominant response is incorrect
  d All of the above are true

3 An alternative explanation for social facilitation is due to arousal being caused by the splitting of attention between the audience and the task. This is referred to as:
  a Mere presence
  b Evaluation apprehension
  c Distraction-conflict
  d None of the above

4 According to Steiner's task taxonomy, when a group's output is equal to the output of a selected group member, this is called what type of task?
  a Additive
  b Disjunctive
  c Conjunctive
  d Compensatory

5 Three track teams with four runners each compete in a 400m race. The times for team A are 46 seconds, 47s, 47s, 49s; the times for team B are 44s, 45s, 49s, 53s; the times for team C are 45s, 45s, 46s, 51s. If the race is set up as a conjunctive task, which team wins?

   a Team A
   b Team B
   c Team C
   d It's a tie!

6 One explanation of social loafing claims that people loaf in a group because they are unclear as to what is expected of them. This is referred to as:

   a Output equity
   b Evaluation apprehension
   c Matching to standard
   d Social impact theory

7 Which of the following isn't a way to reduce social loafing?

   a Ensure individuals work in slightly larger groups than normal
   b Assign individuals to tasks that they find intrinsically interesting
   c Ensure that each individual's contribution to the group output can be identified and measured
   d Assign individuals to groups containing people that they like and respect

8 Group polarization is the tendency for groups of individuals to make more extreme decisions than they would on their own. One theory suggests that this is because they pay attention to the content of the discussions that they have with other individuals in the group. This is referred to as:

   a Social comparison theory
   b Persuasive arguments theory
   c Didactic engagement theory
   d Intergroup differentiation theory

9 Which of the following is not an antecedent of groupthink?
- **a** Homogeneity of members
- **b** Illusion of invulnerability
- **c** Cohesion
- **d** They all are

10 A 'mindguard' is a feature of which symptom of groupthink?
- **a** Overestimation of the group
- **b** Closed-mindedness
- **c** Pressures towards uniformity
- **d** Actually it's not a symptom but instead it's a way of preventing groupthink from occurring

12

Leadership

Exactly who makes a good leader is a matter for some debate. Some say John F. Kennedy was a good leader, but he made many mistakes and was perhaps less than perfect with regards to his private life. Some say Sir Alex Ferguson was a good leader, but it is questionable whether his talent was domain specific to football. Some say Adolf Hitler was a good leader, and he certainly pulled Germany out of a deep recession and returned it to prosperity, but after that ... well, probably not! Defining who is and who isn't a good leader is certainly a tricky question, but social psychologists have attempted to answer the age old question of whether some individuals are born to be leaders, or whether individuals can actually learn to be leaders. They have also examined many other aspects of leadership, such as whether there are links between personal characteristics and good leadership, what types of behavioural styles are employed by leaders, and the extent to which the situation can affect who becomes a leader. This chapter investigates the many facets of leadership.

Defining leadership

Many politicians have attempted to define leadership over the years. Dwight D. Eisenhower referred to leadership as '… the ability to decide what is to be done, and then to get others to want to do it'. John F. Kennedy claimed that he wanted to '… be a President who is a Chief Executive in every sense of the word – who responds to a problem, not by hoping his subordinates will act, but by directing them to act'. Margaret Thatcher referred to leadership in terms of power when she said, 'Being powerful is being like a lady. If you have to tell people you are, you aren't'. Whilst there are many more pithy but relevant quotes, these three highlight some interesting aspects of leadership that will be addressed throughout the chapter: leadership as a type of social influence (Eisenhower), different styles of leadership such as autocratic vs. laissez-faire (Kennedy) and leadership as being a type of power (Thatcher). There are many psychological definitions of leadership, all slightly different but with many addressing core aspects of the role, such as having the ability to influence others (see Spotlight below).

Spotlight: Defining leadership

Chemers (2001) refers to leadership as: 'A process of social influence through which an individual enlists and mobilizes the aid of others in the attainment of a collective goal.' (p. 376)

Haslam, Reicher and Platow (2011) claim that: 'Leadership … is not simply about getting people to do things. It is about getting them to want to do things. Leadership … is about shaping beliefs, desires and priorities. It is about achieving influence, not securing compliance.' (p. xix)

When talking about leadership, it is important to have in mind various leadership roles. This could include president or prime minister, football manager, scout leader, film director, chief executive or middle manager of a large or small company, and so on. Good theories of leadership should be able to encompass the diverse nature of the role.

Leadership as power

It has been argued by some that leadership is the exercise of power, and many types of power have been cited as playing a role in leadership. These include:

▶ **Reward power:** Leaders provide their followers with what they want, such as a pay rise or a promotion, or take away what they don't want, such as unpleasant working conditions.

▶ **Referent power:** This type of power is wielded if the leader is respected, and acts as a role model for the group by emphasizing the group's identification. For example, it could be argued that the Queen of the UK has referent power.

▶ **Informational power:** Leaders with this type of power have access to privileged information and use it for persuasion purposes, such as a CEO with insider information about their company.

▶ **Legitimate power:** This type of power is bestowed with rank, and as such is contingent on the leader retaining their current position. An example would be ranks within the police or armed forces, or a leader of a country.

▶ **Expert power:** Individuals with this type of power are recognized as leaders within their specific domain who possess a superior ability, such as a professor of psychology. Their power is typically wielded within a confined field.

▶ **Coercive power:** Leaders using this type of power use threats and punishment to ensure their followers do as they are told. Wielding this type of power typically leads to negative feelings from followers.

It may be the case that different leaders wield different types of power at different times. In the case of managers, the more senior they become, the more likely they are to wield reward, referent, and coercive power. Knowing the different types of power that leaders might wield can show us how leaders can influence others, but it does not tell us many other things about them, such as who they are, how they behave, or how the situation they find themselves in affects their leadership role.

Characteristics of a leader

The 'great person' theory of leadership suggests that a leader is born and not bred; that is, they are naturally a leader as opposed to learning to be a leader. The popularity of this approach to leadership tends to fade in and out across the years, and it may also depend on the books that you read. It is possibly a question that will never be answered conclusively, but nevertheless psychologists have looked at individual character and personality traits which have been linked to successful leaders.

Key idea: The 'great person' theory of leadership

The notion that a leader is born not bred, and consequently that leadership is a skill that cannot be learned.

The physical appearance of an individual can have a strong influence on how we perceive them as a leader, and we may in fact judge their competence based on their looks rather than their ability (see Case study below). Overall, leaders tend to be slightly taller and heavier than their followers. The age of a leader tends to vary dependent on the group (e.g. political, business or social), but findings suggest that political and business leaders tend to be older than their followers. For example, some recent findings suggest that less than 0.1 per cent of corporate executives are under the age of thirty, but almost 75 per cent are aged fifty or older.

In terms of intelligence, leaders are slightly more intelligent than their followers, and there is a general preference for this to be the case. However, if they are perceived as being too much more intelligent, an element of distrust may creep into the minds of their followers. **Emotional intelligence** (EI) is also a useful attribute for a leader to possess. It has been found to be linked with effective leaders, as they are able to anticipate potential problems, better understand the relations of their group's members and are more able to communicate their ideas efficiently. They are also more able to control their own emotions successfully.

With regards to gender, their representation as leaders is extremely unbalanced with men being far more prevalent as leaders. The results of one study suggested that people are generally more comfortable with men as leaders than women. Researchers asked either men or women to take charge of a group for a task, and then surreptitiously filmed the faces of the 'followers': there were more smiles when a man was the leader and more frowns when a woman was the leader.

However, there is a suggestion that the nature of the leadership role might affect the gender of an appointed leader: when an organization is in crisis the selected leader is more likely to be female (a phenomenon referred to as the glass cliff), but when the organization is successful, the leader selected is more likely to be male. In terms of leadership style, experimental studies show that women adopt a more relationship-oriented style whereas men seem to be more task-oriented (see below). However, when observed in organizations, these differences change: whereas men continue with their task-oriented style, women were seen to evidence both a task-oriented and a relationship-oriented style of leadership (probably the best of both worlds).

Case study: Judging potential leaders by their appearance and not their ability

A study by Antonakis and Dalgas (2003) investigated whether voters chose politicians based on ability or appearance. Taking competing pairs of candidates from the 2002 French parliamentary elections, Swiss adults (naive to the actual results of the French elections) were shown the faces of the two politicians and asked to rate which of the two they perceived as being the most competent. Results showed that over 70 per cent were able to predict the actual winner based on appearance alone. The researchers

With regards to the personality of leaders, early research found no strong links between successful leaders and personality traits. However, more recent research suggests that effective leaders have been found to show elevated personality scores on measures of extraversion, conscientiousness, agreeableness, and openness to experience. Other findings suggest that those who emerge from a group as a leader rate more highly in intelligence and in the traits of masculinity and dominance. However, the personality of a leader may depend on the gender of their followers, as one study suggested that when the group was all-female, emergent leaders tended to rate as being more intelligent and androgynous (showing high levels of both the male leader tendency to be task focused and the female leader tendency to be person-centred).

Behavioural styles of a leader

Whilst the characteristics and personality traits of a leader may tell us something about who leaders are, it still does not tell us exactly what they do. Good leadership may not be about who an individual is, but how they behave. A classic study addressing this issue was conducted by Lewin, Lippit and White (1939); they attempted to find out which of three types of leader behaviour – autocratic, democratic or laissez-faire – was the best. The setting for the study was an after-school club run for boys. The boys were divided into three groups and each group spent seven weeks with an individual leader who was trained in one of the three styles of leadership. One of the strengths of the study was that after the seven-week period was over, the individual leaders were trained in a different style of leadership which they adopted for the next seven weeks, and so on. Thus, for each period they behaved in a different way, meaning any findings of the study must have been due to the behavioural style of the leader and not due to their individual characteristics.

During the seven-week period, the boys were engaged by their leader to complete different tasks. The *autocratic leader* was very directive, telling the boys what they were going to be doing and who would be doing what. They also remained quite aloof from the group. The *democratic leader* was much more prepared to discuss any decisions that needed to be made, and acted like a regular group member. The *laissez-faire leader* basically left the boys to their own devices, only answering direct questions and having only a minimal level of interaction with them.

Key idea: Leadership styles

An autocratic leader is directive towards followers; a democratic leader consults and seeks consent from followers; a laissez-faire leader shows disinterest towards followers.

At the end of the three rotations of leadership styles, the results were analysed and differences were found in measures such as the levels of efficiency of the groups, the satisfaction with belonging to the group and levels of aggressiveness displayed by group members. Lewin, Lippit and White concluded (unsurprisingly) that the optimal style of leadership was that shown by the democratic leader. However, this does not tell the full story. Whilst the groups with the democratic leader showed higher levels of friendliness, spent as much time working when the leader was present as when they were absent, and showed the lowest levels of critical discontent, the groups with the autocratic leader actually spent the most time working of the three groups when their leader was present (though their levels of working were the lowest of the three groups when their leader was absent). This suggests that if group output is a key performance indicator of a group (as opposed to, say, satisfaction), then an autocratic style of leadership may have its merits (though the groups with this type of leader did also show high levels of hostility, negativity and scapegoating, therefore this type of leader might not have a long-term future with a group).

One of the interesting things about this study is that it suggests that leadership style can be learned and is not actually set at birth. In addition to these three styles of leadership, research has suggested that other leadership styles are prevalent.

Based on his work with interaction process analysis, Bales (1950) concluded that individuals were either *task specialists* or *socio-emotional* (person-centred) *specialists*. The task specialists were normally the biggest participators in group activities, and their behaviour was mainly focused on task interaction activities; this type of leader also tended to exhibit more of an autocratic style of leadership. The socio-emotional specialists were more likely to pay attention, and respond to, the feelings of other group members; they also tended to exhibit a more democratic style of leadership. Interestingly, he conceived of these two leadership styles existing as mutually-exclusive behaviours – leaders were either one or the other.

At about the same time, the Ohio State leadership studies were being conducted, and were investigating leadership in mainly military and industrial groups. They found two main themes emerging which bore a striking resemblance to the two behaviours identified by Bales; they referred to them as:

1 *Initiating structure* (the equivalent to a task-centred specialist)

2 *Consideration* (the equivalent to a socio-emotional specialist)

The interesting difference was that these two themes were measured on two separate scales, from low to high; thus you had a rating on each. This meant that it was possible to be high in both initiating structure and consideration (and thus presumably a good leader), whereas Bales claimed that you could only have one style or the other, though he did concede that it was possible to be rated on a continuum between the two extremes.

Two other styles of leadership are also worthy of mention, namely transactional and transformational leadership. **Transactional leadership** refers to a leader who treats their relationship with their followers as a simple transaction, whereby expectations and shared goals are defined in advance, rewards are promised, and given, for good behaviour, and punishment is meted out for digressions from the expected behaviour. If the transactional leader is an *active* one, they watch and search for deviation from the rules and standards expected by their followers and take corrective action; if the leader is a *passive* one, they intervene only when standards are not met. Although it sounds like a transactional leader is uninspiring (compared to a transformational leader – see below), in many situations it is just what a group (whether it be a small company or a pack of cub scouts) may need if things are going well and running smoothly.

Key idea: Transactional leadership

A traditional style of leadership that advocates the attainment of a collective goal through the rewarding of desired behaviours and the punishment of undesired behaviours.

A *transformational leader*, on the other hand, by the very force of their personality, tends to have a profound effect on their followers. This type of leader inspires people to change. According to Bass (1990) (see below), transformational leaders have a number of key qualities which include:

▶ **Charisma:** they provide vision and a sense of mission to their followers; they gain the respect and trust of the group and instil in it a sense of pride. In terms of traits and characteristics, they are self-confident, determined, have good verbal skills, high energy levels and a keen intellect.

▶ **Inspiration:** they supply intellectual stimulation to those around them and are able to communicate their ideas simply but effectively.

▶ **Individualized consideration:** each follower feels that this type of leader gives them their individual attention (even though this may not actually be the case).

Transformational leaders can vary in their personal styles, but have the ability to raise standards in the group that they lead. A word that is used a lot to characterize them is 'maverick', as they are much more likely to engage in risky behaviour than transactional leaders. One of their assets is that they feel able to reject conventional methods when they believe it will pay dividends to do so. However, whilst they tend to show superior performance in uncertain or crisis situations, they are not always appropriate; in a stable situation, the last thing a group may need is a transformational leader who may feel the need to 'shake things up'.

> '... transformational leadership ... occurs when leaders broaden and elevate the interests of their employees, when they generate awareness and acceptance of the purposes and mission of the group, and when they stir their employees to look beyond their own self-interest for the good of the group.'
>
> (Bass, 1990, p. 21)

Situational effects on leadership

Whilst the ways in which leaders behave may have a profound effect on their effectiveness, the environment in which they find themselves should not be ignored. There may be functional demands of a situation which will affect the performance of a leader, and indeed may dictate who the leader is. For example, in Sherif's summer camp studies (see Chapter 14 for a fuller explanation of these studies), when the group of boys were in a peaceful, non-conflict situation, their notional leader tended to be a less aggressive, and a more 'bookish' individual. However, when there was the opportunity for competition, their role was usurped by a bigger, more athletic individual who the others felt was more equipped for the situation. Real world events have also shown exactly this, for example Winston Churchill was considered a great wartime leader but a less than adequate leader during times of peace.

Experimental studies have also shown that the leader of a group depends on the situation in which the group finds themselves. One study gave pairs of high school students three tasks to complete: an intellectual task, a clerical task and a mechanical task. It found little evidence to suggest that the same person emerged as the leader in each situation, and notionally this would seem to contradict the idea that leaders are made (as in the 'great person' theory).

Generally speaking, the most effective leader in a given context is the person who is best suited to help the group to attain its goals. Nevertheless, it is likely that there is some interplay between all of the factors covered so far (characteristics, behaviour and situation), and contingency theories of leadership address this idea.

Contingency theories of leadership

Probably the most famous of the **contingency theories of leadership** was put forward by Fred Fiedler (1965), and is referred to as the 'least preferred co-worker (LPC)' contingency theory. Its premise suggested that the effectiveness of a leader was contingent upon the match of leadership style with the situation in which they found themselves.

Key idea: Contingency theories of leadership

Such theories suggest that the effectiveness of a leader depends on the interaction of the person with the situation in which they find themselves.

The first stage of this theory involved measuring an individual's leadership style, and for this Fiedler relied on the dichotomy of a task-focused vs. a person-centred approach. Individuals were asked to imagine a person with whom they had the most difficulty working (their LPC), and were then given a series of 18 scales on which to rate their LPC. The scales (1–8) represented a series of personality characteristics and were labelled at the ends (e.g. unpleasant–pleasant; cold–warm; guarded–open; nasty–nice). The range of possible scores was 18–144, with a high score (>64) representing a person-centred leader and a low score (<57) representing a task-focused leader. Fiedler believed that this leadership measure represented a fixed-personality characteristic (though this is questionable given current personality theories, along with the fact the Lewin, Lippit and White were able to train individuals in three different styles of leadership, and with Bass also claiming that individuals can be taught to become transformational leaders).

Fiedler had already identified three elements regarding the situation in which a leader might find themselves. These were:

1 Leader-member relations (good/bad)

2 Task structure (structured/unstructured)

3 Leader's position of power (strong/weak)

The situation was labelled on each of the three elements, giving eight possible outcomes, which Fielder referred to as octants. The eight octants were classified on a scale of high situational control (octant I) through to low situational control (octant VIII). He predicted that when the situation was highly favourable (octants I, II and III) or highly unfavourable (octant VIII), the most effective leader would be a low LPC (task-oriented) leader. However, when the favourability of the situation was middling, then a high LPC (person-oriented) leader would be more effective.

The final task for Fiedler was to correlate the leader's group effectiveness (using some performance criteria) with the leader's LPC score and map the findings on to a slightly-complicated looking graph (see Spotlight below). Fiedler claimed his results supported his theory, and that it was therefore possible to predict what sort of leader would be effective in a given situation. As predicted, it appeared that a task-oriented leader was the most effective in octants I, II, III and VIII; he claimed that this was because the group relations were already so good or so bad that no amount of person-oriented behaviour could make the situation any better. However, a person-oriented leader appeared more effective in octants IV, V, VI and VII when the situation was in the mid-range of acceptability (e.g. there were some positive and negative aspects of the situation). He claimed that this was because such a leader would bolster the group relations and this in turn would lead to an enhanced performance.

Overall, there is reasonable empirical support for Fiedler's model, though octants II and VII did not quite map as predicted. However, critics have questioned the seemingly arbitrary ordering of the three situational factors; in any other order, the model loses its shape and predictive nature (though Fiedler did mount a reasonable defence for why the situational factors should be listed in their given order). Fiedler's measure of leadership style has also been questioned on many counts. First, his choice of the LPC scale to measure effective leadership seems odd, and it may not in fact be measuring what Fiedler claimed it was measuring. Secondly, with regards to its test-retest reliability, it was not always the case that an individual registered the same leadership score when retested at a later time, thus calling into question the stability of his leadership measure and with it the models predictive power. And finally, the eagle-eyed reader will have noticed that the scoring on the LPC (i.e. <57 or >64) seems to miss out a series of possible leadership scores – what type of leader are you if you score 60 on the LPC scale? Instead, it has been suggested that a trichotomy of leadership styles should be used (i.e. including a 57–64 category) which might add to the predictive power of the model. However, in spite of the criticism, the model may have some interesting applications given that it appears reasonably able to predict the most effective leader for a given situation.

Spotlight: Fiedler's contingency theory:

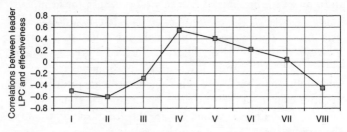

Leader-Member Relations	Good	Good	Good	Good	Bad	Bad	Bad	Bad
Task Structure	Structured		Unstructured		Structured		Unstructured	
Leader's Position of Power	Strong	Weak	Strong	Weak	Strong	Weak	Strong	Weak

LPC Fiedler's LPC model
Based on Fiedler (1964).

Other contingency theories do exist, such as Hersey and Blanchard's (1993) situational leadership theory. This theory suggests that the two different styles of leadership (person-centred and task-directed) are needed dependant on the stage of a group's (or follower's) development (referred to as *maturity*). Maturity can refer to the level of commitment to the group's task, and also to the levels of competence of the group or followers (with mature members of the group possessing the requisite skills and knowledge to achieve the group's goals). The theory advocates that a task-centred style of leadership is required when there is a low level of commitment to the group, or when competence levels of members are low. As these two factors increase, the leader should move from a *directive* style to a *coaching* style (high on both styles of leadership). As the group progresses beyond this level, it is possible for a leader to lessen both styles (though task-directed is lessened first), and as the group becomes 'moderately mature', a person-centred style is most effective for the *supporting* style. Finally, when the group is fully mature, a *delegating* style of leadership is most effective. The leader is thus required to adopt four different styles depending on the level of the group's development.

Whilst it can be seen that there are a variety of factors affecting a given leader's effectiveness (e.g. individual characteristics, behaviour, situation and a combination of all three), there is still the question of how leaders come to be leaders.

Leadership emergence theories

In many cases, leaders are elected (e.g. politicians) or earn the rank by meeting a set of criteria (e.g. military leaders). However, in other cases this is not so. A number of theories have tried to explain how individuals emerge from a group to take on the mantle of leader. One such theory was proposed by Hollander (e.g. 1958), who claimed that a potential leader first has to build up *idiosyncrasy credit* within a group before they can lead it. As seen in Chapter 10, group members are subject to norms in order to regulate their behaviour, and this also includes leaders of groups. However, leaders are also agents of change, moving their groups in different directions and perhaps even attempting to change the group norms themselves (think Tony Blair and his idea of 'New Labour'). In order to be able to do this, Hollander claims that they first have to build up credit, and only when they have sufficient credit can they 'cash it in' to attempt to make changes. According to the theory, there are a number of ways that credit can be accumulated:

▶ By conforming initially with the group norms, and behaving as a model group member (Tony Blair was a model Labour rank and file member).

▶ By having the competence to fulfil the group objectives (Tony Blair was seen as intelligent and capable).

▶ By identifying strongly with the group (Tony Blair was seen as being committed to Labour and its ideals).

Additionally, if the individual is eventually elected as leader of the group (as Tony Blair was), as opposed to being given the position, they will gain additional credit. The more credit an individual is perceived to have, the more likely they will be accepted as the group's leader, and the more able they are to effect change (and hence Tony Blair was able to change radically the Labour party).

A further idea of how leaders emerge is based on *social identity theory* (see Chapters 2 and 14). According to this idea, membership of a group is important to the self-definition of an individual. Individuals identify themselves with groups, and eventually categorize themselves as being members of those groups as they discover that they share many traits and ideals with the other group members. As membership becomes more important, individuals will identify more strongly with the group. Over time, each individual develops a clear idea of what a model group member should be like (referred to as a *prototypical member*) and the group as a whole will likely reach agreement on this. Any group member evidencing characteristics approaching those of a prototypical member (it may actually be the case that the perfect group member doesn't exist) will have a greater chance of being accepted as the leader, and is more likely to emerge as the leader.

As well as exemplifying what the group stands for, any successful leader will also be able to show that they also represent how their group is different to other groups. A successful leader will promote the values of their group and show less acceptance and tolerance of rival groups. In fact, intergroup considerations need careful monitoring when determining the effectiveness of leaders – weak leaders seem more conciliatory than strong leaders. In fact, leaders who are in danger of losing the support of their members could do worse than to create conflict with a rival group to bolster their support (consider this idea in light of Margaret Thatcher's decision to declare war on Argentina when it invaded the Falkland Islands, rather than opting for a diplomatic settlement).

A final idea, which is worth considering for the way it explains why women are underrepresented as leaders and not always respected when they do assume such a role, is Eagly's **social role theory**. Applied to leadership, this theory argues that individuals have stereotypes about the way that a leader is meant to behave (e.g. focused on the task at hand, strong, directive), and these behaviours, in turn, are seen as being more typically male than female. Therefore, as these expectations match more with a male gender role stereotype than a female one (which is seen as more sympathetic, gentle, and feminine), when people consider who should become a leader, they are more likely to think of a man than a woman. Consequently, when a woman does achieve a leadership role, not only are they judged by a male standard, but if they should achieve it by acting in the way expected of a male leader (e.g. task oriented), they are more likely to be criticized for betraying their expected gender role which suggests they should be more nurturing and person-centred. Under such expectations and pressure, it is unsurprising that many women are not selected as leaders, or in fact actively avoid leadership roles.

Key idea: Social role theory

The idea that society determines the sex differences in an individual's behaviour, as opposed to it being a biological determinant.

Summary

That there are many good leaders in the world is beyond doubt, but what makes them good leaders is certainly a difficult question to tackle. As we have seen, some suggest that they are born to be leaders, or at the very least have the characteristics that make them more likely to be a leader in the first place. Other theories would claim that the way in which they act is the determinant of whether or not they are an effective leader. And yet others declare that the situation in which they find themselves is the crucial factor in determining their leadership effectiveness. On balance, it is likely to be a combination of some, or all, of these factors that will eventually determine whether or not they are judged a good leader.

However, given the highly applied nature of the topic of leadership, it is certainly worth stopping to think for a moment as to how the current political leaders of your country (or indeed any other leader that you can think of) fit in with the theories and ideas described in this chapter. It should be borne in mind that these theories and ideas need not only be accurate, but should also apply to many different types of leader (from Kennedy and Hitler through to your local scout or guide leader).

Food for thought

If you are a leader of a group, try to determine your style of leadership – is it as simple and straightforward as the typologies outlined in this chapter. If not, try to understand why not. If you're not a leader (or even if you are), look at the leader of any group to which you belong, and attempt to evaluate their style of leadership based on the theoretical perspectives in this chapter. Will the information in this chapter help you to become a more effective leader?

Dig deeper

Ayman, R. & Korabik, K. (2010). 'Leadership. Why gender and culture matter'. *American Psychologist*, **65(3)**, 157–170.

Bass, B. M. (1997). 'Does the transactional-transformational leadership paradigm transcend organizational and national boundaries?' *American Psychologist*, **52**, 130–139.

Eagly, A. H. & Johnson, B. T. (1990) 'Gender and leadership style: a meta-analysis'. *Psychological Bulletin*, **108**, 233–256.

Haslam, S. A., Reicher, S. D. & Platow, M. J. (2011) *The New Psychology of Leadership. Identity, Influence and Power*. Psychology Press.

Fact-check

1 An admiral in the Royal Navy wields which one of the following types of power?
   a Referent power
   b Expert power
   c Legitimate power
   d Coercive power

2 A senior manager of a company possesses secret insider knowledge regarding the finances of his company, which in turn will affect its share price when it floats on the stock exchange in ten days' time. He offers to share the information with one of his employees in return for the completion of an unpleasant task. The manager is wielding what kind of power here?
   a Expert power
   b Informational power
   c Reward power
   d Coercive power

3 Which of the following EI traits has been found to be linked with effective leadership?
   a The ability to understand the relationships within their group
   b The ability to anticipate potential problems before they occur
   c The ability to control their own emotions successfully
   d All of the above
   e None of the above

4 Which of the following is not true with regards to gender and leadership?
   a There are more female leaders than male leaders
   b A male is more likely to be selected as a leader in a crisis situation than a female
   c In lab experiments, males are likely to adopt a more relationship-oriented approach to leadership than females
   d Actually, they are all true
   e Actually, none of them are true

5 Which of the following is not a personality trait on which most leaders have been found to have raised levels?
   a Conscientiousness
   b Psychopathy
   c Extraversion
   d Openness to experience

6 According to the study by Lewin, Lippit and White, which type of leader was responsible for their group being the most productive whilst they remained in the room?
   a Autocratic
   b Laissez-faire
   c Democratic
   d There was no difference between the three types

7 According to Bass, which of the following is not a key quality of a transactional leader?
   a Charisma
   b Inspiration
   c Individual consideration
   d They are all key qualities
   e None of them are key qualities

8 What is the correct order of the three key situational elements identified by Fiedler in his contingency theory of leadership?
   a Task structure; leader's position of power; leader-member relations
   b Leader's position of power; leader-member relations; task structure
   c Leader-member relations; task structure; leader's position of power
   d Leader's position of power; task structure; leader-member relations

9 Hersey and Blanchard's situational leadership theory claims that the maturity of the group (or individual) dictates the style of leadership required. Which style of leadership requires high levels of both task-directed and person-centred leadership?

   a Directive style

   b Coaching style

   c Supporting style

   d Delegating style

10 Member prototypicality is a feature of which one of the following theories of emergent leadership?

   a Idiosyncrasy credit theory

   b Social identity theory

   c Social role theory

   d None of the above

13

Prejudice

Prejudice is a term that is often bandied about without too much thought – we talk about racial prejudice (racism) and sexual prejudice (sexism); prejudice against young parents and people of different religions; prejudice against people with a disability or against older people; we talk about prejudice against people of a different class (classism) or from a different country (nationalism). Prejudice, it seems, is all around us. This chapter looks at the psychology of prejudice in terms of how it comes to exist, how individual factors might affect it, and how it might be possible to reduce it.

What is prejudice?

'If a person is capable of rectifying his erroneous judgments in the light of new evidence he is not prejudiced. Prejudgments become prejudices only if they are reversible when exposed to new knowledge. A prejudice, unlike a simple misconception, is actively resistant to all evidence that would unseat it. We tend to grow emotional when a prejudice is threatened with contradiction. Thus the difference between ordinary prejudgments and prejudice is that one can discuss and rectify a prejudgment without emotional resistance.'

Gordon Allport (1954b)

One of the first psychologists to attempt to define and explore the topic of prejudice was Gordon Allport (his 1954 book, *The Nature of Prejudice*, is considered to be a classic in the field). With regard to ethnic prejudice, he referred to it as being 'an antipathy based upon a faulty and inflexible generalization'. Whilst this seems to be a sound basis for the beginnings of a definition, one prominent expert in this field (see Spotlight below) claims that to call something 'faulty' must imply that we have a way of determining whether or not the thing in question is correct – which much of the time we do not. (For example, whilst some less enlightened members of society may refer to those of another race, culture or nationality as being 'lazy', there is no real way of determining whether or not this is actually the case). This typifies the difficulty that we have within social psychology of determining the exact nature of prejudice: we might feel as though we know what it is, but actually it can be as difficult as nailing down jelly.

Nevertheless, a traditional view of prejudice considers it to be an attitude that is held towards a specific group; as with most attitudes (see Chapter 7) it is thought to have three components:

1 An *affective* component – this involves holding strong feelings (which are usually negative) with regard to the target group.

2 A *behavioural* component – the way in which one intends to behave towards the target group.

3 A *cognitive* component – the thoughts and beliefs that one holds about the target group.

This view is by no means held by all researchers within the field.

Distinct from prejudice is the concept of **discrimination**, which generally refers to some form of action. So, where prejudice is an attitude held by an individual or a group, discrimination is the translation of that attitude into a form of behaviour.

Spotlight: A definition of prejudice

Brown (2010, p. 7) defines prejudice as 'any attitude, emotion or behaviour towards members of a group, which directly or indirectly implies some negativity or antipathy towards that group'.

This definition is interesting in that it does not cover 'positive' prejudice (for example, nepotism).

The topic of prejudice holds an interesting place in social psychology: it is certainly a topic in its own right, but it also overlaps with many other aspects of the subject; for instance, intergroup relations (ingroups and outgroups – see Chapter 14), stereotypes (see Chapter 4), aggression (see Chapter 9), self-perception and attributions (see Chapters 2 and 3), and attitudes (see Chapter 7).

Key idea: Discrimination

Traditionally, discrimination is the behavioural (overt) expression of a prejudice.

Specific types of prejudice: racism

As intimated at the beginning of the chapter, there are many types of prejudice, such as ageism and sexism, however **racism** has been a particularly difficult challenge for society. Defined as prejudice and discrimination on the basis of ethnicity or race, racism has been prevalent throughout history. Practised in its most destructive form, it can lead to genocide, as seen all too recently in places such as Bosnia, Rwanda and Iraq. Whilst we might like to think that we are coming to terms with racism with a more enlightened outlook from society in general, it may be that there is a new form of racism emerging. It is certainly the case that, due to prevalent tolerant societal norms, it is no longer acceptable to use racial slurs or any form of ethnic derogation (in fact it is illegal).

When asked about racial attitudes on questionnaires, people readily offer acceptable answers. However, there is a worry that racism has simply been driven 'underground', and has perhaps changed in its nature. This new form of racism has been referred to by several different names, including aversive racism, symbolic racism and ambivalent racism. Whilst these different forms have slightly different definitions, they all share the view that individuals are caught between deeply-held emotional views towards minority groups, and the more egalitarian views of society. The challenge facing social psychology is how to detect the different types of prejudice (such as racism) in all their forms, explain it, reduce it, and ideally eradicate it.

Key idea: Racism

Prejudice and discrimination against others on the basis of their ethnicity or race.

Measuring prejudice

Until relatively recently, the most common way to investigate the prevalence of prejudice was to measure the *explicit attitudes* of people towards a specific group (such as immigrants). This was typically done through the use of a questionnaire. However, due to a combination of strong societal norms that call for equality and tolerance, and the inherent need for individuals to feel liked by others, this method runs the risk of a 'social desirability' bias. Of course, social psychologists have found ways to circumnavigate this type of bias by using methods such as '**the bogus pipeline**'.

Key idea: The bogus pipeline

A method based on leading people to believe that a polygraph can accurately monitor their emotional responses; this allows researchers to measure their real attitudes.

However, a more recent and innovative way to measure prejudice is to tap into the *implicit attitudes* of individuals. These are unintentional attitudes which have a degree of automaticity in their activation when in the presence of the target group: this could be in the actual proximity of a group member or when something representing the group is present. One common measure is the Implicit Association Test (see Spotlight below). It is generally thought that implicit attitude measurements have a couple of advantages:

1 It isn't subject to social desirability.

2 It is better used in cases where it is not societally acceptable to express negative views about a specific minority group.

Spotlight: Measuring implicit attitudes of prejudice

Using the Implicit Association Test, individuals are asked to categorize stimuli from either their own group (e.g. native British) or a target group (e.g. Romanian immigrant), alongside positive or negative stimuli (for example, words with positive or negative associations, such as 'dynamic' or 'lazy'). The speed with which they do so is measured (referred to as a reaction time task). Results suggest that individuals are quicker to associate their own groups with positive stimuli and outgroups with negative stimuli. This quicker reaction time indicates an implicit bias.

It was long believed that explicit attitudes were able to change relatively easily, but that implicit attitudes were more rigid and less easy to change. However, recent research has suggested that this may not be the case, and that current events can influence implicit attitudes more easily than thought, and in a positive way. It is also believed that behaviour is affected in different ways according to whether the attitudes held are explicit or implicit: in the former case, the behaviour tends to be more conscious and deliberate; in the latter case the behaviour is a little more subtle and indirect such as nonverbal behaviour (for example, avoiding eye contact, hesitations during speech, and the distance held from outgroup members).

Individual personality traits and prejudice

When attempting to explain the existence of prejudice, it would be sensible to start with an individual explanation as it seems clear that some people show more prejudice than others. This led early researchers to consider the **authoritarian personality** trait as an explanation for prejudice. Theodor Adorno and his colleagues developed the 'F-scale' as a means of measuring it (the 'F' denoting fascism). Predicated on Freudian psychoanalytic theory, it was believed that those scoring highly in authoritarianism did so because they were raised by overly-strict parents. Having no way to express their hostility towards their parents (for fear of sanctions), such children were forced to look for other outlets for their repressed aggressive tendencies, and as such they tended to target weaker targets; this trait persisted into adulthood. Those with an authoritarian personality also tended to bestow an overly deferential outlook towards authority.

Key idea: Authoritarian personality

A prejudiced personality type based on psychoanalytic theory, and thought to have its origins in childhood.

Examples of questions from the 'F-scale' include: 'People can be divided into two classes: the weak and the strong'; 'Obedience and respect for authority are the most important virtues children should learn'. Respondents were asked to rate their response to each of the thirty questions on a six-point scale from 'Disagree strongly' to 'Agree strongly'.

However, as an explanation for prejudice, the authoritarian personality ran into two fundamental problems. The first suggested that empirical evidence for such a trait was less than convincing: for example, it was unable to predict racism in South Africa in the 1950s. Secondly, it is almost inconceivable that, when we see ethnic cleansing perpetrated by one nation on another, the entire aggressor nation was raised by overly-strict parents. Finally, it is not always the case that those raised by a harsh parental regime go on to be overly harsh themselves.

Nevertheless, the observation remains that some people are more prejudiced than others, and some are more liberal, which again suggests that individual personality may play a role.

An alternative personality trait which has been linked to prejudice is **social dominance orientation**. This is derived from social dominance theory which claims that there is a tendency for human societies to be based on a hierarchical structure: that is to say, there will be a ranking of groups within a given society in terms of their dominance. Within those groups, at one end of the spectrum, there will be individuals who have ways, and the need, to subjugate the members of lower-ranked groups; at the other end, there will be individuals who are less likely to exploit these differences in group rankings, and who will instead attempt to lessen the differences between groups.

Key idea: Social dominance orientation

The degree to which an individual embraces the concept of society being based on a hierarchical structure, and rejects a more egalitarian outlook.

Social dominance orientation measures the place where an individual falls on such a scale. The theory suggests that those with a need to subjugate are much more likely to be prejudiced than those at the other end. However, unlike the authoritarian personality measure, the SDO scale has no clear overriding rationale on which the theory is based.

The SDO scale comprises 16 statements which purportedly measure whether or not an individual is for or against the desirability of group inequality. Example statements include:

▶ Sometimes other groups must be kept in their place.

▶ Some groups of people are simply inferior to other groups.

▶ We would have fewer problems if we treated people more equally.

▶ All groups should be given an equal chance in life.

Each item was scored on a 1 (very negative) to 7 (very positive) scale, with some items being reverse-scored.

Generally speaking, there is some evidence to suggest that there is a link between SDO and prejudice (for example, in the form of racism, sexism and nationalism): the correlation tends to be around 0.50, which is considered to be quite strong. Other findings suggest that: men score slightly higher on SDO than women; individuals scoring high on SDO are more likely to seek out professions in which some form of hierarchy enhancement is prevalent; low SDO scorers tend to prefer professions in which they can work towards minimization of group hierarchies. Some critics have questioned whether SDO is actually a stable personality factor, or whether it should be considered to be more of a measure of social attitude.

Overall, attempts to explain prejudice in terms of personality traits have come in for a number of criticisms:

▶ It underestimates the power of the social situation in which an individual finds themselves; that is, the attitudes of the people around us and the groups to which we belong. For example, studies of students have found that personality traits, such as authoritarianism, can change (e.g. go down) simply by housing them in more liberal dormitories for a year.

▶ Studies of highly prejudiced populations (such as South Africa and Southern states of American in the 1950s where there were high levels of anti-black discrimination) have found that whilst there was a strong link between personality traits such as authoritarianism and prejudice, the levels of authoritarianism found were actually not all that different from populations where prejudice was found to be at much lower levels. This suggests that prejudice was much more likely due to the prevailing societal norms than it was to individual differences.

▶ It is difficult to explain how prejudice found in an entire population or society can actually be down to individual differences. In effect, it would be saying that thousands, and possibly tens of thousands, of people are different on so many other personality traits, such as introversion-extraversion, agreeableness, and the like, but they all happen to be the exactly the same on personality traits linked to prejudice.

▶ From a historical perspective, it has been found that prejudice in individual societies can emerge in a very short space of time, such as anti-Japanese sentiment in the USA following the bombing of Pearl Harbor, or Islamophobia following 9/11; as such, it is unlikely that individual personality traits can really account for such situations.

More typically, prejudice tends to be seen as an intergroup process (see also Chapter 14), and there are a number of theories that attempt to explain prejudice from this perspective.

Intergroup explanations of prejudice

There are a number of different theories that can account for intergroup explanations of prejudice, and these have been covered in other chapters looking at aggression and intergroup conflict. However, it is worth briefly reprising some of them here as a reminder.

The 'frustration-aggression hypothesis' (see Chapter 9) puts forward the idea that a frustrating situation, such as a poor economic climate, can lead to aggression; importantly, the aggression tends not to be targeted towards the cause of the frustration, which is usually a more powerful target, but instead is likely to be displaced towards an easier and weaker target, such as an ethnic minority. Essentially, the weaker group becomes the scapegoat and the target of prejudice.

Relative deprivation theory suggests that prejudice may be due to one group feeling that they are less well-off compared to another group, and resentment due to this state of affairs may emerge in the form of prejudicial attitudes and behaviours towards the other group. Fraternalistic relative deprivation would certainly account for feelings of prejudice between groups (see Chapter 14).

Key idea: Relative deprivation theory

The theory suggests that prejudice is caused by individuals or groups feeling that they have less than that to which they are entitled.

Realistic group conflict theory suggests that when groups are in competition with each other for scarce resources, the groups that miss out may well be resentful towards the groups that secure the resources, and hence prejudice may ensue. Similarly, one group may feel that they are entitled to the resources and should not be in competition for them; thus they may feel resentful towards the competing group(s) and hence prejudicial feelings may ensue (see Chapter 14).

Reducing prejudice

A number of theories have been put forward as ways in which prejudice can be reduced. The most prominent, and successful, of these theories is the **contact hypothesis**. In essence, this idea states that in order to reduce prejudice, there needs to be contact between the two groups (i.e. the group showing prejudice and the minority group that is the target). However, the name of the theory is a little misleading, according to Allport who was an architect of this idea, in that there are certain conditions of the contact that need to be in place for the reduction of prejudice to be achieved:

▶ There need to be prevailing social norms in place to promote equality between the two groups. For example, if laws are in place to stop discrimination then the required attitude change is far more apt to occur, and this change will likely come about based on Festinger's cognitive dissonance theory – if we are forced to behave in a certain way by society, it is likely that our attitudes will soon align with our behaviour in order to reduce the dissonance that we feel;

▶ When the contact does come about, the social status of the two groups must be equal. There can be no perceived subordination of one group to the other;

▶ The contact must be predicated on the need to achieve a common target or goal. That is, there must be a good reason for the two groups to come into contact with one another – namely a need to co-operate with one another. Prejudice reduction is also far more likely to occur when there is success in achieving the common goal; failure to do so may potentially worsen the situation;

'One of the most long-lived and successful ideas in the history of social psychology has been the so-called contact hypothesis (Allport, 1954). Its central premise is that the way to reduce tension between groups is to bring them into contact with one another. However, the phrase "contact hypothesis" is something of a misnomer because it implies that mere contact is sufficient a panacea. As Allport noted, this is far from the case.'

(Brewer & Brown, 1998, p. 576)

Key idea: The contact hypothesis

The idea that, under optimal conditions, contact between two groups can reduce the prejudice felt by one of the groups towards the other.

Further conditions have been added by theorists since the days of Allport, one of which is *acquaintance potential*. This condition ensures that the contact occurs often enough, and for long enough, in order that meaningful relationships have the opportunity to develop between individuals of the two groups.

Indeed, research has shown that finding out that members of your group have friends in the other group can improve relationships with the other group further.

Of course, there may be situations where direct contact between the two groups is not possible. However, work on '*indirect contact*' has shown that if this is the case, under certain circumstances, it may still be possible for the contact hypothesis to work its magic. For example, if you know that other members of your group have friendships with individuals in the 'outgroup', then this can be sufficient to reduce your prejudice; this is referred to as *extended contact*. However, there may be situations where you know no one who has friendships with members of the other group: in this case, it has been shown that simply imagining (in a reasonable amount of detail) a positive contact with a person from the 'outgroup' can help to reduce prejudice; this is referred to as *imagined contact* and works due to the activation of, and increased access to, concepts linked to successful interactions. Additionally, in light of the rise of the Internet, social media (such as Facebook), and online communities and discussion forums, more recent work has started to test the *virtual contact hypothesis*, whereby online contact is used to reduce prejudice. This type of contact has many advantages, one of which is that it is able to bring together people who might not have been able to meet face-to-face, and another is that it is possible to remove all of the trappings of status that might have been a barrier in direct contact situations. It is early days but some results are quite promising.

With regards to the efficacy of the contact hypothesis, a meta-analysis by Pettigrew and Tropp (e.g. 2006) of the findings from over 500 studies suggested that, when group members were able to meet face-to-face, prejudice was reduced in 94 per cent of cases. Generally speaking, the more contact there was, the less prejudice there existed between groups. Additionally, findings suggested that contact was most effective in work and social settings and least effective when groups visited another group's country. In terms of cultural effects, the contact hypothesis was found to be most effective in places such as America, Europe, Australia and New Zealand, but was less effective on the

African and Asian continents. Contact was found to be effective in the reduction of prejudice between heterosexuals and homosexuals, and harmful attitudes were also lessened in terms of racial and ethnic prejudice.

Whilst the contact hypothesis enjoys good empirical support, and has good practical applications, it has not been without its detractors, and a number of criticisms have been levelled at the theory – though most of the criticisms have been addressed subsequently. For example, it wasn't clear as to how exactly the positive effect would generalize to the two groups beyond the contact situation. That is, it is all very well to have a good relationship between a black person (let's call him Jack) and a white person (let's call him Jim), but how would this improve the relationships between Jack and other white people, or vice versa? The danger of 'subtyping' was also present in that Jack might consider Jim to be unrepresentative of whites in general, and therefore simply an exception to the rule. However, research has shown that so long as the people in the contact situation are seen as representative (i.e. typical) of their groups, and that the different aspects of their groups (i.e. their race) are prominent, seen in a positive way, and not down-played, then the benefit of contact should endure.

A second criticism was that the contact hypothesis had become too convoluted, in that too many conditions were being applied to the contact situation before it could be successful; these included factors such as the need for a common language, that the contact should be voluntary as opposed to being prescriptive, and the background economy should be flourishing. However, a modification of the theory to suggest that such conditions were not essential, but instead only desirable, satisfied the critics. The more desirable conditions that were present, the more likely the contact situation would be to reduce prejudice.

Summary

There can be no doubt that the world would be a better and safer place in which to live if there was no prejudice. Regrettably this is not the case currently, but it is a laudable goal, and to this end social psychologists have attempted to define and quantify prejudice as a first step. It is not always easy to achieve this as overt prejudices may simply have been driven underground, and thus have become harder to detect and therefore require more sophisticated methods. However, by understanding the origins of both individual differences and group explanations of prejudice, it has become possible to devise interventions, such as the contact hypothesis, to help reduce intergroup prejudice. Nevertheless, more work is needed to understand, and combat, the changing nature of prejudice.

Food for thought

Identify a prejudice that seems largely to have disappeared over the last few years. With reference to this chapter, devise a way to determine whether this is really the case, or whether it has just been forced underground. Then, identify a new type of prejudice prevalent today and determine how it might be reduced.

Dig deeper

Brown, R. (2010) *Prejudice: its Social Psychology*. Chichester: Wiley-Blackwell.

Devine, P. G. (1989) 'Stereotypes and prejudice: Their automatic and controlled components'. *Journal of Personality and Social Psychology*, **56**, 5–18.

Dovido, J. F., Hewstone, M., Glick, P. & Esses, V. M. (Eds.) (2013) *The SAGE Handbook of Prejudice, Stereotyping and Discrimination*. Sage.

Pettigrew, T. F. & Tropp, L. R. (2006). 'A meta-analytic test of intergroup contact theory'. *Journal of Personality & Social Psychology*, **90**, 751–783.

Fact-check

1 Which of the following is not a type of prejudice?
- **a** Racism
- **b** Genocide
- **c** Nationalism
- **d** All of the above are, in fact, types of prejudice

2 Who was one of the first psychologists to attempt to tackle the topic of prejudice?
- **a** Muzafer Sherif
- **b** Theodor Adorno
- **c** Rupert Brown
- **d** Gordon Allport

3 A way to measure prejudice by tapping into unintentional automatic attitudes is by using the:
- **a** Bogus pipeline
- **b** Authoritarianism scale
- **c** Implicit association test
- **d** Minimal groups paradigm

4 Which of the following is not an assumption of the implicit association test for prejudice?
- **a** Individuals are quicker to associate their own groups with negative stimuli
- **b** Individuals are quicker to associate outgroups with negative stimuli
- **c** Individuals are quicker to associate their own groups with positive stimuli
- **d** Individuals are slower to associate outgroups with positive stimuli

5 Adorno's authoritarianism scale is based on a:
- **a** Cognitive theory
- **b** Psychoanalytic theory
- **c** Evolutionary theory
- **d** Biological theory

6 The link between social dominance orientation and prejudice tends to be:
   a Quite weak, with a correlation of 0.1
   b Of medium strength, with a correlation of 0.3
   c Quite strong, with a correlation of 0.5
   d Very strong, with a correlation of 0.7

7 Which of the following is not a valid criticism of attempts to explain prejudice through personality traits?
   a It overestimates the power of the social situation in which the individual finds themselves
   b Whilst there is a clear link between authoritarianism and prejudice, the levels of authoritarianism found in a prejudiced population are not always considerably different to authoritarianism levels found in a population where no prejudice is found
   c It is difficult for a prejudiced society to be explained in terms of the majority of their population scoring high in personality traits linked to prejudice
   d From a historical perspective, prejudice has been found to emerge within a comparatively short period of time and therefore cannot be due to personality differences in its population

8 Which of the following is not a condition for the contact hypothesis to predict the successful reduction of prejudice?
   a Prevailing social norms, such as legislation, need to exist in order to promote equality between the two groups
   b The status of the two groups must be that of equals when they meet
   c The contact between the two groups does not need to have a specific reason for it to take place
   d The contact needs to occur often and long enough for meaningful relationships to develop

9 When two groups are unable physically to come together in a contact situation, it may still be possible for prejudice to be reduced if members of one group know that one (or more) of their number have friendships with an individual in the 'outgroup'. This is referred to as:

   a Displaced contact

   b Imagined contact

   c Minimal contact

   d Extended contact

10 According to the meta-analysis by Pettigrew and Tropp, with regards to the effectiveness of the contact hypothesis, which of the following is not true?

   a Face-to-face contact reduced prejudice in 94 per cent of cases

   b Contact was more effective when group members visited the other group's country

   c Contact was more effective in Europe than in Africa

   d Contact was effective in reducing prejudice between heterosexual and homosexual groups

14

Intergroup relations

Groups, it seems, are extremely good at fighting with each other. It may be that the groups are gangs, rival corporations or nations, but nevertheless conflict seems almost inevitable. If you were asked to compile two lists, one which catalogued as many examples as you could think of when groups had come into conflict, and the other list covered examples of when groups has co-operated, it wouldn't be too hard to guess which list would be the longest. Regrettably history is full of examples of group conflict. This chapter starts by looking at just how easy it is for groups to form an 'us' and 'them' mentality, before looking at some theories which attempt to explain why intergroup conflict occurs. It will finish by investigating ways in which conflict between groups can be reduced.

'Whenever individuals belonging to one group interact, collectively or individually, with another group or its members in terms of their group identification, we have an instance of intergroup behavior.'

(Sherif, 1966, p. 12)

Investigating intergroup conflict

One of the first researchers to study this phenomenon was Muzafer Sherif in a series of ground-breaking field studies referred to as the 'summer camp' studies. Using the backdrop of an American summer camp (where teenage boys are sent away for a time during school holidays to engage in outdoor activities and give their parents a few weeks rest), Sherif and his colleagues manufactured a situation where a group of approximately twenty boys were arbitrarily split into two groups – sometimes down the middle of existing friendships. In another of the studies, there were two summer camps in the same national park and (by design) the two groups of boys only became aware of each other after a week.

The objectives of the research were threefold:

1 to observe group and friendship formation;

2 to observe the effects of introducing competition between the groups;

3 to study factors that might have an effect of reducing any conflict that arose during the first two stages.

Very quickly after the two groups had been artificially created, distinct group behaviour was observed. The boys gave names to their groups (for instance, Eagles and Rattlers; Bulldogs and Red Devils; Panthers and Pythons) in order to differentiate themselves from the other group, they made icons to represent their groups and displayed them above the doors to their dormitories. The division of the boys also had the effect of ensuring that most friendships soon became within-group (the **ingroup**), and any existing friendship with members of the other group (the **outgroup**) were suspended.

Suggestions for some form of competition were soon requested from both sets of boys and the researchers duly obliged by organizing tug-of-war contests and games of baseball. It was decided that the winning team would be awarded a cup, and members of the winning team would also be awarded individual prizes of penknives. The losers received nothing. It was noted that as soon as competition was introduced, intense rivalry between the two groups ensued: this consisted of derision of the outgroup in the form of name-calling, and it even deteriorated into physical violence in the form of the group icons being attacked by their rivals, and blows being traded when the prizes were stolen from the winning team (Sherif and his colleagues were a little too successful at creating a conflict situation).

Key idea: Ingroup and outgroup

An ingroup refers to a group to which an individual belongs, and an outgroup refers to a group, or groups, to which the individual does not belong.

The minimal group paradigm

One of the many interesting things about the summer camp studies was the ease with which **social categorization** occurred (ingroups and outgroups), and the two rival factions formed. However, another set of studies, equally as ground-breaking as Sherif's, was to throw even more light on the ease with which this type of categorization could occur.

Key idea: Social categorization

The way in which people are classified as being members of different groups.

Henri Tajfel conducted a set of experiments (see Case study below) to examine the minimum conditions under which ingroup favouritism might occur, that is where individuals show a preference for members of their own group over members of an outgroup. This has come to be known as the *minimal group paradigm*, and it shows that *mere categorization* (just knowing that someone belongs to your group, but without knowing anything about them) is sufficient to bring about an intergroup bias and prejudicial tendencies i.e. you favour those in your group over those not in your group.

This has been shown to be a very robust finding, although it was not without its critics who claimed that the findings could be due to *belief similarity*; that is, knowing that others in your group are similar to you (in this case, liking for the same type of paintings could have been the basis for the ingroup favouritism). To try to address this alternate explanation, Tajfel and colleagues conducted a similar study, but this time the children were allocated to two groups based on the flip of the coin (and this was made explicit to the children), meaning that no belief similarity could exist. However, whilst the amount of bias evidenced by the children towards their group members was reduced considerably, it certainly did not disappear entirely. It can therefore be concluded that whilst belief similarity can increase intergroup bias, it is certainly not a necessary factor to do so: it seems that mere categorization is still sufficient to lead to some degree of ingroup bias.

Causes and explanations of intergroup conflict

One of the common causes of intergroup conflict has been identified as *relative deprivation*. Such deprivation does not need to be absolute, but instead it is comparative. When a group of people thinks that it is not getting all that it expects and believes that it deserves, then a state of relative deprivation exists. Davies (1969) proposed the **'J-curve' hypothesis** to illustrate how people project expectations into the future based on their past experiences. For example, if a group of workers have received a three per cent pay rise each year for the last five years, then it's not unreasonable for them to believe that they will also get a three per cent pay rise next year – this is their expectation. However, if they actually then get only a one per cent pay rise in the following year, then they will experience relative deprivation. And according to this idea, it is inevitable that some form of conflict will follow.

Case study: Tajfel's minimal group paradigm study

A group of schoolchildren were shown a number of slides depicting paintings by either the artist Klee or Kandinsky, and then asked to express a preference for one or the other. It was suggested to the children that they would be allocated to a group based on their choice, but, in actuality, they were *randomly* assigned to one of the two groups (Klee or Kandinsky) regardless of their preferences (though the children were not aware of this). Individually, the children were then given a number of matrices (a sample matrix is shown below), and told that each column in the matrix represented a number of points that could possibly be given to two anonymous individuals who were only denoted by the 'painting group' to which they belonged and an arbitrary number (e.g. Klee group #72). For each matrix, the children were asked to put an 'X' by one of the columns to designate how they would like the points to be distributed.

	(b)					(a)							
Klee Group #72	25	23	21	19	17	15	13	11	9	7	5	3	1
Kandinsky Group #47	19	18	17	16	15	14	13	12	11	10	9	8	7

The allocation tasks given to the children were designed to measure discrimination (the prejudice shown) between an individual's own group (the 'ingroup') and the other group (the 'outgroup'). In the sample matrix above, an individual in the Klee group was asked to make an allocation between two anonymous individuals – one belonging to their own group (Klee Group #72) and one belonging to the other group (Kandinsky Group #47). If they chose a column where there was little, or no, difference between the allocations of points to the two individuals (e.g. the column marked 'a'), this would suggest no prejudice was present. However, if a column was chosen where there was a marked difference in the point distribution (e.g. the column marked 'b'), then this would indicate that some form of prejudice was present. Such prejudice would be remarkable given that:

▶ group membership was arbitrary;
▶ each individual did not know who else was in their group;

- there was no interaction between the group members;
- the individuals to whom the points were being distributed were anonymous;
- the group had no history and there was no prospect of a future for the group.

Tajfel was not expecting to find any prejudice at this point in his experiments, as the groupings were as basic as groups could possibly get; he was simply intending to use the task as a baseline to which he could add other factors until prejudice did start to occur. However, his findings were quite unexpected: he found that there was a consistent trend for participants to choose a column which allocated more points to the anonymous individual who was a member of their own group (as opposed to a column giving an equal distribution of points). Tajfel's findings have been interpreted as a show of how easy it is for some form of prejudice to occur.

Key idea: J-curve hypothesis

A graphical representation of how relative deprivation occurs when attainments no longer meet expectations.

Research has identified two different types of relative deprivation. These are:

- **Egoistic relative deprivation:** this is the idea that an individual perceives that they are deprived compared to their fellows; for example, a worker doing the same job and with the same title might feel deprived if they were earning less than someone else with the same job and title.

- **Fraternalistic relative deprivation:** this suggests that members of a group feel deprived compared to members of a different group, or compared to what it believes that it is entitled. For example, a group of workers who only receive a one per cent pay rise might feel deprived when their managers receive a five per cent pay rise, or when they have received a three per cent pay rise previously but only a one per cent rise this year.

Research suggests that fraternalistic relative deprivation is a more predictive indicator of social unrest (such as demonstrations and law-breaking) than egoistic relative deprivation (which is more likely to lead to individual stress symptoms such as lack of sleep and headaches).

However, for fraternalistic deprivation to be developed fully and lead to action, there are four additional factors that should be taken into consideration:

1 There needs to be a strong identification with the group to which an individual belongs. For example, a relatively new recruit to a group may not feel as great an affiliation to the group as do longer-term members, and this may prevent them from joining in with any collective group action.

2 There must be a feeling held by the members of the group that any action contemplated would actually have the desired effect in terms of reducing the perceived deprivation. Any considered actions should also seem to be both practical and viable in terms of leading to the desired change.

3 Generally, there is a feeling that *distributive injustice* is an important factor behind fraternalistic relative deprivation; that is to say, the group has less than it is entitled to compared to either its expectations or to other groups. However, a second form of injustice – *procedural injustice* – may also play a role; this is where there is a perception that the group has been the victim of unfair procedures. The latter form of injustice has been found to be a strong predictor for action, though it can sometimes be very difficult to untangle the two different types of injustice when trying to interpret the cause and effect of any intergroup behaviour.

4 It depends on the nature of the ingroup–outgroup comparison; that is, it depends on who a group compares itself against to measure the deprivation. Typically, groups compare themselves against similar groups, for example residents in one town are more likely to compare themselves to those in a similar town, when considering whether the council services they get are acceptable and whether they need to stage any form of protest. However, the most

prominent form of intergroup conflict will occur when comparisons are made between distinctly different groups (e.g. blacks vs. whites in 1960s America).

The consideration of all of these factors will lead to a better understanding of when unrest and disruptive behaviour is most likely to occur.

A further reason for why conflict between groups might occur comes directly from the findings of the summer camp studies by Sherif and his colleagues. They formulated the **realistic group conflict theory** which argues that conflict stems from competition for scarce resources (see below). In the case of the summer camp studies, the scarce resource was the prizes on offer which could only be awarded to one of the groups; however, the theory suggests that scarce resources could equally be represented by food, territory, wealth, power, natural resources, energy and so forth. Hence this theory seems to be able to explain real world occurrences of conflict and prejudice; for example, the reason there may be prejudice towards, and conflict with, immigrants is the perception that they take jobs, and other benefits (such as medical and monetary resources), away from the indigenous population, thereby representing a competition for limited resources.

'The realistic group conflict theory provides a powerful explanation for many instances of intergroup discrimination and prejudice. Moreover, it has the advantage of being able to account for changes in levels of prejudice over time or across different social contexts; such changes can often be attributed to changing economic and political relations between the groups concerned.'

(Brewer & Brown, 1998, p. 565)

Key idea: Realistic group conflict theory

The notion that conflict between groups is due to competition for scarce resources which if one group possesses the other group cannot have.

A key idea in this theory is the concept of *interdependence*, whereby scarce resources, or mutually exclusive goals, are the target of one or more groups. If one group gains the resources or achieves the goals, then the other group misses out and is likely to suffer as a result. If this is the case then intergroup conflict is likely to occur. This has been demonstrated in many studies, both in the field (such as the summer camp studies) and in the lab (such as Zimbardo's prison studies).

Overall, realistic group conflict theory seems to be good at explaining conflict in the real world; however, that in itself is a slight weakness as it could be the case that there are many other factors present in different settings that might also explain the conflict. Additionally, it is also the case that some form of conflict or competition can occur when group goals are not interdependent, or when groups are non-competitive (as seen in Tajfel's minimal group paradigm above), or even sometimes when the groups are actually co-operative.

There does seem to be a clear contrast between the two preceding explanations for intergroup conflict. Relative deprivation suggests that social comparison with a targeted outgroup is the reason for conflict. Conversely, realistic group conflict theory suggests it is the competition for real and valued resources that is the reason for the conflict.

However, a further explanation for why intergroup conflict occurs may be because members of a given group want to feel that their group is superior to other groups, which in turn will make the individuals within the group feel better about themselves. Thus Tajfel and Turner proposed **social identity theory** as an explanation for intergroup conflict.

Social identity theory uses the idea that there are two facets of an individual's identity – their personal identity and their social identity (see Chapter 2). The former relates to their personality traits and their interpersonal relationships, whereas the latter refers to the groups to which they belong. Social identity theory suggests that we define ourselves by the groups to which we belong (ingroups) or don't belong (outgroups); this is referred to as **self-categorization**. The more successful and prestigious the groups are to which we belong, then the better we feel about ourselves (e.g. the higher our self-esteem). However, regardless of the success or prestige of our group, if our social identity comes under threat, then action may need to be taken against any outgroup that is posing the threat.

Key idea: Self-categorization and social identity theory

Self-categorization refers to the way in which an individual thinks of themselves as belonging to different groups. This categorization helps to define who they are as a person and gives them a social identity (as opposed to a personal identity) in terms of their group memberships.

Social identity is just one aspect of group membership that may escalate intergroup conflict. Many other aspects of group life can also help to increase the likelihood of conflict, and a review of Chapters 10 and 11 will illuminate this proposition further. For example, *group polarization* (in terms of decision making) may lead to a more extreme (polarized) view of any outgroups being discussed. Similarly the concept of *groupthink* may lead a group into conflict with another because alternative options were not considered. Chapter 9 on aggression may also offer clues as to why conflict can become more inevitable if we consider Berkowitz's idea that environmental cues lead to a more aggressive stance (e.g. *the weapons effect*): for example, one might question the wisdom of a group meeting in a place referred to either as a 'war room' or an 'emergency briefing room' when considering its response to the actions of an 'outgroup'. Intergroup relations might be better served if such places were renamed as 'peace rooms'.

Improving intergroup relations

In light of the ease with which conflict may occur between rival groups, social psychologists have also focussed their attention on ways in which to prevent or reduce conflict, and a number of effective ways have been identified.

One of the primary ways in which to reduce conflict between two groups is to introduce *superordinate goals*. This idea arose from Sherif's summer camp studies when they were looking for ways to reduce the conflict between the two groups of boys. A superordinate goal is a task that can only be accomplished if both sides work together. For example, Sherif and his colleagues arranged a situation whereby both groups of boys were being transported on a lorry that broke down. The only way in which they could get back to camp was if they worked together to pull the lorry (neither group could achieve this feat on their own). Other superordinate goals created by Sherif included getting the boys to work together to find out the reason for why the water supply to the camp had ceased, pooling their money to hire a film that both groups wanted to see, and preparing meals together. Of course, it is unlikely that just one instance of a superordinate goal will be effective at reducing conflict, and many may be needed. There are two important points to consider with regards to the successful functioning of this method:

1 It is important that neither side could achieve any of the tasks on their own (or at least not easily).

2 It is important that the goal is achieved successfully, as working together but failing can actually exacerbate the conflict.

In terms of the theoretical reason for why this strategy might work, it is likely that the social identity of the groups is being rewritten: instead of belonging to two distinct groups, one group has been formed (to achieve the task) to which all members belong. Another theory that relates in some way to this method for reducing conflict is the contact hypothesis (see Chapter 13). However, some aspects of the contact hypothesis are also appropriate for consideration in terms of superordinate goals, such as ensuring that members of both groups mingle with one another during the accomplishment of a goal in order that they learn about one another and to promote opportunities for friendships to form.

A number of cognitive methods have also been utilized to reduce conflict. The first is **decategorization**, which is almost the opposite of social categorization. This method, sometimes referred to as **personalization**, works by attempting to get the members of the conflicting groups to think about the outgroup members as individuals. For example, one study merged two groups (who were in conflict) and gave them problems to solve; in one condition, the participants were told to focus on solving the problems, and in the other condition they were told to focus more on getting to know one another. Results suggest that the latter condition de-escalated the conflict far more effectively than the former, though it didn't completely resolve it.

Key idea: Decategorization

Reducing the effect of social categorization as much as possible by re-emphasizing the individuality of each member in the group and reducing the importance of the group.

A second method attempts to get the two groups in conflict to move away from thinking of themselves as two groups and to think of themselves as one group instead; this is referred to as **recategorization**. This can be achieved in a number of ways, one of which is to manipulate environmental cues, such as giving the new group one name and reducing the space between members when they are brought together. In one of the summer camp studies, Sherif and colleagues introduced a common enemy to the two groups (in that specific case, it was the Red Devils and Bull Dogs) and this had the effect of bringing about a recategorization of the groups' identity.

Key idea: Recategorization

Reducing the effect of social categorization by reworking the groups in conflict into one group.

A third method, referred to as **cross-categorization**, makes the individuals in the conflicting groups aware of their other group memberships i.e. other groups to which they belong. Whereas other types of categorization (e.g. decategorization and recategorization) attempt to unite the individuals within one group, cross-categorization attempts to reduce the salience of the problematic group membership by emphasizing less problematic group memberships. For example, in the summer camp studies, it might have been possible to reduce conflict by getting the boys to form new groups based on the place where they lived. Of course, this does require an initial willingness from individuals to undertake this cognitive restructuring of their situation, and this may not always be possible.

Key idea: Cross-categorization

Reducing the effect of social categorization by emphasizing an individual's membership of other social groups unrelated to the group in conflict.

A further method for improving intergroup relations is *mediation*, whereby a third party is employed to help both sides to move towards a mutually acceptable goal. It is important that the mediator is seen to be impartial by both sides and has sufficient power (e.g. to bring about a solution, and to put pressure on any side that shows intransigence). It is also necessary that the positions of both sides in the dispute are quite close.

Although only a small number of ways for reducing intergroup conflict have been covered here, there are certainly many more that have been tested. The general trend for creating such methods tends to be that if it is possible to theorize why conflict occurs in the first place, then it is possible to use these theoretical perspectives to *reduce* conflict. Thus we have seen how social identity theory and social categorization have been used to create interventions. This is also the case for other social psychological theories and ideas. For example, as covered in previous chapters, the norm of reciprocity plays a very strong role in motivating human behaviour (e.g. social influence, prosocial behaviour, etc.), and it is no surprise therefore that it forms the basis for a conflict reduction intervention referred to as G.R.I.T. (graduated and reciprocated initiatives in tension reduction). When employing this method, one of the conflicting groups announces publicly that it will make a small concession in the conflict and then follows through with the promise.

This then puts pressure on the other group to reciprocate – and as we have seen, the need to reciprocate can exert a very strong influence indeed.

Summary

Understanding intergroup behaviour is important given the nature and prevalence of conflict in the world today. By understanding both the minimal conditions that might cause some form of intergroup bias to exist, and the reasons and explanations for why intergroup conflict might occur, it is possible to conceive of ways to reduce conflict. Whilst it might be overly optimistic to believe that conflict can ever be eradicated, it is reassuring to know that there are methods to reduce it when it does transpire, and that this reduction can be applied to both children (who may not know any better) and adults (who probably should know better).

Food for thought

Imagine that you are the Secretary General of the United Nations. It has come to your attention that two of your member states are teetering on the brink of all-out conflict. How would you apply the information in this chapter to prevent that from happening. Would your strategy differ if it were two factions within a member state, and if so, why?

Dig deeper

Forsyth, D. R. (2014).*Group Dynamics*.6th Edition. Wadsworth.

Hogg, M. A. & Abrams, D. (2001). *Intergroup Relations: Key Readings in Social Psychology*. Routledge.

Turner, R., Crisp, R., Hopthrow, T. & de Moura, R. (2015). *Group Processes and Intergroup Relations*. Blackwell.

Fact-check

1 The principle researcher involved in the summer camp studies, which studied the roots of intergroup conflict, was:
   a Henri Tajfel
   b Muzafer Sherif
   c Philip Zimbardo
   d John Turner

2 The way in which group favouritism could occur simply through mere categorization was studied in the:
   a Summer camp studies
   b Relative deprivation theory
   c Minimal group paradigm
   d Realistic group conflict theory

3 One of the criticisms of the minimal group paradigm was:
   a Tajfel was not a social psychologist
   b The matrices used were invalid
   c The effect found could be due to belief similarity and not mere categorization
   d They were all valid criticisms

4 The 'J curve' is incorporated in which one of the following?
   a Relative deprivation theory
   b Minimal groups paradigm
   c Realistic group conflict theory
   d Social identity theory

5 If relative deprivation is experienced compared to a fellow worker, this is referred to as:
   a Fraternalistic relative deprivation
   b Comparative relative deprivation
   c Parallel relative deprivation
   d Egoistic relative deprivation

6 Which of the following is more predictive of the occurrence of social unrest?
   a Fraternalistic relative deprivation
   b Comparative relative deprivation
   c Parallel relative deprivation
   d Egoistic relative deprivation

7 Which of the following could not be a scarce resource according to realistic group conflict theory?

   a Food

   b Territory

   c Natural resources

   d All of the above are, in fact, possible scarce resources

8 Social identity theory suggests that we define ourselves by the groups to which we belong or don't belong. This is referred to as:

   a Self-categorization

   b Cross-categorization

   c Recategorization

   d Decategorization

9 Bringing two groups together to achieve a goal that neither could achieve alone is referred to as:

   a Recategorization

   b A superordinate goal

   c Cross-categorization

   d G.R.I.T.

10 The norm of reciprocity plays a key role in which one of the following methods aimed at reducing intergroup conflict?

   a Recategorization

   b Superordinate goals

   c Cross-categorization

   d G.R.I.T

15

Social psychology in action

And so we have just about reached the end of our whistle-stop tour through the realms of social psychology. I trust that you have learned lots, and have started to find the subject as fascinating as I have over the past twenty years or so. One message that I have tried to highlight and reiterate throughout the book is that social psychology is a very applied subject: it has the power to impact on the world in very real, and hopefully beneficial, ways. Therefore I just wanted to take a last opportunity to promote this message by taking a very brief look at some additional areas in which social psychology has been shown to have an impact, starting with the legal system.

The legal system

Whilst legal systems may vary across the world, they all have one thing in common – they involve people. And as you know by now, where people are involved, social psychology has much to say. The focus here is on one small aspect of the legal arena, namely the courtroom. In many countries, such as the UK, America, Canada, Australia, and New Zealand, the jury system is used, whereby (usually) twelve good persons and true listen to the facts of a case in court, and then based solely on those facts, they reach a verdict on the guilt or innocence of the defendant – or do they? Well, not according to some social psychological studies.

There has been a lot of research to suggest that when the evidence is weak, many extra-legal factors can bias a jury's decision. For example, a large body of evidence suggests that there is a real effect (albeit a small one) of the appearance of a defendant on a juror's decision-making process: the more physically attractive a defendant, the more lenient they are likely to be treated, whether this means being found 'not guilty' or being given a shorter sentence. However, it has also been found that this bias might be mitigated by the type of crime committed. For instance, if the crime is one in which the defendant may have used their physical attractiveness to achieve their nefarious ends (such as fraud), then the opposite might happen and they are more likely to be found guilty than innocent, and their punishment will be more severe.

Additionally, the size of the jury has also been found potentially to have an effect on the outcome of a trial. A jury usually comprises twelve people, but in America in the 1970s, it was decided that in order to cut costs, some juries would be reduced to six persons; the assumption was made that twelve- and six-person juries would have functional equivalence (e.g. they would reach the same verdicts). But research suggested that this was not the case: amongst other things, twelve-person juries were found to deliberate longer and were able to recall more of the evidence than six-person juries (which presumably is a good thing), and equally they were more likely to result in a hung jury (which is certainly an important result if you are a defendant). The conclusion drawn by many social psychologists suggested that this cost-cutting exercise was not in the interests of justice.

These two factors alone (interpersonal perception and group dynamics) suggest that social psychology has much to contribute to the functioning of the legal system.

Health

A vast amount of money is spent each year to promote healthy behaviour, whether this involves attempting to get people to stop smoking, increase their condom usage, or to take more exercise. However, trying to change the attitudes and behaviour of the masses is a tricky undertaking and it would be useful to know the most effective form that such a campaign should take. Some recent research, tackling smoking behaviour, pitted a number of different message types against one another in an attempt to answer this question: for example, the researchers used two types of messages that told participants 'Why' they should quit (one used emotional testimonies from those who had lost loved ones to smoking-related diseases, and the other used graphic images of what smoking could do to various body parts); one type of message that told participants 'How' to quit (including messages about how difficult it was to quit, and examples of people who had quit successfully); and combinations of the two types. Their results suggested that the 'Why' to quit advertisements were much more effective in predicting positive attitudes and intention to quit smoking than the 'How' to quit message.

Another area which has been investigated is the way in which a social network can have an effect on the health of an individual. There is certainly evidence to suggest that people with larger social networks live longer than those with smaller networks. Similarly, some research has found that getting support from others can have a very real positive effect on our response to disease and illness. For example, women who felt that they were socially connected with others were likely to respond more robustly to diagnoses of breast cancer than those who weren't.

In one study, participants with breast cancer were assigned randomly to one of two conditions: those who participated in weekly sessions in therapy groups (comprising other breast cancer patients) which gave emotional support (along with teaching a self-hypnosis strategy for the pain) and those who didn't. The results showed that women in the support group condition survived on average 18 months longer than those who were not members of a support group.

These two factors (persuasive messages and group membership) also show what social psychology can contribute to the health arena.

Everyday life

Imagine you are opening a new cheese shop – if you were looking to maximize your profits, what would be your best strategy: offering a large range of cheeses or a small range of cheeses? Not sure? Well, turn the problem on its head – imagine you are a shopper, you have a penchant for cheese and you've heard that a new cheese shop has opened in town. Do you think you would be more likely to buy from a shop which has a wide selection of cheeses, given that conventional wisdom suggests that having more choice is better, or from a shop which has a narrow selection? Well, you'll be pleased to hear that social psychologists have investigated this area (well, not cheese specifically) and have an answer for you.

Two researchers conducted an experiment in an existing shop that sold a variety of luxury goods (over 300 types of jam, about 250 mustards, and a wide variety olive oil). They set up a display of jams in front of the shop and allowed customers to taste them: the crucial factor was whether there was a selection of six or 24 jams on display. Anyone taking part in the tasting session was given a money-off voucher that could be used to make jam purchases in the shop (the vouchers were coded to allow the researchers to know in which of the two tasting conditions the participants were involved). Interestingly, they found that, whilst having 24 jams as part of the session drew in more potential tasters, it was the six-jam session that produced more customers in the long-run (about 30 per cent of these customers went on to make a purchase, compared to only 3 per cent of customers in the 24-jam condition). It seems that people can suffer from 'decision paralysis' when they have too much of a choice, thus refuting the idea that to have more choice is necessarily better. Social psychologists studying areas such as the self and social cognition have shown that individuals don't always make rational or optimal decisions, and certainly individuals are not always aware of the basis for the decisions that they make.

There are certainly many, many other studies that could have been included here to illustrate the way in which social psychology impacts on our daily lives. However, the hope is that you have now had your appetite well and truly whetted, and that you will be driven to find these multitude of studies on your own. And who knows, one day you may well be conducting the research that will be used as illustrations of 'social psychology in action' in books such as this one.

Dig deeper

Duke, J. C., Nonnemaker, J. M., Davis, K. C., Watson, K. A. & Farrelly, M. C. (2014). 'The impact of cessation media messages on cessation-related outcomes: Results from a national experiment of smokers'. *American Journal of Health Promotion*, **28(4)**, 242–250.

Iyengar, S. S. & Lepper, M. R. (2000). 'When choice is demotivating: Can one desire too much of a good thing?' *Journal of Personality and Social Psychology*, **79**, 995–1006.

Mazzella, R. & Feingold, A. (1994). 'The effects of physical attractiveness, race, socio-economic status, and gender of defendants and victims on judgments of mock jurors: A meta-analysis'. *Journal of Applied Social Psychology*, **24(15)**, 1315–1344.

Saks, M. J. & Marti, M. W. (1997). 'A Meta-Analysis of the Effects of Jury Size. *Law & Human Behavior*, **21(5)**, 451–467.

Spiegel, D., Bloom, J. R., Kraemer, H. C. & Gottheil, E. (1989). Effects of psychosocial treatment on survival of patients with metastatic breast cancer. *Lancet*, *2*, 888–891.

Answers

Chapter 1
1 a
2 b
3 c
4 b
5 c
6 d
7 d
8 b
9 a
10 c

Chapter 2
1 d
2 d
3 e
4 b
5 a
6 c
7 c
8 d
9 e
10 d

Chapter 3
1 d
2 b
3 a
4 b
5 c
6 d
7 a
8 c
9 b
10 a

Chapter 4
1 c
2 b
3 c
4 e
5 b
6 a
7 b
8 c
9 c
10 c

Chapter 5
1 d
2 c
3 d
4 b
5 a
6 b
7 b
8 b
9 d
10 b

Chapter 6
1 c
2 c
3 b
4 c
5 d
6 a
7 d
8 b
9 d
10 a

Chapter 7	Chapter 9	Chapter 11
1 e	1 c	1 a
2 c	2 a	2 d
3 b	3 d	3 c
4 c	4 d	4 b
5 a	5 a	5 a
6 b	6 b	6 c
7 d	7 d	7 a
8 c	8 c	8 b
9 d	9 b	9 b
10 a	10 a	10 c

Chapter 8	Chapter 10	Chapter 12
1 a	1 b	1 c
2 e	2 d	2 b
3 b	3 c	3 d
4 c	4 d	4 e
5 d	5 b	5 b
6 c	6 b	6 a
7 d	7 a	7 e
8 a	8 d	8 c
9 c	9 c	9 b
10 b	10 c	10 b

Chapter 13	Chapter 14
1 b	1 b
2 d	2 c
3 c	3 c
4 a	4 a
5 b	5 d
6 c	6 a
7 a	7 d
8 c	8 a
9 d	9 b
10 b	10 d

References

Introduction:

Allport, G. W. (1954a). 'The historical background of modern social psychology'. In Lindzey, G. (Ed.) *Handbook of Social Psychology* . 2nd Edition. (Vol. I, pp. 3-56). Addison-Wesley.

Brewer, M. B. & Brown, R. J. (1998). 'Intergroup relations'. In Gilbert, D. T., Fiske, S. T. & Lindzey, G. (Eds.) *The Handbook of Social Psychology*. 4th Edition. (Volume II, pp. 554–594). McGraw-Hill.

Chapter 1

Aronson, E., Wilson, T. D. & Brewer, M. B. (1998). 'Experimentation in social psychology'. In Gilbert, D. T., Fiske, S. T. & Lindzey, G. (Eds.) *The Handbook of Social Psychology*. 4th Edition. (Volume I, pp. 94–142). McGraw-Hill.

Chapter 2

Tesser, A. (2001). 'Self esteem'. In Tesser, A. & Schwarz, N. (Eds.) *Blackwell Handbook of Social Psychology: Intraindividual Processes*. Blackwell Publishing.

Cortes, K., Kammrath, L. K., Scholer, A. A. & Peetz, J. (2014). 'Self-regulating the effortful "Social Dos"'. *Journal of Personality and Social Psychology*, 106(3), 380–397.

Chapter 3

Choi, I., Nisbett, R. E. & Norenzayan, A. (1999). 'Causal attribution across cultures. Variation and universality'. *Psychological Bulletin*, 125, 47–63.

Jones, E. E. & Harris, V. A. (1967). 'The attribution of attitudes'. *Journal of Experimental Social Psychology*, 3, 1–24.

Chapter 4

Hamilton, D. l. & Gifford, R. K. (1976). 'Illusory correlation in interpersonal perception: A cognitive basis of stereotypic judgments'. *Journal of Experimental Social Psychology*, 12, 392–407.

Kahneman, D. & Tversky, A. (1972). 'Subjective probability: A judgment of representativeness'. *Cognitive Psychology*, 3, 430-454.

Chapter 5

Baumeister, R. F. & Leary, M. R. (1995). 'The need to belong: Desire for interpersonal attachment as a fundamental human motivation'. *Psychological Bulletin*, 117(3), 497–529.

Rubin, Z. (1970). 'Measurement of romantic love'. *Journal of Personality and Social Psychology*, **16**(2), 265–273.

Sternberg, R. J. (1986). 'A triangular theory of love'. *Psychological Review*, **93**(2), 119-135.

Chapter 6

Asch, S. E. (1955). 'Opinions and social pressure'. *Scientific American*, 193, 31–35.

Milgram, S. (1963). 'Behavioral study of obedience'. *Journal of Abnormal and Social Psychology*, 67, 371–378.

Milgram, S. (1974) *Obedience to Authority*. Tavistock.

Chapter 7

Eagly, A. H. & Chaiken, S. (1993). *The Psychology of Attitudes*. Harcourt Brace Jovanovich.

Maio, G. R. & Haddock, G. (2010). *The Psychology of Attitudes and Attitude Change*. Sage.

Smith, M. B., Bruner, J. S. & White, R. W. (1956). *Opinions and Personality*. Wiley.

Levine, R. (2006). *The Power of Persuasion. How We're Bought and Sold*. Oneworld.

Gass, R. H. & Seiter, J. S. (2011). *Persuasion: Social Influence and Compliance Gaining*. Fourth Edition. Pearson.

Chapter 8

Batson, C. D. (1998). 'Altruism and prosocial behavior'. In Gilbert, D. T., Fiske, S. T. & Lindzey, G. (Eds.) *The Handbook of Social Psychology*. 4th Edition. (Volume II, pp. 282–316). McGraw-Hill.

Eagly, A. H. (2009) 'The his and hers of prosocial behavior: An examination of the social psychology of gender'. *American Psychologist*, 64(8), 644–658.

Chapter 9

Baron, R. A. (1977). *Human Aggression*. Plenum.

Krahe, B. (2013). *The Social Psychology of Aggression*. Second edition. Psychology Press.

Bushman, B. J. (2002). 'Does venting anger feed or extinguish the flame? Catharsis, rumination, distraction, anger, and aggressive responding'. *Personality & Social Psychology Bulletin*, 28(6), 724–731.

Chapter 10

Levine, J. M. & Moreland, R. L. (1998). 'Small Groups'. In Gilbert, D. T., Fiske, S. T. & Lindzey, G. (Eds.) *The Handbook of Social Psychology*. 4th Edition. (Volume II, pp. 415–469). McGraw-Hill.

Brown, R. (1999). *Group Processes: Dynamics Within and Between Groups*. 2nd Edition. Blackwell publishing.

Johnson, D. W. & Johnson, F. P. (1987). *Joining Together: Group Theory and Group Skills*. 3rd Edition. Prentice Hall.

Miller, D. (2003). 'The stages of group development. A retrospective study of dynamic team processes'. *Canadian Journal of Administrative Sciences*, 20(2), 121–143.

Chapter 11

Levine, J. M. & Moreland, R. L. (1998). 'Small Groups'. In Gilbert, D. T., Fiske, S. T. & Lindzey, G. (Eds.) *The Handbook of Social Psychology*. 4th Edition. (Volume II, pp. 415–469). McGraw-Hill.

Janis, I. (1982) *Groupthink*. Houghton Mifflin

Chapter 12

Chemers, M. M. (2001). 'Leadership effectiveness: An intergrative review'. In Hogg, M. A. & Tindale, R. S. (Eds.) *Blackwell Handbook of Social Psychology: Group Processes*. Blackwell.

Haslam, S. A., Reicher, S. D. & Platow, M. J. (2011). *The New Psychology of Leadership. Identity, Influence and Power*. Psychology Press.

Bass, B. M. (1990). 'From transactional to transformational leadership: learning to share the vision'. *Organizational Dynamics*, 18(3), 19–31.

Fiedler, F. E. (1964). 'A contingency model of leadership effectiveness'. In Berkowitz, L. (Ed.) *Advances in Experimental Social Psychology* (Vol. I, pp. 149–190). Academic Press.

Chapter 13

Allport, G. W. (1954b). *The Nature of Prejudice*. Addison-Wesley.

Brown, R. (2010). *Prejudice: Its Social Psychology*. Wiley-Blackwell.

Brewer, M. B. & Brown, R. J. (1998). 'Intergroup relations'. In Gilbert, D. T., Fiske, S. T. & Lindzey, G. (Eds.) *The Handbook of Social Psychology*. 4th Edition. (Volume II, pp. 554–594). McGraw-Hill.

Chapter 14

Sherif, M. (1966). *In Common Predicament: Social Psychology of Intergroup Conflict and Cooperation*. Houghton Mifflin.

Index